D1621961

Service Orient or Be Doomed!

Service Orient or Be Doomed!

How Service Orientation Will Change Your Business

JASON BLOOMBERG
RONALD SCHMELZER

WILEY

John Wiley & Sons, Inc.

Library of Congress Cataloging-in-Publication Data

ISBN-10: 0-471-76858-8
ISBN-13: 978-0471-76858-6

Printed in the United States of America

10 9 8 7 6 5 4 3 2

HD 30. 213
.B58
2006

Contents

Preface

Have you ever wondered why business books and periodicals rarely talk about technology? Business books do go so far as to credit technology with helping to make businesses work, and the business news covers technology *companies,* but never talks about the technology itself. Is it because publishers think that technology is just too, well, *technical* for a business audience? Or because they think that technology isn't a relevant or important topic for business discussions? Or, perish the thought, maybe these business publishers themselves don't discuss technology because they were the jocks back in high school, and technology has always seemed to be of interest only to the nerds.

In this book, *Service Orient or Be Doomed! How Service Orientation Will Change Your Business,* we take aim at all three of these positions and lay each of them finally to rest. First, we make the case that technology is vitally important to today's business. Dot-com bubble or not, every company those business periodicals cover uses technology throughout the organization.

Companies often think that business and technology are two different worlds, with different languages and priorities. Nothing, however, could be further from the truth. We explain that technology is actually a *business* concept. It's not some other world, a black box full of strange people who speak a different language. On the contrary, technology is a business resource, just like any other resource a company might leverage to meet its goals.

Until now, books aimed at leveraging technology to solve business problems have been lumped into two categories: technology-focused books that only pay lip service to business woes or business-focused books that overly simplify the technology problems that companies must solve. Even worse, business books often fall into one of three common traps: consultant-speak, MBA-speak, and books that talk down to the popular market. Not so with this book.

We even debunk the silly jocks versus nerds dichotomy and help even the most muscle-bound of you out there to unleash your inner nerd. Perhaps one reason the business/technology divide has grown so large is that, time and again, authors who try to talk about technology to a business audience commit the most venal of sins: talking down to their audience. Their reasoning is that they can take any technology concept and simply *dumb it down* enough, and they'll have a business book. It's the worst example of revenge of the nerds—assuming the jocks are simply stupid. No wonder nobody buys such books!

You have our promise, therefore, that there's no dumbing down going on in this book. Our approach to the topic of Service Orientation is that this is a *business* book about *business concepts,* where the business concept at hand is how companies can best leverage technology resources to meet their business goals. In fact, we eschew the distinction between business and technology altogether. Instead, we talk about a range of business problems that are preventing companies from being efficient and competitive and then discuss the new approach we call Service Orientation to leveraging business resources to solve those problems.

Now, don't get us wrong—there's plenty of technology in this book. After all, technology is pervasive in today's companies, and as we'll discuss, poor approaches to technology are the primary source of the business problems we'll seek to address. If something's broke, you gotta fix it, so yes, we need to talk tech. But you won't find jargon for jargon's sake, and we'll never dumb anything down. In fact, we watch for jargon, and whenever any creeps into the text, we call it out into a *Jargon Watch*—a sidebar that explains the term just in case it's unfamiliar. If you recognize the term, you can simply skip over the Jargon Watch.

Jargon Watch: Jargon

Jargon is a specialized vocabulary intended for a particular area of interest. Every profession and academic pursuit has its own jargon, from medicine, to factory floors, to computers. When a group of people within a single such area of interest use jargon among themselves, everything's fine. However, when specialists in one area use their own jargon with people outside their group, they often come across as condescending—unless they take the time to define the terms they're using to their audience.

The fact of the matter is, we need to talk about Service Orientation, because we need to free this powerful concept from the clutches of the techies. Service Orientation and the related technology concept *Service-Oriented Architecture* (SOA) are new approaches for businesses to leverage technology in a flexible, agile manner. Until now, however, discussions of

SOA have been in the technology realm. As a result, most books about SOA are very technical and don't place SOA in a business context. Surprisingly, however, Service Orientation isn't a technology concept at all. It's a *business* philosophy and approach—a new way of thinking about organizing the business and its processes.

It seems that techies within every enterprise (and many smaller firms, as well) are all abuzz over this new approach to organizing their technology. And yet, the business folks are largely unaware of what all the fuss is about. This lack of awareness wouldn't be such a big deal, except for the fact that Service Orientation is a business concept, not a technology one. Some of the techies get this point, but many do not, and even fewer businesspeople understand the power of Service Orientation.

That's why we wrote this book. We're quite serious about the title—if you don't Service-orient your company, you will not be able to compete with the organizations that do. So, to avoid the doom around the corner, flip to the next page and start your Service Orientation journey!

CHAPTER 1

The Business Inflexibility Trap

Business books today are a sorry lot indeed. Sandwiched between the get-rich-quick manuals and the even-losers-can-get-a-job tomes, today's business library is a dreadful mix of business school doublespeak and trite platitudes. Sure, you want to be more productive, more effective, more efficient, and more profitable—pick your adjective, and then choose your book. Maybe it's full of cases, like so many courses on the road to an MBA. Or maybe it's full of quaint distillations of wisdom. Either way, the chance that reading a particular book will actually help you address whatever intractable problems you face at work is an unlikely proposition at best.

At the bottom of the barrel of the business book world are those books that attempt to talk about *information technology (IT)*. After all, what business manager in her right mind doesn't roll up her eyes at the thought of a business book that deigns to address issues of technology? After the last decade's plethora of books on digital-this and E-that, and that ridiculous "New Economy" thing (what were we thinking?), the whole idea of a business book that even brings up the topic of IT causes publishers to run screaming.

There is an enormous irony in this sad state of affairs. That irony arises from the simple fact that IT is more important to business than it ever was. Name your business goal—productivity, profitability, efficiency, what have you; today, they all depend on IT. You'd think that publishers, authors, and especially business book readers would eventually get wise to this fact. The industrial age is long gone, folks! We live in the information age, so get with it! If you as a business reader don't first fathom the problems that IT causes the business, then how will you ever come to understand how IT might actually help you solve the problems facing business today? And we hope you've evolved past the stage where you would rather put your head in the sand than try to slog through a book that had anything to do with technology. If not, then, well, the books on the shelf below might be right for you. Yes, we mean the even-losers-can-get-a-job shelf.

Jargon Watch: Information Technology

Information refers to understandable content that one individual communicates to another. We generally understand information to contain some measure of meaning, thus distinguishing it from *data,* which are the basic nuggets of content—some with meaning, some possibly sheer gibberish. *Data* is the plural of *datum,* one of those nuggets. Nobody ever uses the word *datum* anymore; we only bring it up here to explain why we talk about data as the plural of something. Not that it really matters!

Information technology, then, is all the various and sundry pieces of hardware and software that deal with information: computers, networks, applications, databases, and so forth. Information technology (abbreviated IT, always pronounced "eye tee" so as not to confuse it with the pronoun) broadly refers to the entire world of computer stuff, including the companies and people that deal with such things. Sometimes IT refers more narrowly to the application of such technology in business. In this book, we generally stick to the broader meaning, encompassing the world of computing. If we're talking about the use of IT in business, we'll say so.

The problem with business books about IT is that they're not really business books about IT at all. They are technology books aimed at a business audience. Big difference! Authors of such books figure that if they can just dumb down the material enough, even you, poor dear business reader, will be able to follow what they are saying. Techies like to think that they're smarter than everybody else, after all. Otherwise, why would college students transfer from computer majors to business ones, and not vice versa? IT is really hard stuff, you know, and by comparison, all this business stuff is soft. (We hope you can recognize the sarcasm in this paragraph!)

The fact of the matter, of course, is that business is harder than they think, naturally, and furthermore, IT is frankly easier than they would have you believe as well. These technology books aimed at business audiences typically fail to ground their arguments in the basic business realities—the business drivers that form the impetus for everything companies do. Typical business/IT books take the approach: "Here's some great technology, now let's see what we can do with it," rather than: "Here are some difficult business problems, let's come up with a great way to solve them."

Needless to say, we wouldn't be faulting such books unless we thought this book avoided the same traps. Well, you'll be relieved to hear that this book isn't about IT at all. It's all about business. When we talk about IT, we're talking about a set of business resources available to solve business problems. Fundamentally, this book takes a close look at certain key business problems and then explains a broad-reaching but practical approach for addressing those problems that leverages IT, among other types of resources. We call this approach *Service Orientation*—a vision that can dramatically impact your business tomorrow; a vision that doesn't center on IT, but rather centers on the business and its problems.

THE MOTHER OF ALL BUSINESS PROBLEMS

As a way of getting the business-centered discussion going, we focus attention squarely on the "mother of all business problems" that, at a fundamental level, covers all the rest. That one mother of a problem is *inflexibility*.

We consider inflexibility to be the überproblem of business today, because basically, if companies were flexible enough, they could solve all of their other problems, since no problem is beyond the reach of the flexible company. If only companies were flexible enough, they could adjust their offerings to changes in customer demand. If only they were flexible enough, they could build new products and services quickly and efficiently. If only they were flexible enough, they could leverage the talent of their people in an optimal manner to maximize productivity. And if only companies were flexible enough, their strategies would always provide the best possible direction for the future. Fundamentally, flexibility is the key to every organization's profitability, longevity, and success.

At the core of every organization's inflexibility is human nature. People are only just so flexible, after all, and groups of people tend to be less flexible than many of the individuals within the group. There are many reasons for this human inflexibility: fear of the unknown, resistance to change, limited attention spans, and our core personal motivations to follow enlightened self-interest and avoid discomfort and risk. As organizations form and grow, these basic human characteristics become institutionalized in the corporate culture and the overall behavior of the organization as a whole. In fact, the success and failure of many companies depends on their founders' tolerance for change, incorporated into the culture and traits of the company. Organizations run by such risk-inclined, flexibly minded souls pass along those personality traits to their organization, and as a result, their companies are more flexible than those that are not.

Lest you think that this book is actually a psychological treatise rather than a business book, rest assured that we won't be delving much further into the human psyche. We will, however, spend a good amount of time discussing techniques organizations can use to address the human issues of inflexibility. When the conversation comes around to the topic of leveraging IT, these inflexibility issues cut two ways. On one hand, we will spend time talking about how organizations can best use IT in flexible ways, and on the other hand, we will also discuss how IT itself can help organizations be more flexible.

Service Orientation, in fact, neatly addresses both issues: flexibility *of* IT and flexibility *with* IT. These two themes entwine themselves through the chapters that follow. As you read through this book, look for ideas for dealing with inflexibility in all its forms. Expect to learn new approaches for leveraging IT and other business resources to meet business needs in environments of change. You may even come away with a new way of thinking about IT. You won't, however, find quaint platitudes or MBA-speak here.

ONE CONSTANT IS CHANGE

At the core of the concept of flexibility is the notion of *change*. Businesses are under constant pressure—that's why we call work the "daily grind." The pressures on today's executives are enormous: They must cut costs and make do with existing resources, while at the same time serving customers better, satisfying shareholders, being more competitive, and responding to the business's strategic priorities. The realities of the current world add regulatory and compliance pressures on top of these basic business motivators—with the penalty of loss of liberty, if not profit. Basically, executives must do more with less, not just right now, but also into the future as business needs change and new ones develop.

As the ancient Greek philosopher Heraclitus once noted, "Change alone is unchanging." Even today, change is the one constant in all the pressures on the business. Change occurs throughout today's modern enterprise. Business as well as human and technological factors are all at the root of the change facing today's organizations. At the macro level, broad economic forces including globalization and eBusiness are accelerating the pace of change. Businesses once thought of as mature, like the book-selling business or textile manufacturing, now experience significant pressure to change the way they are run. Globalization leads to fierce competition, which in turn leads to shortened product cycles and reduced prices, as companies look to gain advantage over their competition. Companies that can't evolve their business model quickly soon find themselves facing extinction.

In addition, customer requirements are changing at an ever-increasing pace. The wealth of available information, the plethora of competitive offerings in the global marketplace, as well as newfound gains in productivity are driving customers to demand more from their suppliers at ever-lower prices, squeezing margins thinner and thinner. In response to these heightened customer demands, businesses must improve their offerings, and this leads to a recurring cycle of heightened customer demand, competitive pressure, and global competition.

Furthermore, customers increasingly demand access to information and products in ever more convenient forms. Although telephone and direct mail might have been a good way to reach your customers up until the 1970s, they are no longer sufficient today. Web sites, once seen as a curious add-on to the business, are now seen as a necessity. E-mail is making the fax machine obsolete. New developments in electronic forms and automated procurement may finally make the paper-based office history (or maybe not, but you get the idea). These technological factors exert additional pressure on the business to innovate. Fail to innovate and your customers will find other businesses that provide better value and are more convenient to work with.

The Change We Know and the Change We Don't

Secretary of Defense Donald Rumsfeld once famously quipped: "There are known knowns. These are things we know that we know. There are known unknowns. That is to say, there are things that we know we don't know. But there are also unknown unknowns. There are things we don't know we don't know." Even though it might take a doctorate in linguistics to properly understand what he's trying to say (intentional obfuscation on his part?), we can rephrase this quote and apply it to business in this way: There are those changes that the business knows about ahead of time, including new technologies, ongoing business pressures, compliance mandates looming on the horizon, and so forth. And there are also those changes that we know will happen eventually, such as rises in energy and labor costs, although we don't know precisely how or when they might happen.

However, the most significant changes are the ones that businesses can't foresee. No one could have known the impact that the Internet has had on businesses or how global terrorism has changed the way we think about risk. Major economic, political, and even geologic shifts can have significant and unpredictable impact on today's businesses. Those businesses that are the most capable of dealing with those unpredictable changes have the best chances of survival. So, it pays to think of change as a positive force in business, since responding to change and leveraging change for competitive advantage are the keys to continued success.

How We Get Locked In: The Change Conundrum

Organizations' resistance to change results from the simple fact that people are resistant to change. Basically, humans are creatures of comfort. Do you remember when you were in elementary school and on the first day you had to select which desk to sit at? From that point on, for the rest of the school year, you would sit in the same seat—partially out of habit and partially because of comfort. How earth-shattering it was to come into class one day and find some other kid sitting in your seat! That one event was probably your first exposure to change that left a bad taste in your mouth.

Despite the evolutionary forces that brought about the human race, people do not like change. People maintain the same haircuts, daily routines, morning coffee runs, clothing styles, and other habits, and generally loathe any changes to those routines. If humans are resistant to changing the most trivial of daily activities, imagine the resistance to something more threatening, such as changes to the way the business is run. In fact, the only change people like is the kind they get from a cashier! The problem is that no change can happen without risk—and people generally don't like taking risks.

This resistance to change is engrained in corporate culture in a number of places.

Companies establish processes early on in their history and rarely change them, even in the face of compelling reasons to do so. People get used to the same old procurement, human resource, manufacturing, customer support, and management reporting processes and are very resistant to changing them, even if newer, more cost-effective processes are available. What once was supposed to be a stop-gap process to solve a single problem quickly evolves into "the way things are done," giving employees comfort in doing things the same way, despite evidence to that things really should be done differently. This seemingly irrational dedication to existing processes prevents companies from becoming flexible.

Jargon Watch: Corporate Culture

The Merriam-Webster dictionary defines a culture as the "patterns, traits, and products considered as the expression of a particular period, class, community, or population." Certainly, then, any group has a culture—whether it is explicit and intentional or an accidental by-product of the behavior of a group. Therefore, corporate culture consists of those patterns, traits, and by-products of how a company does business. Corporate cultures, like yogurt cultures, are productive to growth only when environmental factors are right. Build them wrong—for instance, by letting corporate culture develop as a by-product of the irrational behavior of the chief executive—and you have a stinky mess.

But locking in obsolete processes is only one of the ways that businesses become inflexible and resistant to change. Over the years, companies have invested heavily in technology solutions to various business problems yet have found themselves automating the same, rigid processes they had before. Nevertheless, once IT departments implement such technology solutions, their corporate champions defend them as if they were beachheads on Normandy during D-Day. Even when a given technology implementation is clearly failing or is a source of ongoing cost, complexity, and difficulty, the implementers will continue to defend their desire to spend money on the technology until forced to do otherwise. As a result, these ineffective, inflexible implementations rapidly become the legacy technology that tomorrow's solutions have to deal with. Like a bad remodeling job, these technologies simply get wallpapered or carpeted over, leaving some later, unsuspecting homebuyer to deal with the mess. The inertia of doing things the way "they've always been done" makes companies ineffective, inefficient, and inflexible.

Planning for Change Is Preparing for the Future

Feeding into the resistance to change in today's organizations is the snake oil that new-age business gurus and overpaid management consultants have been peddling over the past few decades. Reengineering, as you may remember, was a phenomenon of the 1980s and early 1990s that offered great promise of increased efficiency and customer focus, but in reality was a mixed success that came to be a euphemism for downsizing and of the susceptibility of management to fads in general. In retrospect, one of the main reasons why reengineering wasn't a greater success was because businesses didn't have the tools to deal with the resistance to change that permeated their organizations. Instead, the limitations of IT and the cultural resistance to change constrained the ability of business to adapt.

The general failure of reengineering illustrates the impossibility of separating the notions of change and progress. Without change, there can be no progress. So, to be able to make progress, companies must deal with their cultural resistance to change. Taking the first step of tackling the fear of change will bring you closer to surviving the changes you know and those you don't. It would be wonderful if we had some sort of magic formula for dealing with this resistance—some snake oil better than the other guy's snake oil, as it were. Well, we don't. Instead, we accept this fundamental aspect of human nature and provide an approach for improving flexibility in your organization *in spite of* the cultural resistance to change, rather than trying to pass off some technique for changing human nature.

This approach—Service Orientation—takes advantage of IT, even though traditional technology solutions have generally locked in inflexibility, rather than helping to solve the problem of resistance to change. The secret to this refreshing, if not downright incredible, claim centers on the fact that we aren't simply proposing a technology solution to the problem. Instead, we're proposing a new approach for business to leverage IT, combined with a new approach for organizing IT resources for improved flexibility.

COMPLIANCE CONUNDRUM

Expecting an organization to be less resistant to change is like expecting people to lose weight or quit smoking. Everyone agrees on the need for change, to be sure, and there's even a general understanding on how to go about such changes (although people may disagree on the specifics), but change nevertheless is extraordinarily difficult. Furthermore, most people who have the need to lose weight or quit smoking have generally made the attempt, often many times, and the vast majority have failed. So too with organizations when they face necessary changes.

Ironically, studies have shown that even after serious heart disease, people resist lifestyle changes, even though their doctors tell them they are far more likely to die if they don't make those changes. This desperate scenario plays out in the business world as well. Rather than face a life-or-death scenario, however, companies face the grim prospect of noncompliance with new regulations that make their businesses—and even their freedom—disappear.

Why do we discuss regulatory compliance at this point? For one thing, compliance illustrates a specific issue that is top of mind for most businesses today. But more important, the issue of regulatory compliance is a great place to begin the discussion of the resistance to change in organizations, because compliance issues are clear examples of arbitrary, incontrovertible forces of change on the business. Regulations and other change factors that come from outside the direct influence of business management are fundamentally arbitrary, because legislatures can concoct or amend them at will for any number of political or economic reasons. Furthermore, global companies must submit to regulations in every region they do business in, a fact that adds to the capricious nature of the regulatory picture.

Regulations also represent ongoing change. After all, would you be willing to bet that the current regulations that apply to your organization are now set in stone? Of course not. In fact, you can count on new rules and changes to existing rules, and you can also count on those changes to be inherently unpredictable—a great example of unknown unknowns. Furthermore, the world has evolved into a place where lawsuits and summary judgments that can impact personal and business freedom are a daily occurrence. To limit financial and personal liability, and to provide some sense of security in an inherently unpredictable world, we've become even more regulation-dependent. Unlike in the past, when laissez-faire, or the explicit noninvolvement of government in business affairs, was the order of the day, today companies find that a wide range of regulations that protect individuals, corporations, shareholders, and governments from liability govern and constrain them.

Finally, regulations are generally nonnegotiable. In other words, your organization *must* abide by them, or suffer consequences that you must avoid at any cost, such as going out of business or, even worse, going to prison. Companies do not have the luxury of setting limits on how much they will spend to bring themselves into compliance with new regulations. Instead, they must simply bite the bullet and spend that money. There is no monetary return on investment (ROI) for such expenditures—ROI in this case means "risk of incarceration." And just as regulations impose arbitrary change on companies, so too can other uncontrollable transformations impact the business. The more that people think of regulations as a way to structure their business for arbitrary change, the better able they will be to deal with any number of different forces impacting the business.

Managing Risk in a Risky World

Business change always involves risk, and people always try to avoid excessive risk. The constant refrain of the naysayers of change says that all change is risky. "It's too expensive . . . too complex . . . too much trouble . . ." We've all heard it before. The irony of the situation is that such naysayers are right: change *is* risky. The question is whether changing is more or less of a risk than avoiding change. In the world of compliance and regulatory pressures, the answer is obviously that change lowers risk and that not changing actually increases the quantifiable risk facing companies. It's the nonquantifiable changes that give indigestion to the risk-adverse naysayers.

The real question facing companies is how to measure risk. Companies that are able to quantify their risk can prioritize their various choices and come up with a plan for dealing with change. Unfortunately, measuring risk is rarely straightforward. Most risks are simply unquantifiable and therefore difficult to prioritize. How can a company judge the relative priorities of compliance with a regulation relative to responding to competitive pressures? In one instance, the company is able to avoid a fine or jail time, but then the business might fail. In another, the company maintains market share, only to receive penalties from the government.

Regulations Require Specific IT Capabilities

If you look at many of today's newer regulations, including Sarbanes-Oxley, the PATRIOT Act, Basel II, the Health Insurance Portability and Accountability Act (HIPAA), and others, you should notice an important pattern.

These twenty-first-century-era regulations expect and demand a range of IT capabilities from the companies they apply to. Many drive corporate visibility into finances, operations, or both. Others regulate privacy and confidentiality, and in the case of HIPAA, the regulation specifically applies

---

Jargon Watch: Regulatory Alphabet Soup

Every country has its own regulations, and many regulations are international. Among those regulations that are motivating substantial change in many of today's companies are:

- *Sarbanes-Oxley Act of 2002* (Sarbanes-Oxley, SarbOx, or SOX): Regulates how U.S.-based public companies must manage and store financial records, both paper and electronic, as well as certification of financial reports by chief executive officers (CEOs) and chief financial officers (CFOs), as well as a laundry list of rules about executive loans and compensation and auditing. Executives can go to jail for violating this one.
- *The Uniting and Strengthening America by Providing Appropriate Tools Required to Intercept and Obstruct Terrorism Act of 2001* (PATRIOT Act): Revised rules involving information-gathering and criminal procedure with respect to cases of suspected terrorism in the United States. This act is particularly controversial, and Congress may decide to amend it at some point.
- *Basel II*: Rules put together by central bankers from around the world aimed at producing uniformity in how banks and banking regulators approach risk management across national borders.
- *American Health Insurance Portability and Accountability Act of 1996* (HIPAA): A set of rules that health plans, doctors, hospitals, and other healthcare providers must follow, including requirements for using standard formats for electronic data interchange and a range of privacy rules governing the protection of patient records.

Needless to say, there are hundreds more.

these concerns to electronic transmissions. As a result, such regulations are examples of changes to the business environment that companies *must* respond to, and they *must* use IT to meet the requirements of the regulations to avoid substantial financial and personal penalties. Not only is nonimplementation of these regulations as a result of resistance to change not an option, but resistance to applying IT to solving the problems of change is not an option either.

These regulatory issues represent arbitrary forces of change on business that both directly impact IT as well as require changes in IT in order to satisfy the new set of requirements facing the business. Regulatory changes, however, are only one piece in the puzzle of change that companies face today. Compounding these problems are competitive pressures, changes in customer demand, the continual push to increase shareholder value and profits while driving down costs, and more. Companies not only must respond to such forces, but must be able to respond better than their competition, or they risk being the other guy's lunch.

Faced with these diverse pressures coupled with the human resistance to change, where is a CEO going to look for relief? Although the answer lies in IT, it doesn't rely on the inflexible IT of today. Organizations must organize their IT and how their business leverages the resources of IT to respond more quickly to change and to leverage change for competitive advantage. In other words, companies must implement more *agile* IT approaches to make their business more agile.

NEED FOR BUSINESS AGILITY

Given the requirement for change plus the resistance to change, how can companies even attempt to make progress? If business agility is the secret to being successful in environments of continual change, then it makes sense for us to take a close look at just what agility is. Fortunately, we have billions of years of experience to learn from: lessons from nature. And the lesson we can learn from nature is: Adapt and be agile or die.

As Charles Darwin explained in *On the Origin of Species,* agility includes the notion of *adaptability,* or fitness for survival in the face of change. In fact, Darwin said that the *fittest* species were those that survive, not the ones that were the strongest. Mammals survived when dinosaurs didn't because the mammals were the species that were able to deal with unpredictable change. Even with their significant numbers, resources, and size advantages, dinosaurs had only a limited ability to adapt to circumstances. When an asteroid suddenly hit the planet, the ensuing climatic change was too much for them to cope with, and they died out.

Many businesses are literally like dinosaurs in this regard: Companies tend to stick with the status quo until changes in their environment force them to react. The world and markets can shift significantly in a very short amount of time, driving businesses slow to adapt to extinction and rewarding nimble, agile ones with success. Slow-adapting companies scramble to stay afloat, while their more nimble competitors all of a sudden get the opportunity to capitalize on whatever is new.

However, the newly successful and agile companies often establish their own status quo, and the process repeats itself many years later. How can businesses aim to survive, even in environments of unpredictable change? The answer is *business agility*. The question then becomes: How can companies progress from the inflexible, change-resistant form they are in now to become businesses that can survive dramatic change? In other words, how can companies become more agile?

Defining Business Agility

We define *business agility* as the ability to respond quickly and efficiently to changes in the business environment and to leverage those changes for competitive advantage. Companies that can make effective use of a changing environment are better able to compete and thrive in any business climate. The most important aspect of this definition is the fact that it comes in two parts: the ability-to-respond part and the leverage-change part. The ability to respond to change is the reactive, tactical aspect of business agility. Clearly, the faster and more efficiently companies can respond to changes, the more agile they are. Achieving rapid, efficient response is akin to driving costs out of the business: It's always a good thing, but has diminishing returns over time as responses get about as fast and efficient as possible. Needless to say, your competition is also trying to improve their responses to changes in the market, so it's only a matter of time till they catch up with you (or you catch up with them, for that matter).

The second, proactive half of the business agility equation—leveraging change for competitive advantage—is by far the most interesting and powerful part of the story. Companies that not only respond to changes but actually see them as a way to improve their business often move ahead of the competition as they leverage change for strategic advantage. And *strategic* advantages—those that distinguish one company's value proposition from another's—can be far more durable than tactical advantages, such as better responsiveness to change.

One great example of the ability to leverage change for strategic advantage was MCI's "Friends and Family" offering launched in 1991. MCI offered discounts to customers who joined groups of other MCI customers. The competition was caught flat-footed, because their technology was unable to provide a competitive offering for years to come. MCI had introduced a change into the marketplace, leveraged it for competitive advantage, and made hundreds of millions of dollars as a result.

Debuzzifying Business Agility

Unfortunately, the term *agility* has become a buzzword in many circles. We want to deflate that buzz-balloon here and now. Some people define agility as simply being an alignment of the objectives of different, disparate parts of the organization, such as business and IT. However, companies have been attempting such alignment for years, without any impact on their agility. It's one thing to try to get different groups together to discuss their differences and come up with joint plans, and another thing for the business to operate as one cohesive whole, moving on a dime to adapt to new needs. So, alignment is certainly one part of, but not the same as, business agility.

Another key concept that comes up in conjunction with agility is the notion of *synchronicity*, implying that multiple things all happen at the same time, we hope with the same intent. Synchronized swimming is a good example of complex systems made simple through the sheer act of good timing and well-communicated intentions. However, synchronicity by itself cannot guarantee agility, because the organization must still be able to react to new, unpredictable stimuli. So, companies can have both alignment and synchronization and still be caught entirely by surprise by some change in their environment. Basically, companies require approaches to deal with unplanned changes. Fortunately, we'll be giving you some of those techniques in this book.

Impediments to Agility

Business agility, of course, isn't easy—if it were, you wouldn't need to read this book. Let's take a look at the key impediments to making business agility happen in today's companies. Most of these impediments fall into three broad categories:

1. *Complexity.* Today's enterprise environment contains many different people, processes, and departments that work in many different, and often conflicting, ways. The situation is even worse on the technology side of things. To deal with ever-increasing complexity in IT, companies must hire large, multiskilled teams to develop, deploy, and manage layers upon layers of IT infrastructure accumulated over time, through mergers and acquisitions, management changes, and multitudes of individual initiatives and tactical solutions to short-term problems. Considering

that many large organizations have been layering on such complexity for decades, it's no wonder that many enterprises have an intractable mess on their hands.

2. *Inflexibility.*   With complexity comes inflexibility. As pointed out earlier in this chapter, virtually every enterprise has existing processes and technology that are challenging to upgrade, difficult to improve, and, worst of all, impractical to replace. Companies tend to fall into the "if it works, don't screw with it" mode of thinking, which works well when business requirements don't change but significantly impedes agility when companies are faced with new situations.

3. *Brittleness.*   The flip side of inflexibility is brittleness: the risk of failure and other problems that result from excessive complexity and inflexibility. Because many companies grow organically over time, especially those that are prone to mergers and acquisitions, their organizations are often tangled spaghetti of different processes and technologies. As a result, when circumstances force them to change the status quo, they must either undertake expensive, risky improvement projects or simply make do with processes and technology that no longer meets the needs of the business. It is this risk inherent in making changes to complex, inflexible parts of the business that impedes the efforts of many companies to be more agile.

Clearly, the larger an organization is, the more challenging agility becomes. Big company management typically has poor visibility into the various aspects of the business that are changing and those that they need to modify. Layers of decision making, approvals, and ingrained processes bog down the impetus for change in the company. Just as it takes miles for a supertanker to change direction, large companies are inhibited by virtue of their own size. Disparate technologies impede the rapid implementation of changes, and cultural resistance to change is rampant in large companies where being invisible and "not making waves" is often a daily mantra for middle management.

However, small companies are not immune to the challenges of business agility either. Many small companies can't deal with unplanned change because they simply have insufficient resources, they're operating at their maximum capacity, or their centralized management is simply resistant to change. The challenge for companies both large and small, then, is to develop a culture, infrastructure, and resources that enable them to change on a dime as changing needs emerge.

CHAPTER 2

If You're in a Hole, the First Thing to Do Is Stop Digging

Isn't it interesting how some problems only continue to get worse over time? It is as if the problems have some mind of their own and grow like weeds in a well-fertilized lawn. Some problems seem to happen in spite of all of our efforts to prevent them, like that poor chap Murphy immortalized into his law "Whatever can go wrong will go wrong." However, although we can't avoid all our problems in life, at least we can avoid making them worse.

Case in point: the "Big Dig" boondoggle of a civil engineering project that took place in Boston starting in the mid-1980s. A project with the seemingly simple goal of reducing traffic congestion by moving high-traffic corridors under the overcrowded streets of the city of Boston ballooned into a multidecade, multibillion-dollar blunder that to this day has yet to be completed. With billions already invested in this project, there seems to be no other option but to invest billions more. Alas, it seems that our IT systems are often Big Dig boondoggles of their own. Somehow, we must emerge from our black hole of spending—and the best way to do that is to stop digging the hole deeper.

IT DECISION MAKING'S FATAL FLAW

Businesses, like people, are complex organisms. The larger the business, the more complex it becomes, by virtue of its numerous moving parts. However, what makes businesses complex are not just the number of employees, systems, and processes they are composed of but also the sheer number of decisions that their people make on a daily basis. In fact, instead of examining the parts of a business, an alternative way to look at a business is to take a close look at the way that people make decisions and the impact those decisions have on an organization's long-term success.

People throughout an organization make decisions, with different amounts of impact on the company's success. Big ones, such as decisions to acquire other firms or enter new markets, can in turn spawn hundreds of other, smaller decisions. Other decisions, such as whether to take a lunch break, are less critical but still impact the business, especially if the people taking the break are responsible for a vital task. However, it is the totality of *all* the decisions that people make, regardless of where in the organization they emerge, that determines a business's overall success. In particular, decisions made by different parts of the organization are often in conflict with each other, leading to wasted effort and, of course, much-dreaded inflexibility. Obviously, to counter the plague of inflexibility, we must first understand the decision-making process in the organization, especially as it applies to IT.

A decision is a real, tangible thing—that's why we say we *make* a decision rather than *think* a decision. Decisions have real outcomes and tangible consequences, and people have a wide range of motivations for making decisions, many of which have nothing to do with long-term business goals. Given that decisions are tangible things, it's clear that the more decisions people make, the more potential for problems there are.

People always make decisions in light of the facts that are apparent at the time as well as their own motivations. The more facts that they know or the more facts have proven themselves over time to be correct, the easier making a decision becomes. The more that people's motivations are in line with the business, the greater the likelihood that their decisions will result in positive benefits for the business. However, in light of few facts and poor alignment with business goals, decision making in IT has proven to be problematic, at best.

Why Incremental Decision Making Leads to Exponential Problems

IT executives approach spending with the best of intentions and with the desire to solve the problems that senior management and market conditions mandate. And this is where the problem begins. As technology continues to mature at a rapid and unrelenting pace, any technology purchasing decision made today will necessarily be obsolete by tomorrow. Given the pressure to solve big problems with limited facts and inflexible technologies, it is often easier to make smaller, incremental decisions than it is to rethink a corporation's overall IT goal and structure. However, some managers feel that it is simpler to make decisions without thinking through all the resulting consequences.

Furthermore, the IT decision-making process is fraught with emotion in ways that imperil the well-being of the corporation. No one likes to be wrong, so when facts change and a decision proves to be mistaken, many IT managers will simply redouble their efforts to prove that their decision was right rather than take a step back, change their minds, and make a new decision based on the new facts. The motivation to save face versus the motivation to do "what's right" therefore hurts IT significantly. And the promises of technology vendors that claim to solve recurring IT problems sway many IT managers, or at least extend the tenure of their ill-advised decisions. This inertia toward recurrent decision making that continues in a poor direction becomes an IT "religion" that often pits rational, business-led thought against emotional, egotistic resistance.

But IT decision making's fatal flaw is one that takes into consideration only today's requirements. Such shortsighted decisions necessarily result in inflexible, brittle systems that become loaded with emotional baggage and inertia. Just as in developing countries, where independent individual decisions to connect one building's electrical supply to another results in a chaotic, fragile mess, shortsighted decisions plague today's IT organizations. Even though the decisions may solve today's problems, they result in a mess that eventually requires the total replacement of the existing system.

Where Has All the Planning Gone?

The truth of the matter is that the senior management in most companies doesn't have the stomach to make investments that go beyond problems that affect one or two quarters. There's simply too much risk involved in engaging in multiyear, total-company alignment initiatives, especially given the reality of constant change. And so, although companies desire long-term flexibility, they in fact reward short-term decision making that addresses only today's requirements.

Companies reward short-term, incremental decision making in a number of ways. First, they want to quickly turn their IT investments into realizable business gains and move on to the next project as promptly as possible. When these projects relate to products or services a company offers, we call this a desire for fast *time-to-market*. When these projects solve internal problems or address general business requirements, we say that businesses desire quick *return on investment*. And so organizations reward developers and IT staff when they achieve those goals as rapidly as possible, even if the approach they take compromises long-term flexibility.

Companies also motivate their IT organizations to spend as little as possible to solve the given problem at hand. Cached in business code-word phrases such as lowest *total cost of ownership* (TCO), the desire to spend very little often comes at a compromise to long-term viability of the systems that they are implementing. It's much cheaper to repair a broken window with tape or fix a car with bailing wire and chewing gum than it is to replace the broken parts. Although those low-cost solutions might indeed solve the problem at hand, they will come back to bite a company in the rear when inevitable changes stress those short-term solutions to the breaking point.

And yet, even though IT managers might be aware of the shortcomings of a narrow focus, they do nothing to mitigate the potential damage, because nobody is rewarding them for doing so. Very few businesses reward IT management for spending more than absolutely necessary to solve a problem in a more robust way or to take longer than necessary to build a more robust solution that might be able to meet unforeseen needs. The prevailing wisdom for most IT organizations is to move as quickly and spend as little as possible today, and to push potential problems into the future for someone else to solve. (Sounds like how we got into the Y2K mess, doesn't it?)

Breaking the Cycle of Shortsightedness

However, we're not suggesting you ignore the business goals of fast time to market, speedy return on investment, and overall low total cost of ownership. Those are all noble and mandatory goals for businesses. It's not the questions you're asking, rather it's the time frame in which you're seeking the answers. Are companies interested in fast time-to-market for just one project or for *all* their projects going forward? Do businesses want the lowest total cost for just that one particular implementation or to reduce the ongoing cost of *all* their future implementations? Are companies most interested in realizing a quick business return for one particular investment or for all investments going forward? Clearly, the optimal answer realizes benefits both in the here and now as well as in the not-too-distant future.

Understanding how to make the right decisions to realize the most benefits both now and in the future is the trick that's required to implement the next wave of IT solutions and is an essential prerequisite of Service Orientation. In this book we hope to convince you that the technology required to implement the vision of flexible business that can respond to unpredictable change doesn't matter as much as the decision-making process you should use to implement technology as a whole. The proper decision-making process will determine the very success of your business and will bring you that much closer to realizing the vision of a flexible and agile business.

THE IT "RATS' NEST"

Sigmund Freud once conjectured that at our core, we're all animals, and our primitive desires motivate us in all of our activities. Obtaining food, securing a family, and procuring shelter are certainly such core desires. As a result, it's no surprise that people like the idea of building comfortable nests for themselves. For instance, the notion of building a "nest egg" and returning home to the family nest (unless your children have left, in which case, you are an "empty nester") are all comforting thoughts to people.

It is no surprise, then, that we find nests rife in IT systems in the organization; and these nests are not a desirable kind by any means. In the course of building the sort of systems that satisfy the basic desires of IT, we have developed a "rats' nest" of systems, processes, and relationships among them that threaten to strangle all the flexibility out of business. What do we mean by a rats' nest, and how did we get here in the first place?

Interconnectedness of Systems

As we discussed earlier, most IT decision making is of the short-term, incremental, and shortsighted kind. Early on in a company's life, IT management tends to make simple, straightforward decisions to solve current problems with specific answers, but over time, incremental solutions to new problems increasingly require some level of dependency on previous solutions. And so, although little complexity or interdependency exists in the first set of systems a company might implement, over time these incremental decisions result in a spaghetti of connections, processes, and technical dependencies that only grow *more* complex.

In fact, computer scientists often speak of complexity problems like the one we just described as a problem that grows in *geometric,* or "*n*-squared," complexity over time. Some problems double in complexity as you double the number of elements that contribute to them. For example, remembering a list of 20 people's names is twice as difficult as remembering a list of 10 names. Such linear problems are reasonably manageable; you need to have only incrementally greater resources to deal with such problems that grow incrementally.

However, other problems grow with the *square* of the number of elements that contribute to them. For example, more than four times as many handshakes are required in a group of eight people to shake each other's hands as there are in a group of four. So, in this case, doubling the size of the problem *quadruples* the complexity at hand. For example, if you wanted to connect two computers, you would have a system that looked something like that shown in Exhibit 2.1(a). So far, so good. Add a third computer, and you have Exhibit 2.1(b). Not too complicated, right? Okay, add a fourth, and you get Exhibit 2.1(c). Now we're getting a bit messy. Note how we need six arrows to connect four computers? Well, let's cut to the chase. What if you had dozens or even hundreds of different things to connect? Exhibit 2.1(d) shows a vastly simplified look.

That's what we mean by the rats' nest: If you don't have some sort of organizing principle, then even though each incremental change might be simple and straightforward, over time the sum total of all such changes gets out of hand. Clearly, these problems become not only more complex, but more expensive and hopeless over time. Businesses eventually won't be able to survive with problems that continue to grow at geometric rates.

And yet the problem of interconnected systems and processes is exactly the type of problem that grows with geometric complexity. The more systems people build and the more processes they develop, the more they depend on previous solutions and processes. As they continue to solve more problems incrementally, the number of dependencies increases geometrically, to the point where companies now spend most of their time managing the interconnections and dependencies than managing the systems and processes themselves.

We call this situation a rats' nest because rats aren't known for their cleanliness or orderliness. And so a great analogy to describe the sort of interconnected mess of systems and dependencies is the sort of messy nest that a rat would make. Birds' nests are great for soup. Rats' nests are good for nothing (except maybe baby rats). Just so with IT. We must not only deal with the decision-making process that results in rats' nests of systems, but we must also come up with a way to untangle the complex spaghetti of dependencies so that we don't have to resort to throwing away the whole mess and starting from scratch. Furthermore, we also need to figure out how to avoid creating rats' nests in the future.

Rats' Nests and Return on Investment

The reason companies build rats' nests in the first place is quite straightforward: Each individual decision is the least expensive, most expedient choice they can make at the time. And after all, isn't everybody supposed to choose the least expensive, most expedient option whenever they're faced with a decision? The surprising fact is that adding up several least expensive, most expedient options doesn't yield either the least expensive or most expedient overall long-term solution. On the contrary, rats' nests are among the most expensive, time-consuming parts of IT today. So, why do we keep making decisions and investments the way we do?

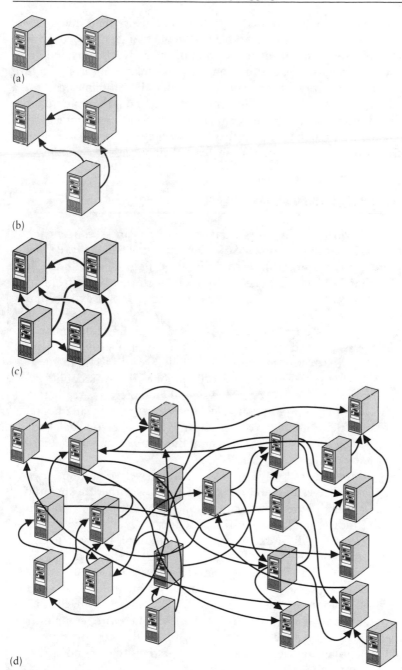

FIGURE 2.1　How to Build a Rats' Nest

The answer has to do with the way companies justify their investments. Despite the relentless and unpredictable nature of change, many companies seek comfort in some sort of quantification of their investments and gains from those investments. The desire to quantify the unknown through return on investment calculations is very understandable. If companies can get a grasp on how much they're spending on something, and if they can quantify what sort of return they are getting, either through top-line revenue growth or bottom-line cost reduction, then they believe they can make sound business decisions that are guaranteed to increase their success.

Jargon Watch: Return on Investment

Return on investment (ROI) is a fairly simple business concept for quantifying the business value of some investment. Technically, ROI is a measure of a company's ability to use its assets to generate additional value for shareholders. To calculate ROI, divide the net profit from an investment by the net worth of the assets invested, and express the answer as a percentage.

An ROI calculation exercise consists of determining how much a company must invest to realize some quantifiable business gain. However, software, hardware, and solutions vendors bandy about the term *ROI* as if it were some simple-to-identify number that you could easily glean from a spreadsheet or a Web site. In fact, there are really two kinds of ROI: the kind you can calculate *after the fact* using actual numbers and the kind that you can postulate *before* you make the investment. The problem is that neither of these ROI numbers matches reality when it comes to IT.

Many companies fail to accurately, quantitatively determine how much a given IT investment returns to the business, either through the addition of top-line revenue or the elimination of bottom-line cost. In fact, the business often fails to justify the effort to quantify the return, and so after-the-fact ROI calculations are actually a rarity. Furthermore, before-the-fact ROI calculations are too often pie-in-the-sky theoretical values that companies scarcely, if ever, achieve in reality. There are simply too many factors and unknown quantities that affect a business's ability to realize a promised ROI, so most before-the-fact ROI calculations are wishful thinking at best. Therefore, companies must rethink their approach for calculating the ROI for IT investments in light of ongoing change and the ability of systems to respond to that change economically.

In fact, businesses regularly think in terms of ROI. Companies determine whether to hire people based on their return to the business, build factories based on their contribution to the top line, and outsource business processes that can reduce their operational expenses. Thus, it's no surprise that companies want to apply the same rationale to IT systems. The problem is that ROI calculations typically focus on the short term—this month or this quarter—and only occasionally as much as a year. In addition, although the number and complexity of factories and marketing campaigns are fairly limited and well understood, the number of IT systems and business processes number in the hundreds, thousands, or perhaps even millions. In many cases, it simply isn't possible to calculate the required total investment in a given IT system that takes years to build, let alone quantify the business return of that investment.

However, the problem is not just the inability to pin numbers on complexity. More often than not, management gets in the way of realizing any ROI from an investment. Cultural resistance to change, emotional religious wars, shortsighted planning, and unintentional sabotage by misguided middle management often impede the ability to complete an investment according to a well-thought-out plan. And if a company can't even complete a project according to its wishes, how could it ever hope to get a planned return?

An even bigger problem is that the calculated ROI for a project is meaningful only if an investment is independent from other, ongoing investments an organization is making. What happens when two concurrent projects, each with its own planned ROI, are in fact dependent on each other in ways that are not well understood? How will those dependencies increase cost, and hence investment, more than anticipated? And even worse, how will interdependencies negatively impact the realization of business return? How can companies deign to pin an ROI on multiyear projects that involve so much complexity and interdependency that the organization is lucky even to complete the project, let alone have it deliver real value?

The IT rats' nest not only harms companies' ability to respond to unpredictable change, but makes the task of ROI calculation an impossibility. The challenge of determining the "I," or investment part of ROI, the impossibility of determining the "R," or return, and the inability to calculate long-term ROI in the face of geometric complexity makes ROI meaningless in an environment where businesses rarely understand the full scope of the interdependency of their systems.

WHY ARE THE NERDS SITTING AT THEIR OWN TABLE?

We have a confession to make. We were among those nerds you remember from high school. You know the type: finished calculus in tenth grade, won the state math contest, took courses at the local college while in high school, and not only won but *ran* their school's science fairs. Now, before you roll your eyes (oops! too late!), let us make our point. Back then, nerds like us were ostracized, relegated to chess club limbo, while everybody else went to parties, got in trouble, and basically acted like regular high school kids.

Now that we're all adults, that old social division from high school still haunts us in the form of "technical" and "nontechnical" people. Look inside any company or on any job board, and this division is readily apparent. A techie's resume is chock-full of acronyms, and careers tend to progress by tackling increasingly more complex projects. However, a nontechnical person's resume is supposed to focus on money saved or earned: "reduced cost by 20%" or "increased revenue by 15%" are the nontechie's equivalent of "developed J2EE-based server solution using WebLogic." The nontechnical person frequently runs the company or manages the largest budget, while the techies are relegated to the part of the business that incurs the costs and spends time on the technical details. Yup, the nontechies are still the captains of the football team while the nerds are still in the business equivalent of the chess club.

For many organizations, this technical versus nontechnical dichotomy is actually getting wider. Ask a typical executive what Linux or J2EE or ERP or (insert technical term here) means, and the best answer you're likely to get, if you don't just get a blank stare, is some high-level simplification. The

---

Jargon Watch: Techie

The term *techie* is a colloquial term for *technologist,* who is a person with a deep understanding of technology and who applies that understanding in work. Needless to say, there are many less complimentary terms for techies, including *nerd* and *geek,* but we'll generally try to avoid these terms in this book since, after all, we're techies ourselves.

The opposite of techie for the purposes of this book might be *businessperson.* There are fewer derogatory terms for such folks, although *suit* comes to mind as a popular one, as in "the meeting was filled with geeks and suits." To be fair to all the suits out there, we'll avoid using this term as well.

business press isn't a big help either. You would think that *The Wall Street Journal,* for example, would talk about IT issues from a perspective that a nontechie would find compelling, but you'd be hard-pressed to find anything but a superficial discussion of the latest IT trends and some examples of how certain businesses benefited in this most business-oriented of business periodicals. After all, the paper wouldn't want to get too technical for fear of losing its audience. How then are businesspeople going to understand the power, complexity, and risks facing IT, if they can't understand the techies, and the business press gives them nothing but superficialities? The answer is, many won't, at least not until it's too late.

Merging Worlds of Business and IT

Techies usually get a sense of empowerment from the knowledge that they simply know how things work—at least, how technical things work. Now, if you're a techie, this is no excuse to gloat; the techie world is no more enlightened about business than the business world is about technology. For many techies, the business world is a necessary evil that's most useful for generating paychecks. Many techies wouldn't admit it out loud, but their jobs would be so much damn *easier* if only it weren't for all the users! (A *user,* after all, is a techie's term for "everyone who's not a techie.") When technologists do delve into business issues, it's often on a simplistic level, for example, when data-centric folks think about customers as sets of data fields rather than as living, breathing humans with unique concerns and motivations. A techie revels in the complexity of object-oriented systems and database optimizations but can't tell a general ledger from a General Mills' cereal box.

Now that we've alienated both our business and technical readers, let's get to the critical point: *It doesn't have to be this way.* Although clearly, people must specialize in their field of interest, regardless of whether it is technical or nontechnical, there is a large gap in the business world when it comes to business-savvy technologists (or technical businesspeople, if you will) and technologies that are firmly rooted in the nontechnical side of the business. After all, there's no getting around the fact that technology is becoming increasingly pervasive in the business world, and likewise, there's no avoiding the fact that IT must respond better to the changing forces of business.

There's no reason why businesspeople can't have a reasonably good understanding of technology and why technologists can't likewise have a pretty good grasp of business. In fact, many people actually do have such an understanding, and they are the ones who are often the most successful at companies that leverage IT for critical business value. Many of today's software applications and systems would have been considered too complex for business users only a few decades ago. A generation ago, highly trained professionals who wore lab coats managed computer systems in the department known at the time as *data processing.* Hardly any techies got close enough to the systems to get any value from them, let alone business users. Had someone in executive management proposed letting business users control their own information, the lab coat–wearing techies would simply have laughed. Today's computers, however, while thousands of times more powerful than the computers of the data processing days, are significantly more simple and easier to understand, and thus well within reach of businesspeople. As such, we can afford now to think of putting the power of computing in the hands of the nontechies.

Such technology-savvy business users are often called *knowledge workers* or *information workers,* pointing out the fact that dealing with information is a key part of their day-to-day work. These people not only use their computer and other high-tech gizmos on a daily basis, but they're actually *comfortable* doing so. They are advanced users of the applications most valuable to them, and they have a reasonable understanding of the distributed technology behind the scenes. Even though they may not know all of the technical details of how those systems work, they are experts at wringing the last bit of productivity and efficiency from them.

Likewise, there is a rising class of business-savvy technologists as well. Many of these people began their careers as "hard-core" techies, but then moved into a more business-oriented role. They often have titles of *analyst* or *product manager* or the like, and they are able to leverage their deep technical understanding of IT to better address the business issues at hand in their work. Chief information officers almost always fall into this category, and an increasing number of chief executive officers do as well.

If these knowledge workers and business-savvy techies can do it, well, why can't you? Or more to the point, why *don't* you? After all, these crossover professionals often get paid more and have better long-term career prospects than either low-tech businesspeople or business-adverse techies. With all the ways to improve your skills, through formal training, working with a particular mentor, and extracurricular learning through books, Web sites, and the like, there is little excuse for nontechie business folks not to improve their knowledge. The more that techies get involved with the day-to-day operations of the business, and the more that nontechies explore the ways that IT can make them more effective, the more that the worlds of business and IT will merge.

Why Crossover Professionals Are So Important

The reason why we're taking the time to discuss the issue of business-savvy techies and tech-savvy businesspeople is because the long-term trend in the business world is toward a future where there's no separation between business and technology in the typical enterprise. In this vision, all technology is simply a business resource to meet business needs, just like office furniture or human resources or finance. Furthermore, the day-to-day work of businesspeople will become steeped in technology—a trend we're seeing today, with all the phones, CrackBerries, and the like that today's business executives have to carry with them at all times. It will simply become impossible for businesspeople to run their daily lives without deep immersion in technology, and it will be impossible for the technical part of a business to operate without a strong business mandate.

Consider the hypothetical scenario in which everybody in your organization is equally proficient in business and technology, so that there is no need to separate the two types of efforts into different groups or departments. Would your company be as likely to go down the IT rats' nest trap we discussed earlier? Remember, the reason people go down the path to the rats' nest is because at every step, they select the cheapest, most expedient option and don't consider long-term gains over short-term benefits. But what if all the executives in your organization understood the value and importance of combining long-term IT planning with short-term goals? What if business users had enough technical acumen to understand the subtleties behind such technology trade-offs? And what if techies knew enough about the business to know when they are playing a losing game of connect-the-system? There's no guarantee, but the chances are significant that your company would never have built a rats' nest in the first place.

Now, that thought exercise is clearly unrealistic on its face because today's business leaders are not proficient in technology, and many technologists simply have no interest in running the business. What's more realistic is to expect *some* executives at *some* companies to really get it—and to build a deep understanding of technological realities into the way they do business. Those technology/business *crossovers* who can build such an understanding will be more successful in their careers than the dinosaurs they leave behind. And companies that can make this change across their organizations will be more competitive, more agile, and, in the long run, more successful than their competitors who are unable to make this shift toward business/technology savvy.

For those of us techies who were stuck in chess club limbo, this broad trend in twenty-first-century business is the revenge-of-the-nerds scenario we so hoped for in our high school years. The popular kids may have gotten all the attention back in high school, but if they weren't able to pick up sufficient technology savvy, then their careers will plateau—and where will their popularity be then? A knowledge of technology will make business folks more popular than ever. For us nerds who build business expertise on top of a technical background, the world is our oyster!

CHAPTER 3

What *Really* Happened to eBusiness

Before we go any further, let's put to bed any discussion of that common consulting-speak cliché, *business-IT alignment*. Speak to consultants about spending money on IT, and they talk about business-IT alignment. Ask chief information officers what they're trying to accomplish, and they might include the term *business-IT alignment* in their strategy discussion. Business-IT alignment supposedly describes the goal of any IT initiative as bringing the capabilities of IT into alignment with business requirements. In a very real sense, then, this book is actually *about* business-IT alignment. So, if that's the case, why are we so eager to bury the term?

The problem with using the *business-IT alignment* term is that alignment simply means bringing different sections of the business together to accomplish some goal. The problems of aligning IT and business are as old at IT itself, and we never seem to make much progress in aligning anything, since corporate inflexibility and resistance to change impedes even the very act of attempting alignment. The elixir of promised agility through business-IT alignment continues to intoxicate businesses, however, when it's time for one more consultant's tired presentation on why some company should spend countless more bazillions of dollars on IT.

Now, don't get us wrong—although *alignment* may be a tired and empty term, there's no question that there has been dramatic progress in IT in the past 50 years and that IT continues to solve an ever-increasing range of business problems. To truly understand that progress, however, it's essential to strip away the platitudes and hype that surrounds the terminology and get down to what problems technology is actually solving and what problems yet remain for us to solve.

EBUSINESS WAS A GREAT IDEA, SO WHAT HAPPENED?

Nowhere has the hype surrounding business-IT alignment gotten so out of hand as with the topic of eBusiness. *eBusiness* is short for *electronic business,*

Jargon Watch: eBusiness and eCommerce

eBusiness refers to the leveraging of IT resources throughout all of a company's business processes. Broader than simply selling stuff online, eBusiness was supposed to transform businesses in their entirety. *eCommerce* is a special, limited case of eBusiness activity that does mean selling stuff on the Web. The most familiar kind of eCommerce is business-to-consumer (B2C). Amazon.com is the most familiar example of a B2C eCommerce company. When eCommerce takes place between businesses, it is business-to-business (B2B).

although the "e" prefix has taken on a life of its own. At its most basic, *eBusiness* refers to enabling a wide range of business functions and business processes that through the use of IT or, more broadly, to companies that have business processes that leverage IT. That definition is really too broad, however, as under that definition just about any company today would qualify as an eBusiness. To give the term more meaning, then, let's define an eBusiness as a company that leverages IT resources throughout all of its business processes—in other words, a company where IT is pervasive in the operation of the organization.

The eBusiness hype machine kicked into full gear in the late 1990s with the rise of the Internet and the World Wide Web. For a while, eBusiness seemed like a fantastic idea. We were building a New Economy, after all—companies could either jump on the eBusiness bandwagon or die a slow, horrible death as Old Economy dinosaurs, according to the marketing hype. We were talking business-IT alignment like never before! According to the media, vendors, and newly invigorated consulting companies, the New Economy would perfectly align business and IT—finally!

Then in 2000, the dot-com crash hit, the bubble burst, and thoughts of the New Economy faded like a bad dream upon awakening. Companies realized that while the boom brought new, useful technologies, their businesses stayed fundamentally the same. The New Economy was really the old economy with the addition of some new technology for reaching potential customers. Many relegated the pie-in-the-sky vision of eBusiness to the dustbin of unrealistic aspirations. Those of us who got caught up, and invested, in the whirlwind of hype saw our stock portfolios dwindle to nothing and went out to try to get a real job once again. eBusiness was dead—or was it?

Jargon Watch: Internet and World Wide Web

Bear with us here—if you already know what the terms *network*, *Internet*, and *World Wide Web* mean, feel free to skip this Jargon Watch. The reason why we explain these things is that we want to ensure everybody has a basic understanding of today's technology. If you know these concepts already, consider this Jargon Watch a review so that we know we're all on the same track.

However, for those of you who have always wondered about the specifics but were afraid to ask, here's a concise set of definitions for you. A *network* is a set of computers (or other devices, such as printers) that are able to communicate with each other via an established set of protocols. The *Internet* is a network of networks across the globe, all linked together via a sophisticated set of standard protocols that provide for interoperability across a wide range of different brands and types of equipment. Originally a U.S. Department of Defense project, the Internet now spans every country and is available for the world to use.

The *World Wide Web*, or the Web for short, is one application of the Internet, but is not the same as the Internet. eMail, for example, is another application of the Internet that is not the same as the Web. The Web is a collection of *Web pages*, which are generally small files on computers called *Web servers* that applications called *browsers* can display. Web pages display text, pictures, and now any number of other media, and they also have *hyperlinks*, which connect pages with one another across the Web. It is this interconnectedness that underlies the true power of the Web.

A collection of Web pages on a Web server is a *Web site*, and most Web sites have *domain names*, such as www.zapthink.com. The domain name is the address of the site, and can tell you how to get to the site from any browser on the Internet. By convention, many domain names end in ".*com*," pronounced "dot com." The term *dot-com* has come to refer to the whole late 1990s Internet build-out/stock market bubble phenomenon. Of course, we know now that domain names had little to do with the build-out and crash that followed, but rather the overpromising and underdelivering of eBusiness was more at fault.

A Closer Look at eBusiness's "Demise"

The story of eBusiness is inextricably intertwined with the period in the late 1990s often referred to as the dot-com bubble. This period, generally considered to have begun in August 1995 with the initial public offering of Netscape and ending in April 2000 with the sudden downturn of technology-related stocks, was actually a "perfect storm" of occurrences that happened to coincide. These three occurrences were the rise of the Internet, the problems associated with computers rolling over from the year 1999 to 2000 (often called Y2K), and the stock market bubble that drove technology and Internet stock prices to outrageous highs.

Any one of these three sets of events would have been enough to drive substantial change in both business and IT. The fact that all three phenomena coincided led to the perfect storm aspect of the period. To understand what happened to eBusiness, therefore, it's important to unravel this tangled knot of history and look more closely at what really happened.

The tale begins with the secret of the World Wide Web's success: open standards. Started by a European physics researcher, the Web grew through the clever use of a small number of standards that enabled any computer on the Internet to access information from any other computer on the Internet set up to be a Web server. In the early days, most Web servers used free software based on these standards, and the early browsers were also free and also relied on these standards. Suddenly anybody in the world could connect to the Internet and view Web pages that anybody else on the Internet could publish. It didn't matter what kind of computer you ran, or which server published the Web pages; it just worked.

At about the same time during the early 1990s, a political and social change also took place—one that people rarely consider important in the growth of eBusiness but that was nevertheless critical: the exponential rise of the adult entertainment industry. When Bill Clinton's administration came to power in 1993, the federal government decided not to enforce a range of obscenity laws, and the adult industry exploded, first with videos, then with CD-ROMs, and soon with the World Wide Web. Make no mistake: The vast majority of eCommerce in the early days of the Web fell into the adult entertainment category (some might say to this day it still does).

For the first time in history, consumers of such material were able to purchase and, er, consume this content in the privacy of their own homes, legally. No trips to the seedy side of town, no risk of public embarrassment. Money poured into the coffers of the pioneers gutsy enough to build out adult businesses on the Web. Soon thousands of other businesses sprang up with Internet-centric business models, and venture capital investors took notice. Rich people would pool their extra funds and call upon investment professionals to put their money into highly speculative investments; that is, those with high risk but also potentially high reward. As the 1990s wore on, the amount of money available for investment skyrocketed, and for a while, it seemed that any college kid with a silly idea could get $50 million. The dot-com boom had arrived.

At this point in the story, madness takes over. In particular, the madness of crowds—that particular form of group lunacy that occasionally afflicts large numbers of people. Basically, if a particular stock price keeps going up for no apparent reason, eventually people lose their incredulity and desperately want to avoid being left out of the rush. After all, if everybody else is getting rich, why shouldn't you? The fact that the Internet itself made trading stocks online possible for the first time only threw gasoline on the fire. More investors than ever before threw more money than ever before into stocks with less fundamental value than ever before. But, as long as people kept throwing money in, the stocks would keep going up.

However, all was not right in this New Economy game of musical chairs. As the pace of change grew ever faster and as start-up companies trumpeted how quickly they could grow, eventually the technology couldn't keep up. The standards behind the Web worked fine for Web pages, and the IT industry was generally able to build out the technology to scale up these Web sites to support millions of users, but these high-volume Web sites were only a part of the eBusiness equation. Remember, eBusiness means leveraging IT in *all* business processes, not only the ones that involve customers sitting in front of their browsers. The rest of the business processes were left in the dust—those processes that involved interactions among computers that didn't necessarily have browsers on them, such as those involved in supply chains and financial transaction processing and the like, and more important, those processes running on systems that the mad rush to eBusiness hadn't yet impacted.

It wasn't obvious at the time, however, that the technology was not yet mature enough to realize the full eBusiness vision. Many entrepreneurs began a new business category known as the electronic marketplace, or *eMarketplace,* with the goal of bringing together buyers and sellers in one industry or another to conduct business automatically over the Internet. Virtually all such eMarketplaces foundered, however, partly because the business model was poorly conceived, but also because there were no *standard* ways to conduct this sort of automatic business.

The answer to this problem, naturally, was to create such eBusiness standards, and many companies got together to hammer some out. However, in spite of the apparent acceleration of business change the dot-com boom engendered, working out standards as complex as these business-to-business ones takes a lot of time—years, in fact. Furthermore, there's no one obvious way to go about it, and many standards efforts petered out as participants realized they were wrong turns. By the time mid-2000 rolled around, the music had stopped, and a few lucky people were able to find chairs, but many had not. Y2K was over, the speculative market bubble had popped, and the rapid pace of change had reached a roadblock. It seemed that eBusiness was dead for sure. As the next chapter explains, however, there's more to this story.

EBUSINESS IS DEAD! LONG LIVE EBUSINESS!

By the depths of the recession of 2001, the madness of crowds, missing standards, and all the games of musical chairs seemed like a six-year-long bad dream. The intoxicating days of irrational exuberance were over, and a long hangover spell quickly set in. To paraphrase Mark Twain, however, the rumors of eBusiness's demise were greatly exaggerated. We couldn't easily toss the proverbial IT baby out with the New Economy bath water. The Internet and the World Wide Web were here to stay and have found their way into corners of every industry. It's easy to forget that prior to the advancements in eBusiness the only way to trade stocks was via a telephone or in person with a broker. Whether it is looking up phone numbers, booking air travel, communicating via e-mail, or conducting research on everything from product purchases to market trends, the Internet has found its way into our everyday lives, both as consumers and as businesspeople.

eCommerce as well is bigger than ever. Most people know about the consumer-oriented eCommerce success stories like eBay and Amazon.com, but B2B eCommerce has penetrated every industry, both for direct trade between businesses and consumers as well as facilitating indirect business among all the participants in a value chain. E-mail and instant messaging further transformed communications within and among businesses, as well as both among consumers and between consumers and the companies that serve them.

The important point to remember is that the Internet didn't just *penetrate* business, it also *transformed* business. The Internet radically shifted the costs of communication, purchasing, and operations for many industries, freeing companies to invest their resources in new ways. The Internet also opened up new avenues of business that were both impossible and unimagined a mere decade ago. The Internet had the power to turn any mom-and-pop shop into a global operation doing business 24 hours a day, 7 days a week. Above all else, it is the fact that this transformation is here to stay that signals that eBusiness is very much alive.

Does eBusiness Equal the Internet?

We've been talking about the Internet as if you couldn't have eBusiness without it. However, that's not strictly true. Our definition of eBusiness, after all, doesn't even mention the Internet—for business to be eBusiness, it must leverage IT across all of its business processes, but that IT may or may not include the use of the Internet. The fact still remains, however, that IT predates the Internet by at least a few decades, and yet the Internet seems to have given birth to eBusiness. So, what's the real story here?

Before the Internet we had the ability for computers to talk to one another, both via local area networks (LANs) like those in individual offices, and wide area networks (WANs) that connected offices together across long distances. What the Internet brought to this world of LANs and WANs was a *standard, free,* and *ubiquitous* way for computers to communicate. Each of these three characteristics is essential for explaining the transformative nature of the Internet, so let's take a closer look.

1. At the core of the Internet is a set of *open standards.* Standards are nothing more than agreements among independent parties about how to go about doing some task. In the technology realm, a standard defines how two technology components will interact with each other. For a standard to be *open,* the process for developing the standard as well as the specifications of the standard are available to anyone who has an interest in using them. The Internet leveraged open standards, so that every piece of software connected to the Internet could work predictably with every other piece, as long as they all follow the same standards. Before the Internet, each LAN and WAN used proprietary protocols, so that one network couldn't talk to another, and every computer on every network had to run proprietary software to use the network.

2. The creators of the standards behind the Internet decided to give their work on those standards away *for free,* rather than charging a licensing fee or royalty for them. If they had decided to charge for them, then what we would have had were just one more set of proprietary protocols that a particular product or solutions vendor owned and controlled. Making the standards free, however, enabled any hardware or software vendor to incorporate them into their products, and before long, everybody was doing so.

3. Soon large telecommunications companies and others built out the infrastructure of the Internet so that it went everywhere. Industrialized nations came first, naturally, but before long, the Internet had penetrated even the most undeveloped of developing countries, making it virtually *ubiquitous.* Now, it's not like different regions had different

Internets, the way that the world handles electrical power or television formats. Instead, the whole world agreed on the *same* Internet.

The Internet, therefore, didn't bring about communication among computers to the world of IT, it simply made the mode of that communication standard, free, and ubiquitous. It is the combination of this new mode of communication combined with the power of the computers themselves that enabled eBusiness.

eBusiness Today

In spite of the dot-com bust and the recession that followed, technology progress continues unabated, as computers get faster, hard drives get bigger, and network bandwidth continues to increase. Roughly speaking, the power of our IT doubles every year and a half, following a rule of thumb developed by Intel's Gordon Moore, popularly known as *Moore's Law.* Moore's Law has been so remarkably consistent over the past 40 years that we're used to it by now.

Jargon Watch: Moore's Law

Postulated by Gordon Moore, chief executive officer of Intel Corporation, in 1965, *Moore's Law* states that the number of transistors per square inch of a computer chip will continue to double every 18 months. Moore's Law—or what you might call corollaries to Moore's Law—go well beyond packing transistors onto chips, something that may be of interest only to semiconductor companies, like Intel, which are in the business of packing transistors onto silicon. How fast those chips go and how powerful they are also doubles every year and a half or so, and other measures of IT capabilities double with approximately the same frequency as well, including hard drive sizes, network speeds, display technology, and more.

Furthermore, as all this power continues to explode, the cost per unit of capability continues to drop dramatically—probably the most important corollary to Moore's Law. Translated into pure business terms, Moore's Law means that the power of a computer will double every 18 months even as the cost of that computing remains stable or even decreases. Moore's Law and its corollaries have come to mean faster, better, cheaper technology on an ongoing basis, with no end in sight. For the purposes of this book, we'll lump together Moore's Law and all its corollaries under the one term *Moore's Law.*

Here's an example of how this law works. Consider the old fable about the man who had to pay a tax calculated in this way: Take a chessboard, and pay one grain of wheat for the first square, two for the second, four for the third, and so on, doubling the number of grains for each square. The man had thought the tax was quite light based on the payments for the first few squares, but by the time the whole board was taken into consideration, he owed more wheat than existed in the whole world. Such is the power of geometric growth that Moore's Law predicts.

As with the poor taxpayer, early in the days of IT we may not have conceived the sheer power that we would be able to place on our desks and carry in our pockets, and we may still find it difficult to predict what power may yet come in the future. Be that as it may, the computer power we have today makes practical tasks considered difficult or impossible a mere handful of years ago. And equally as important, the cost of that computing continues to decrease over time, such that computing power that costs thousands of thousands of dollars a few decades ago now costs mere pennies.

As an example, let's consider the process of financial reporting. Before IT, reporting took a dedicated staff of highly trained accountants to pull together the necessary financial data for a particular month or quarter. In the past few decades, dramatic improvements in computing power as well as desktop software have made the process of financial reporting and charting as simple as creating and manipulating a spreadsheet.

Moore's Law has had its inexorable effect on supply chain interactions as well. Whereas early in the twentieth century, suppliers had to do business via mounds of paperwork and complicated interpersonal interactions, now it's straightforward to automate those same relationships to the point where few, if any, individuals must participate directly in transacting business between suppliers and vendors. Since the emergence of IT, the combination of maturing standards, dramatic improvements in IT infrastructure, and the overall pressure of Moore's Law and its corollaries have led to the practicality of Service Orientation, as we'll explain in more detail later in the book

Whither eBusiness?

In spite of the continued survival of eBusiness, crowd mentality follows a basic pattern of hype followed by antihype. During the dot-com bubble, people felt like fools for staying out of the game and missing out on the riches, but after the dot-com collapse, people felt like fools for ever participating in the craziness in the first place. Such sentiment gives rise to what we like to call antihype, where people irrationally scorn a concept like eBusiness where before they irrationally championed it. Eventually such madness dies down, and people then realize the true worth of eBusiness.

Today, improvements in technology and standards have rejuvenated eBusiness, although people are still reluctant to use the term, due to its association with the dot-com boom. That's fine with us, because while the term *eBusiness* might not sit well with executives in today's businesses, companies today desire the benefits that eBusiness has promised all along. In today's world where even the smallest mom-and-pop operation has its own Web site and uses computers for point-of-sale, communication, keeping the books, and more, it won't be long until the words *eBusiness* and *business* refer to the same thing. At that point, we will have no more use for the term *eBusiness* anyway.

HOW TO THINK LIKE AN EBUSINESSPERSON

All of you techies reading this book might find this particular section boring because it is exclusively for businesspeople—in particular, businesspeople who wish to be *eBusinesspeople*. We've already talked about technology-savvy businesspeople, who not only carry around a menagerie of high-tech doodads everywhere they go, but who are also quite productive in front of a computer. We've called those individuals information workers because of the role that information and, by extension, information *technology* plays in their day-to-day work life.

Well, being tech-savvy is not sufficient to wear the mantle *eBusinessperson*. Just because you can use a computer in your day-to-day life doesn't mean that you can effectively leverage IT for the sort of business advantage that eBusiness espouses. Because in an eBusiness, IT is pervasive in the day-to-day operations of the business, the skills you need to be proficient in eBusiness go beyond checking e-mail from an airport or submitting a complex expense report. Rather, individuals require a new set of skills to understand how to manage as well as implement IT. On the plus side, however, it's not necessary to go out and take a course in computer networking or programming or anything like that. Instead, the core skill to being an effective eBusinessperson is to know how to interact with IT as *business resources*.

To understand what we mean by thinking of IT as a set of business resources, think of an appliance, say, a television set. Inside this television set are all manner of transistors and capacitors and who-knows-what-all, and if you touch the wrong thing, you're sure to be electrocuted. In fact, the TV manufacturing companies are kind enough to put a notice on their devices saying "Do not open—no user serviceable parts inside." Does this warning mean that no one can open the box to repair it? No, it means "Get your hands off this box, you schlub, unless you know what you're doing!" Needless to say, very few people have any business monkeying around inside a TV set. Outside the TV, however, we have very simple output (the screen and the speakers) and almost as simple input (the controls, as well as the connection on the back for the cable). As with any good technology, it's complicated on the inside yet simple on the outside.

Business resources should be the same way. Whether what's inside the box is IT or some other resource that's difficult to understand, such as finance, the interface should be clearly defined, well understood, and simple. If you have to open the box to monkey around with the innards, then something is wrong—not just with the resource itself, but with how your organization deals with resources. After all, not everyone in the company needs to understand every resource to make full and effective use of it.

To clarify this IT-as-TV set metaphor, consider what would happen if you outsourced all your IT capabilities, as some companies choose to do. Now, instead of working directly with the various individuals or departments within your IT department (the doodads inside the TV set, as it were), your third-party IT provider offers a clear set of instructions for how to interact with its firm and a clear expectation of what it will be providing. Maybe phone numbers to call or e-mail addresses to contact or whatever—what's important is that your company's contract with this third-party provider specifies how you will access, manage, and evolve the capabilities the provider offers to your organization. How this provider actually goes about its business is none of *your* business, as long as the provider sticks to its contract and keeps you, their customer, happy. In fact, all the people at this third-party IT provider might be halfway around the world and it wouldn't matter.

Now ask yourself: Does the fact that you've outsourced your IT to a third party matter at all as to how you access, manage, and evolve the IT resources you need? Shouldn't everything work the same regardless of whether the IT guy is in the next office or in India or China or somewhere? If your company is truly thinking of IT as business resources, then it doesn't matter whether you're outsourcing those resources, because ideally, you as the business user shouldn't be able to tell one way or another. In fact, this is the way we think of resources such as shipping and logistics, office supplies, and telecommunication—three business resources a company couldn't live without, but are all supplied by third parties.

Business Application Oxymoron

If you're in a large organization in particular, then this notion of IT as a business resource should sound familiar. After all, most large companies have help desks that work as business resources. With eBusiness, however, the pervasiveness of IT goes well beyond the help desk and the services it provides to you. Specifically, eBusinesses should package *application functionality*

Jargon Watch: Application

The common English meaning of the word *application* is essentially "what you do with something." The earliest computers generally had only one application. For example, the British government *applied* Colossus to Nazi and Japanese code-breaking, so code-breaking was its *application*.

As computers got more powerful and easier to program, their handlers could apply them to many different tasks, so each task was an application. Before long, the word *application* began to mean the same thing as *computer program*, or more specifically, a complete computer program (as opposed to a program fragment whose purpose was to participate in other programs).

Soon personal computers (PCs) came along, and with them a new market for commercial software. At that point, an *application* was a computer program you could buy (or write) that essentially ran by itself on your computer. You might have other software for your computer as well that might help with the operation of the computer or getting it to work with other devices. But applications ran by themselves and did something ostensibly useful.

As networks improved and the Internet evolved, distributed computing became the norm, and now several computers might work together to run a particular application. To avoid ambiguity, some of these distributed applications earned the monikers *business application* or *enterprise application*—not that there weren't business applications in the early days of the PC, but now distributed computing was so complex that it was important to distinguish those applications that actually did something for the business from those that simply kept the lights on and everything working in the IT department.

into business resources for the business to access, manage, and evolve as needed.

Today's business applications can be enormously complex. Applications like *enterprise resource planning* (ERP), which can handle all the accounting, scheduling, and operations for a company, and *customer relationship management* (CRM), which deals with sales force automation, call center operations, marketing, and all the other ways a company interacts with its customers, strike fear into many an IT and business manager alike, because of their sheer complexity, cost, and risk. These applications and others like them have been necessary evils up to this point, in spite of the fact that they contribute enormously to the inflexibility epidemic facing today's IT.

Paradoxically, companies have been unable to treat the functionality these gargantuan business applications provide as *business* resources, because of the sheer scale, complexity, and inflexibility the applications exhibit. It's as if instead of buying your television in simple sets, you bought an enormously complex mishmash of devices that some high-priced consultant had to install and configure, filling up two whole rooms in your house, and then also had to baby-sit the thing to make sure it worked properly. No simple remote control for you, oh no! To use the thing you'd have to work with the consultant to convert your requirements into something the monstrosity could understand, and then if you were lucky, you'd get to watch your TV show hours—or days—later.

There's no way we'd put up with such nonsense when watching TV, and there's no good reason to put up with it when dealing with application functionality at work, either. The secret to eBusiness is packaging up such functionality along with all the other stuff IT does for you into business resources that simplify the complexity that lies underneath and provide clear expectations for how to interact with them and what to expect they will provide. That way, businesspeople can access, manage, and evolve those resources as needed in the business.

eBusinesspeople, therefore, go through their day-to-day work interacting with business resources as needed, including both IT and non-IT resources. If you're planning your sales strategy, say, then you'll do many things including analyzing sales data. Those data are at your fingertips through a business resource. You may use analysis tools, which are also resources. Next, you may formulate a new sales campaign, leveraging customer information provided as a business resource. You then enter the details of that campaign into a business resource, which automates the various steps of the campaign and disseminates your instructions to the various participants, who access them via business resources at their disposal.

In many ways, then, eBusinesspeople are like any other information workers—they leverage IT as a critical business resource in their everyday work. The essential difference that distinguishes eBusinesspeople from people who simply are adept at using technology is how they *think* about IT: For an eBusinessperson, technology doesn't simply represent a set of tools for doing business; rather, IT is an integral part of the business itself.

The specific form each interface takes to each business resource depends on the task at hand. Likewise, the underlying technology should crank away without the businesspeople having to know what's going on behind the scenes. What matters is the *separation*: a clearly defined boundary separating businesspeople accessing business resources from the IT capabilities that make those resources work. This separation is what Service Orientation is all about.

WHY AREN'T THE SYSTEMS INTEGRATORS HELPING ANYMORE?

Becoming an eBusiness isn't an easy task, to be sure, and many companies need outside help. After all, companies have been turning to consultants to help them with both their business and technology problems since, well, the dawn of business and IT, respectively. So it shouldn't come as a surprise to anyone that as eBusiness picked up in the 1990s, many companies turned to consultants for help.

Now, there are many kinds of consultants in this world. Broadly falling under the moniker *professional services,* consultants can offer any manner of different services to the business. Anyone can hang out a shingle and call themselves a consultant, after all. When it comes to *eBusiness consulting,* however, companies face a problem: Is an eBusiness consultant focused on the business or on the technology? eBusiness by definition completely intertwines the two areas, so which kind of consultant do you look for: a business consultant or a technology consultant?

As it happens, the history of consulting contains an important story of how these two broad areas of specialization intertwined in the past. A curious thing started happening in the late 1970s through the 1980s: Accounting firms that had heretofore specialized entirely in business consulting started turning themselves into IT consulting companies. In the late 1970s about eight large accounting firms, with household names like Arthur Andersen and Ernst & Young, were retained by over 90% of the largest firms in the world.

Companies hired accounting firms like these to provide objective, third-party advice and guidance to their business. Corporate executives had to place a significant amount of trust in their accountants, since they were so close to the core of their operations. When an accountant spoke, more often than not, a smart corporate executive listened. Doing more than simply balancing the books, these accountants guided their clients' businesses to improve the way they ran their organization. They were able to offer their customers advice by comparing them to other companies in their industry or in their similar situation. In other words, accounting firms were business consulting firms first and foremost or, more specifically, management consulting firms.

Increasingly, senior management at the largest of companies depended on these accountants–cum–management consultants to provide advice and guidance on improving their procurement processes, optimizing their inventory and manufacturing, and streamlining their operations. Senior management began to become more dependent than ever on these large accounting firms to help them beat their competition by making their business more efficient and satisfying their shareholders. In essence, companies relied on accounting firms to help them improve their businesses, using whatever tools were available to do so.

These large accounting firms, being no dummies when it comes to shrewd business, realized that the trusted position they found themselves in with many top executives at the world's largest firms was a logical path to expanding their own business, by expanding the types of consulting they offered their clients. IT consulting was the natural growth path. Despite the prominence of these big accounting firms in the worlds of financial auditing and corporate tax filing, companies started hiring them to provide IT consulting. Yes, that's right—companies started hiring bean counters to help them with their IT problems. As a result, it is no surprise that as IT became increasingly important to the business, senior management would turn to their accounting firms to find out how they could best apply technology.

Rise of the Systems Integrator

As the large accounting firms were getting into IT consulting, the world of distributed computing was also taking off, first with client/server and then

Jargon Watch: Systems Integrator (SI)

The strict definition of a *systems integrator* is a business that specializes in assembling complete IT solutions for the customers from different vendors' components. Broadly speaking, we call such assembly *integration*. Systems integrators typically do not develop any original applications, but rather focus on the integration of individual components and applications to meet business needs.

However, this definition strays a bit from reality. As systems integrators became increasingly responsible for configuring and customizing complicated enterprise application software, they developed more and more of their own custom applications and utilized less and less off-the-shelf technology. By the end of the twentieth century, it became hard to distinguish between a systems integrator and any other custom software development shop. Given the term's increasing ambiguity, it is quite possible that it might disappear altogether from the IT lexicon in the next few years.

with the Internet. Naturally, companies needed help connecting all the various parts of this complex set of technologies together, and the IT consulting specialty of *system integration* was born. Systems integrators (SIs) emerged in an environment where there were only two types of businesses providing IT solutions: hardware and software vendors with products to sell, and custom development shops that would build what you needed according to the specifications you provided. Systems integrators filled this gap by providing custom-tailored solutions built out of parts that third-party vendors provided.

In the 1990s, money started pouring into the SIs. Companies looked for help to implement enterprise applications, solve Y2K problems, and, yes, implement eBusiness solutions, and consequently, the money just kept coming. One challenge that SIs faced in the heady years of the late 1990s was not having enough people on staff to deliver on the projects they had already sold. As a result of these hiring pressures and the desire to capture as much of the business thrown their way as possible, many of the SIs starting acquiring other SIs.

However, SIs faced an even bigger challenge when it came to eBusiness: In the crazy dot-com days of the late 1990s, hot new consulting firms focused on Web-based solutions took all the attention, casting the SIs as dinosaurs from the old economy. Soon the plethora of small Web consulting firms rolled up into a small handful of large eBusiness consulting firms known at the time as *iBuilders*. iBuilders like marchFIRST, Scient, and iXL trumpeted their New Economy chops, positioning themselves as experts in the world of eBusiness.

End of the iBuilders

So what of the large accounting firms that had moved into the system integration business? Business picked up, to be sure, as their clients caught the eBusiness craze. Frantic that they would lose these clients to the iBuilders, they rapidly built out their SI divisions, emphasizing their depth of expertise in both business and technology over the flash and pizzazz the iBuilders were trumpeting.

Then, of course, the bubble burst. Most of the iBuilders and many others either went entirely out of business or sold out for a song mere months after market capitalizations had reached billions of dollars. It turns out the accounting/SI firms were right: The iBuilders were really only peddling sizzle after all, and the bean counters were the ones selling the steak. Nevertheless, the recession of 2001 hit the bean counters hard as well.

The post–perfect-storm hangover, as well as the corporate accounting and finance scandals that soon followed, hit the large accounting firms where it hurt. To add insult to injury, the federal government woke up to the fact that having the same firm auditing the books, providing advice to top management, and solving IT problems was a huge potential conflict of interest. In 2002, Congress passed the Sarbanes-Oxley Act, which, among many other things, forced accounting firms to spin off their IT consulting arms. Accounting firms were out of the SI business for good.

There is an important irony in this story. The iBuilders trumpeted eBusiness but didn't have either the business or technology chops (or both) to put their money where their mouths were. Contrarily, the large accounting/SI firms did have both business and technology chops, but the fallout from the dot-com bust split them apart. And yet eBusiness today is stronger than ever. What happened?

Companies, after all, still rely on third parties for objective advice as well as guidance on how to improve their businesses, especially in relation to their competition. Today's SIs and business consulting firms are all struggling to find their long-term value propositions in environments that are in constant change. While there is still money in IT implementation, the long-term value for these firms is providing critical expertise in making businesses more agile and flexible. Likewise, although the pure business consulting firms still have traditional markets as well, it's becoming increasingly important for them to have a deep understanding of the role IT plays in business. So, in essence, SIs and business consultants must once again seek to pull together their offerings so that they can leverage IT as one tool in a tool belt of many available tools they might use to solve business problems. After all, this is why SIs got into the IT consulting game in the first place.

The movement away from simply implementing IT to making IT a core part of the business agility value proposition presents both opportunities and threats to consulting firms: On one hand, there will be an increased demand for business-level consulting and guidance in building the agile systems that every eBusiness requires. On the other hand, as companies realize that they don't necessarily have to spend more money on big-bang, high-risk IT projects, the market for pure systems integration will gradually dry up, requiring SIs to change their business focus.

However, such changes are familiar to the IT consulting world, with the shift from client/server to eBusiness/Web technologies and the subsequent downturn. Some SIs won't survive, but others will roll with the changes and come out on top. The key to any consultant's survival in the face of changing customer demands, of course, is to continue to focus on solving customer problems. As those problems change, so must the solutions.

THRIFT: GET USED TO IT

In today's world, it's *hip* to spend money. Most people want big houses, fancy cars, expensive vacations, and the newest gadgets. Television shows like *Lifestyles of the Rich and Famous* didn't detail how the individuals they feature made their millions or billions, but rather how they spend them. Music videos and commercials show people "living the good life" by spending their money, doing things they enjoy without much care for how they might afford them. However, saving money and being frugal is seen as *square*. It's not particularly sexy to live a modest life, buying things only when they're absolutely necessary, and using one's current earnings to guarantee future ones, rather than spending them for today's benefit. Words like *extravagant* are sexy and glamorous, while words like *economical* are as sexy as Margaret Thatcher's drawers.

However, today's companies can't afford to think sexy. Although the television shows and commercials feature the spending habits of the CEOs of many large firms, the companies themselves are responsible to too many constituencies for the particular spending habits of their CEOs to be part of the overall corporate culture. For most successful companies, it's the bottom line that's important. The mantra for those firms is to increase revenues and decrease spending. And it's the decreasing spending part of this mantra that we shift our attention to in this section.

Most executives evaluate the financial health of their companies in a simplistic way, asking how much money they are making and evaluating how much they are spending. Companies divide their various activities into the money-making and money-spending sides of the business. Activities like sales and marketing, although they do have costs associated with them, are connected to the money-making side of the financial equation, while operational costs like human resources and administration are generally associated with the money-spending side of the business. Many firms associate IT spending with operational expenses and thus, often consider it a liability that they want to reduce over time.

IT Spending in the Good Ol' Days: Pay and Pray

In the earliest days of IT, most businesses didn't have a place in their budget for information technology. As a result, companies had to justify the very significant expenditure on mainframe computers and costly application development on a project-by-project basis, implementing IT as a means of automating their heretofore manual core business processes.

Companies continued to consider IT as a part of their operational budgets until the dawn of personal computers and desktop computing. As individuals and groups throughout the company required computing resources, discrete spending on individual projects increasingly contributed to an environment of chaos and disorganization in the corporate environment. With IT becoming increasingly important to the daily operation of the business, companies dealt with this chaos by creating the role of the chief information officer (CIO), who was responsible for exerting strong, rational control over IT expenditures.

For many decades, companies maintained this rational, cost-justified approach to their IT spending. However, this approach would soon be thrown completely out of whack by the perfect storm of the 1990s: eBusiness, Y2K, and the stock market bubble. The first big factor of IT spending was the emergence of the Internet and eBusiness as a new requirement for businesses. The increasing irrationality of the stock markets and rapid emergence of new business models motivated businesses to toss out their old-economy ideas in favor of the supposed promises of the New Economy. Selling goods in stores was now old-fashioned, whereas doing the same online was seen as cutting-edge. As a result, companies felt pressured to spend significantly on eBusiness and Internet-related projects, without feeling the need to justify them with well-founded business plans.

At the same time that companies were spending millions on eBusiness projects, they also undertook multiyear, megabudget IT projects that aimed to significantly improve their operational efficiency as well as their interaction with customers and suppliers. Known as customer relationship management (CRM) and enterprise resource planning (ERP), these large IT projects not only required significant spending on new software licenses, hardware, and professional services, but also required the addition of large numbers of IT staff to deal with the monolithic applications that the company now suddenly relied on. However, despite all this spending and growth, few companies implemented these "big bang" enterprise application projects successfully. According to many studies, fewer than 25% of all ERP projects and 10% of CRM projects netted a positive business return to the enterprise. Yet companies continued to feel pressured to spend on these applications as a result of their almost-addictive dependency to the systems that run their business.

To top it all off, Y2K reared its ugly head. Instead of representing dates with four digits, such as "1998," programmers over the years had used just two. Normally, this wouldn't be a problem, but as companies approached the dawn of the millennium, they panicked, believing that their systems might suddenly get out of whack when the clock rolled over from 1999 to 2000. The media stoked fear into the populace with visions of airplanes unable to fly straight, power grids shutting down, and nuclear reactors suddenly going haywire. Governments required companies to put disclaimers in their financial filings to state their liability to date-related disasters, and many even had to put cute yellow stickers on their products to let customers know that they fixed any date-related coding problems. The survivalists took these moves as omens of impending doom and ran for the hills, shotgun and canned meat in hand, stocking up on gold for the imminent collapse of the world's economic systems.

In reality, Y2K became a motivation for consulting firms, software companies, and businesses of all sorts to wring the last remaining dollars out of companies' IT budgets. Companies rewrote thousands of lines of code in their arcane systems and spent billions of dollars reworking systems that already met existing business needs. It's hard to tell how much of this spending actually helped to avoid a Y2K nightmare. It is clear, however, that the perfect storm of IT motivators of the late 1990s resulted in significant spending that showed little real return for the business. With the collapse of the dot-com boom, this irrationally exuberant IT spending would all come to a sudden and dramatic end.

Thrift: The New Normal

Much—but not all—of the IT spending in the late 1990s was excessive, and certainly, we shouldn't paint all of IT with the broad brush of irrationality. After all, IT evolved to meet business needs, and it's only now that companies are returning to the mandate that their expenditures provide immediate and quantifiable business return. As a result, any new story about IT cannot be about dramatically increasing capital investment. Spending less and getting more is now cool. It's hip to shop at Wal-Mart (okay, maybe Target) and squeeze every penny. Free, open source products are now "in." Removing expensive systems that aren't performing up to snuff is the new mantra. In order to move forward and make progress, companies must do more with what they already have and realize continued benefit from their existing IT investments for years to come. This is one story that today's executives love to hear.

Another word for this frugality of IT spending is *thrift*. The meaning of the word *thrift* has two parts. First is the aspect of simply spending less. Thrifty individuals and companies abhor unnecessary expenditure and demand business justification for all of their spending. However, in some instances, an obsession with cost reduction can be an unhealthy thing. So, we don't want to equate being thrifty with that of simply being *cheap*. Thrifty companies are not penny wise and pound foolish, but instead know when to make the necessary investments to guarantee the smooth and efficient running of their businesses.

Thrift, however, means more than simple cost savings. True thriftiness means making do with what you have and squeezing value out of every asset. Thrifty companies view each investment they make with an eye toward reuse and longevity. Systems that they buy must be able to meet not only current needs, but also future, unplanned ones. Software applications and hardware investments must handle a wide range of requirements without needing expensive rewrites, upgrades, or add-ons. Thrifty companies must demand more from their consulting organizations, IT management teams, and suppliers, and should seek to extract the very last amount of value from their systems until they absolutely must replace them to meet ongoing needs. The agile and hip companies of the future will not only understand thriftiness, but covet and cherish it.

The last IT build-out of the 1990s heralded the beginning of the dot-com boom, where thrift was the furthest thing from most executives' minds. Today, of course, we've come to our senses. This return to business reality is driving the move to agility in the face of continuing downward pressure on IT spending. Instead of a massive build-out or extensive rip-and-replace of existing systems, the new approaches of the future need to thrive on an environment of reusable systems that leverage yesterday's spending. Instead of "staking out new real estate along the information superhighway," as in the good old days, today we're squeezing every bit of business value out of the technology we already have. And that's yet another factor moving us forward to newer, better ways of making IT work for the business, rather than the other way around.

CHAPTER 4

What Do You Want Your IT to Do, Anyway?

Information technology is complicated stuff. Although we've tried to simplify how to interact with IT, there's no denying the complexity of its inner workings. As time goes on, IT becomes more and more complex, as the power of the technology goes up, the number of dependencies and interactions among disparate technologies increases, and as we use that new power to tackle increasingly complex tasks. People, however, have a limited tolerance for such complexity. Sure, there are a few people who desire the latest gadgets and thrive on getting immersed in tech talk, but your average person would just as soon avoid excess complexity.

EVERYONE'S A GRANDMA

If you think about our lives outside of work, technology isn't really that complicated, since the vendors of such technology must serve the lowest common denominator and make their technology so that as many people as possible can consume it. As a result, our environments look little like the Jetsons' world of fancy gadgets and complex controls and flashing lights everywhere you look. Instead, think about where complex technology lies—in automobiles, mobile phones, microwaves, and the like. You can easily see that these devices are complex on the inside yet simple on the outside—simple to learn, simple to operate, and simple to understand (or, at least, the *good* ones are). After all, *simplicity* of design is a virtue, even if the underlying technology is very complex.

Why, then, is so much of the technology we use at work so complicated on the outside? Specifically, the distributed IT we've been focusing on doesn't pass the "grandma test": In other words, your grandma would have a difficult time figuring out how to use it. Grandma, after all, has no problems with phones, microwaves, cars, and even e-mail and the like. (Now, we're not trying to pick on all the grandmas out there, so please don't e-mail us any complaints. The fact of the matter is that we're all grandmas when it comes to using technology.)

There's nothing wrong with Grandma, after all, that she would have a difficult time with IT. The problem lies with the technology. If something is too complicated for its users (including Grandma) to learn, operate, and understand, then something is wrong with it, not with the user. The problem lies in the assumptions that the creators of IT technology make about their users.

Power Paradox

Naysayers may make the point that the grandma test works fine for cars and the like, but that distributed IT is so inherently complicated that its interface

Jargon Watch: Interface

An *interface*, in the IT sense, is that part of a piece of technology that users and other pieces of technology interact with. All technology has interfaces of one sort or another. There must be a way to make the thing do what you want it to, and the only way for a human to interact with a piece of technology is through its interface. People (known by that friendly term, *users*) predictably interact with *user interfaces*. A user interface includes both *input*, like a mouse, the buttons on a phone, and keys on a keyboard, and *output*, including the image on a computer display and the sound that comes out of any manner of devices. A *graphical user interface* (GUI; pronounced "gooey") uses visual icons and metaphors instead of just text to represent the underlying system and is the sort of image you see on all of today's computers, typically with icons, windows, and the like. GUIs are essentially both input and output interfaces, since you type and click on them as well as look at things on them.

User interfaces, however, are not the only kind of interface many types of technology have. Distributed computing requires various pieces of IT to have interfaces that other pieces of IT can interact with. Sounds simple, right? Unfortunately, it is hard to determine how to best build interfaces for IT-to-IT communication. As it turns out, one of the secrets to Service Orientation is to create the right kinds of interfaces and manage them in the right way.

must be complicated as well. That may have been true at some point in the past, but there's simply no good excuse for that belief now. It is indeed a difficult task to make an interface to a complex system simple, but that doesn't change the validity of the grandma test. After all, making mobile phone interfaces simple was pretty damn complicated as well, but people just wouldn't buy them if they weren't easy to use.

Fundamentally, simplicity and power aren't contradictory. Complexity and power may correlate for a time, but that correlation reaches its limit as the system's complexity eventually impedes its usefulness and therefore its power within the organization. Distributed computing has actually reached that limit—and that is the root of the problem this book seeks to address. If we make our technology any more complicated to use, it will actually begin to provide less benefit to the business, in spite of the ongoing pace of technology espoused in Moore's Law. As we discussed in Chapter 3, Moore's Law observes that computing power doubles every 18 months or so. The answer lies not in making the technology itself less complicated. Instead, the answer lies in making its *interfaces* simpler.

Tech Isn't for Techies

Clearly, IT has served a vitally important role in business for over 50 years, but that's not what we're talking about here. We're talking about empowering individual businesspeople and the teams they are members of to take advantage of the full breadth of IT resources within their organization, both to respond to business change and also to leverage that change in their operations. After all, businesspeople don't want to engage in technical discussions. While they don't want to be grandmas, the truth is that businesspeople have no time to be techies either.

What characterizes distributed technology is the fact that there's so much of it. As a result, it's important for people to be able to find the *right* technology for a particular task—the needle in the haystack problem. In order to find the right technology, you must be able to tell different bits of technology apart. For example, if you have 12 different ways to find a customer's information, you need to know which one will give you the information you're actually looking for. Because distributed technology is, well, distributed, the right technology can be difficult even to locate, let alone to use. Therefore, one of the requirements for simplifying an interface is in making the technology easy to find.

Once you have found the correct piece of technology, then—and only then—do you need to know how to use it. The technology in question may have a user interface, in which case you need to be able to use that interface. In the more general case, however, you want the various systems you already are using, and know how to use, to be able to access the remote bit of technology, say, when you want to enter some financial information into your spreadsheet. Where that information is and how the technology works should be hidden from view. You just need to know it works.

Finally, you must be able to extract value from that bit of technology you just found and accessed. After all, your job isn't about using the bit of technology, it's about leveraging the value of that technology in your work. The last thing you want is for the technology to slow you down or get in your way. Remember, the natural state of affairs is that business is always changing, always in flux. Your work changes from day to day, and the tools you use must remain flexible and easy to use so that you can respond to that change and ideally leverage it to provide greater value to your customers. Business agility, therefore, depends on the ability to find, learn about, use, and link IT resources simply and easily enough for your grandma to do it.

MIDDLEWARE: PART OF THE SOLUTION OR PART OF THE PROBLEM?

We're sure you've all heard the old Henny Youngman joke: "The patient says 'Doctor, it hurts when I do this.' The doctor replies: 'Then don't do that!'" In a similar way, today's IT systems are a complex assortment of moving parts that cause recurring, chronic operational pain so intractable that many IT organizations now simply put Band-Aids on the problems without solving the underlying condition. Of course, we are talking about the recurring costs and risk that today's inflexible integration approaches cause.

Jargon Watch: Middleware

Middleware is a term that evolved as the complexity of IT started to rear its ugly head. Middleware is software that provides an intermediate role between two other pieces of software in order to provide data format conversion, business logic translation, or some other value-added role. Some middleware software provides messaging capabilities that connect disparate systems in a reliable manner, and others consolidate data from multiple sources in the enterprise. Many companies program their own middleware in-house, and of course, many software vendors offer packaged middleware solutions. Today it's possible to find a number of flavors of middleware on the market and in IT shops everywhere.

At the center of this discussion of pain is a class of software product commonly known as middleware. *Middleware* has come to mean many different things. In the most general sense, middleware is software that intermediates functionality or data between two otherwise independent and separate systems. In most instances, middleware doesn't provide the actual application that consumers use or the systems of record that store the data and content information. Middleware is essentially the glue that holds together the disparate systems that provide all the various pieces of functionality that distributed applications need to fulfill business requirements.

Glue is good when you need to connect two systems together for them to work, but apply too much glue, or apply it to the wrong places, and you quickly find yourself stuck! Although middleware has helped businesses solve tough IT problems over the past few decades, in many situations, middleware has simply contributed to the problem of business inflexibility, compounding the pain of integration in such a way that simply makes companies want to avoid the use of middleware as much as possible in the future.

Middleware for Your Middleware

Companies require middleware when the systems they want to connect have proprietary interfaces and thus require specifically designed software just to extract even the most basic of information. The rapid build-out of IT capability in the last two decades led to a proliferation of such isolated islands of business functionality, requiring companies to unlock the information from

Jargon Watch: EAI

Enterprise application integration (EAI) is a specific kind of middleware whose primary role is to allow users to connect disparate software applications together at the business logic level. In contrast to connecting businesses together, EAI focuses on the complex interaction between systems that a company directly controls. EAI has become synonymous with complex, costly, and brittle integration, because the approaches that the majority of EAI vendors take offer only solutions to short-term integration challenges, without moving a company toward an infrastructure that allows for dynamic responses to ongoing business change.

the tight grasp of proprietary interfaces in order to provide value to their organizations. Businesses therefore had a hard time getting these systems to do what they wanted, let alone getting them to communicate with other systems to meet new needs as they came up. Middleware, including enterprise application integration (EAI), served a role in helping companies meet the urgent needs of eBusiness, Y2K, and enterprise application development. However, middleware functionality turned out to be woefully inadequate for solving companies' chronic IT problems.

One of the biggest problems that some traditional approaches to integration present is the geometric growth in connections that leads to rats' nests. Although some middleware integration approaches do solve the geometric part of the scaling problem, they don't address the brittle, inflexible nature of the connections between systems. In other words, getting rid of the rats' nest, while definitely an improvement, still doesn't guarantee agility. When business requirements change, the cost and complexity of making such changes are still significant. Compounding the integration problem is the fact that most companies perform integration in an ad hoc manner, narrowly focusing on short-term integration needs rather than long-term solution effectiveness. The end result is a tangled web of brittle connections between systems that are increasingly expensive to maintain and update. It's as if the rats' nest were the natural order of things, and even introducing an organizing force like EAI eventually leads to—you guessed it—a rats' nest of EAI!

The bigger problem—the one that causes rats' nests to reappear—is that companies now think of distributed computing entirely in terms of connecting systems. Rather than focusing on the creation of business logic that meets business needs, companies now create layers of middleware, requiring them to deal with the problem of integrating their disparate middleware implementations throughout their enterprise—middleware for their middleware, if you will. Companies must now spend millions more to manage and integrate the middleware that they have glued in place so well that it is virtually impossible to change or remove. Instant rats' nest!

It simply makes no sense for companies to spend money to get their middleware to work well with other middleware. Why should companies have layers upon layers of glue, each dealing with a specific integration problem? Using middleware to solve acute, localized integration issues is one thing; using it to solve chronic problems that relate to business agility and ongoing flexibility is another! Companies don't need more or better middleware to make their systems more agile. Instead, they need to step back and think through how to build, run, and manage distributed computing infrastructures that are inherently flexible and agile—without adding middleware to their middleware.

Moving Away from an Integration-centric Mentality

Part of the challenge of moving to systems that are inherently flexible is that it requires a shift in the way that organizations think about their IT resources and how they develop and integrate business functionality. It is far simpler to implement, install, and deploy a system in isolation and then think about how to connect it to other systems in the enterprise after the fact than it is to come up with an approach ahead of time that factors in the need for flexibility. In fact, the movement to systems that are flexible and agile requires a sea change in thought.

It is a difficult task indeed to build systems that allow companies to make changes as needed, especially in response to unpredictable business requirements, if you are thinking with an integration-centric mentality that involves connecting systems together in a rigid and brittle way. But the most compelling reason to move away from thinking that middleware will solve chronic IT problems is that it simply costs less over time to adopt agile systems than to glue together isolated ones with middleware. Henny Youngman once joked: "A doctor gave a man six months to live. The man couldn't pay his bill, so he gave him another six months." Believe it or not, companies operate in much the same way with regard to middleware.

Many firms operate on the edge of disaster, with IT systems interconnected in such a tenuous way that significant changes are either too costly or too complex to perform. They continue to spend money on those systems, even as their cost and complexity continue to increase dramatically from year to year. Companies complain that they can't afford any significant spending on strategic IT initiatives, yet they continue to spend out the wazoo for brittle, inflexible layers of middleware that unnecessarily glue them into place. Managers should instead be thinking about *cost recovery*— reducing how much they spend on middleware in order to fund spending on new, agile approaches to IT. In fact, cost recovery is a critical technique for driving change within the IT organization. Through cost recovery, firms can recoup their investments and still move toward IT systems that are flexible and agile.

AUTOMATION PARADOX

Let's take a step back for a moment and take a look at how cost recovery has driven IT innovation through history. Our story starts when industrial automation began in textile mills over 200 years ago with the dawn of the Industrial Revolution and hits full stride in the last century with the evolution of machinery that could automate repetitive human tasks. Once people realized that they could harness the power of moving water, steam, combustion, or electricity to do the work of humans or animals, the pace at which they could improve productivity and reduce costs grew tremendously. The Information Revolution of the mid-twentieth century expanded the power of automation beyond manufacturing and across all parts of the organization, as one IT innovation after another automated an increasingly expanding set of business processes.

The problem with automation, however, is that as each new technology innovation, from the Jacquard loom to the transistor to the World Wide Web, moved businesses up the spectrum of automation, processes become increasingly difficult to automate. Tasks that require human knowledge and logic are among the most difficult to automate. At some point, however, the effect of the new innovation peters out, and people must step in to manually handle the tasks that have been resistant to automation. That is, until the next innovation comes along and changes the game anew.

Workflow Trap

The history of technological innovation, therefore, consists of a gradual automation of tasks or processes. Gradually we're able to automate the easier processes, leaving only those processes that are more difficult to automate. Those processes must remain manual until further innovation enables us to automate them.

If you look closely at this progression of increasingly automated processes, you'll see that few if any processes actually involve no human interaction. Furthermore, even the most manual of tasks typically have automated steps here and there. As a result, the discussion of automation really boils down to a discussion of *workflow,* which we define as a series of human tasks within an organization that produce a desired final outcome. Processing an insurance claim, purchasing supplies, or building a car are all workflows, because they involve people at particular steps in the flow, and they all have a particular outcome. Workflows are a kind of business process, but for now, let's focus on the fact that a workflow requires some element of human involvement.

Some workflows are entirely manual, such as getting someone to approve something, while others are at least partially automated. There's no such thing as a fully automated workflow, however, because human involvement is part of the definition of a workflow. It's also unusual to find a workflow with absolutely no IT involvement these days as well, for example, because IT is so pervasive that that we commonly use e-mail or the Web to execute some otherwise all-human workflow. In many cases, technologists use the term *workflow* to refer to otherwise automated processes that have human steps in them, as though people were plugged into the process. Just like Charlie Chaplin in the movie *Modern Times,* people find themselves enmeshed in the gears of uncaring workflows as the wheels of automation continue to turn. It's clear that those technologists would wish that all humans were more like predictable, machinable gears than the unpredictable, quirky organisms that we actually are.

Whether you've seen *Modern Times* or not, it's a good bet that if Charlie Chaplin is involved, then something is bound to go dreadfully (and hilariously) wrong. In the real world of business, we call such situations *exceptions,* and unfortunately, they're rarely hilarious and are extremely common. An exception is simply an occurrence in a work flow that breaks out of the automated progression of the process and requires a human operator to perform some often unplanned task. Examples of exceptions might be missing information in an insurance claim, a supplier who is out of needed inventory, or an unplanned outage or downtime in an assembly line.

There are basically two ways for a company to deal with exceptions. First, it might plan out its workflows in a fantasy world as if there were no exceptions and then have a way for people deal with exceptions as they come up. Basically, plan for the best-case scenario, and have extra resources (and budget) on hand to deal with the inevitable exceptions that happen. An example might be stopping an assembly line to fix the problem before starting the line up again. The other, more practical way to deal with such exceptions is to plan for them ahead of time, so that dealing with the exception is essentially part of the work flow itself. For example, there should be alternate workflows that deal with what happens when an exception interrupts an otherwise automated workflow, like finding missing information for an insurance claim or locating an extra supplier for a given part. Planning on exceptions is the first step in reducing their number, as anyone who has participated in a quality improvement program will attest.

Today's workflow automation approaches typically focus on executing those workflows under predictable conditions. When something unexpected happens, however, the process throws an exception that a human must deal with—sometimes predictable, but often not. The classic example of exception management in action involves merchandising processes: getting winter coats on a store's racks, for instance. One early cold snap can cause a spike in demand that throws a wrench into the most carefully laid forecasts, and now people have to step into an otherwise automated workflow and deal with the situation. These exception managers must adjust or revise an existing workflow to deal with the problem manually.

Both approaches to tackling exceptions don't address the fundamental problem with workflows in general: They rarely have the flexibility and adaptability that businesses need to fully meet their objectives. The problem with today's workflow automation is that workflow tools aim to fix the workflows in place—what we like to call *pouring concrete* on them. Rather than allowing workflows to change, these workflow automation technologies assume that the workflow you have is the one that you *always* want. Basically, such technologies exhibit a version of the resistance-to-change problem discussed earlier. Processes that were supposed to be ad hoc or meant to solve one problem in one situation soon become the "way things are done." In situations where the business needs are unlikely to change, the poured-concrete approach may be adequate. In reality, however, most businesses require far more flexibility from their workflows, especially as they move up the automation spectrum to those workflows that are more difficult to automate. The problem with the poured-concrete approach to workflow is that it's difficult to predict what will actually happen, in spite of trying to figure out every likely exception ahead of time.

Why Are We Pouring Concrete in the First Place?

If simply automating workflows by fixing them in place doesn't address the needs of the business even when that workflow is sophisticated enough to handle certain exceptions, then why do so many businesses fall into this workflow trap? The answer, unsurprisingly enough, has to do with the limitations of IT. After all, if companies are used to solving problems using only the most expedient approach, connecting their technology together in a shortsighted manner, then there's no way their IT can be flexible or agile enough to support the automation of work flows in a way that actually represents business needs over time.

What we need is a way to reverse the poured-concrete situation. Instead of plugging people into rigid processes à la *Modern Times*, we need a way to plug automation into people's daily work routine. Once people realize that they aren't a resource for the *workflow* to use, but rather automated workflows are among the business resources that *they* can use, then they will be able to leverage the power of IT in a far more flexible manner.

At the basic level, when exceptions like the unexpected cold snap occurs, line-of-business managers, rather than technologists, should be able to call upon a range of work flows and other resources at their disposal to deal with the exception. They can put those resources together in a flexible manner to reallocate IT resources as needed without having to invest thousands or millions more dollars on new IT systems.

So far, so good—now let's take this example to the next level. An enterprising software vendor realizes that exceptions are the rule in most businesses, and industries like retail (or most other industries, for that matter) are subject to the whim of outside forces. The vendor develops an exception management system that automates not just how companies manage exceptions, but also how nontechnical users can assemble the various resources at their disposal, including, but not limited to, exception management tools. This vendor's customers can now handle exception management in a fashion that's more amenable to dealing with change and possibly in a more automated fashion. The exception manager's role now moves away from fighting fires to more strategic assignments, such as further removing costs from the merchandising/exception management system.

Paradox of Agile Automation

The ongoing series of innovations that lead to increasing levels of automation clearly represent progress for the businesses that are doing the innovating. Such progress, however, comes at a price, as the humans involved in those processes find their daily work transformed or eliminated. People, of course, can tolerate only so much punishment. The history of business through the last two centuries documents progress in the human condition as well, from the labor movement to occupational health regulations to the World Wide Web and the global community it fostered. Fundamentally, with each technical innovation, business can progress only so far before people require improvements in the human condition.

The ability to automate workflows in the flexible manner we describe here represents the next step in this progression toward better work for people. No one wants to be a Charlie Chaplin plugged into some automated workflow. Likewise, people generally don't enjoy jobs where they're spending all their time fighting the fires that various exceptions cause. As we move up the automation spectrum, work gets better as business gets more efficient and people become more productive. Today's poured-concrete approach to automation is nearing the end of its usefulness, as competitive pressures put companies with inflexible business processes at a disadvantage.

BUSINESS PROCESS: SWEETNESS AND LIGHT OR EVIL HELLSPAWN?

Successful businesses are built on the principles of delivering great products or services, operational efficiency, excellence in satisfying customers, well-honed sales and marketing efforts, and leveraging relationships with suppliers and partners. Senior managers at most companies think first and foremost about the way they do business, not the individual tasks, resources, activities, or systems that comprise the enterprise. In many industries, such as finance and insurance, how fast they can roll out new products to customers offers a competitive advantage, and how fast they can deliver products and services is directly dependent on the way they run their business. In some cases, customers are purchasing not products or services, but rather the way that the business delivers those products and services.

To make changes to these service offerings, these companies don't necessarily change the product or service itself, but rather the *process* they use to offer the service to the customer. Organizations dedicate considerable sums of money and resources to developing and enhancing their businesses in a constant quest to deliver the best services and products for the least cost. As a result, when companies look to effect change in their organization, they look first at the various activities and operations that comprise the organization and then to the tasks that support those activities. In a world where IT is controlling more and more of those activities, how can a company address its core issues of business agility and flexibility if it doesn't address the activities that are so central to the way the business is run?

What Is a Business Process?

Enterprises can be thought of as an aggregation of processes and the resources that comprise those processes. But what exactly is a business process? The term *process* has many meanings and connotations, depending on the context. Of course, we are not concerned with processes in general, but rather those processes that are relevant to the operations of a business. The dictionary definition of *process* is a "series of actions, changes, or functions bringing about a result." But that definition sounds pretty generic. After all, sneezing brings about a series of actions, changes, or functions, but we don't consider that to be core to the business, do we?

A more concise and appropriate definition of process is one that the Workflow Management Coalition (www.wfmc.org) explained as "a set of one or more linked procedures or activities which collectively realize a business objective or policy goal, normally within the context of an organizational structure defining functional roles and relationships." In this context, for a process to be a *business* process, the business must identify a goal for the process as well as the activities that the process requires to support that goal. If our business goal was to test tissue paper, then perhaps sneezing might indeed be an activity that supports that goal. But a process is more than simply activities and goals; it also involves people. Processes use operations, information, roles, and the sequencing of tasks to carry out specific objectives in the enterprise. It is the role of business management to make sure that the business performs those processes adequately or to change them to meet new business requirements.

It's possible to trace the concept of business process can back to the early 1920s, when "Methods and Procedures Analysis" described ways to "restructure work flows" and improve the operation of business organizations. As a result, there is a rich history of understanding of the interactions between an organization and its processes. In general, we can glean a number of important points from experience and various definitions as they apply specifically to business processes:

- *A process is a collection of activities.*   The concept of *activity* represents the fundamental building block of a business process. An activity represents a unit of work that a user, system, or organization performs. An activity may have some input and output and some associated actions. A process is not a singular activity or action, but a collection of activities and actions that, when tied together in a logical flow, result in an outcome. A business process is merely a succession of activities following a specific control flow.
- *Processes are an inherent part of the enterprise.*   An enterprise cannot function without processes, regardless of whether it formally defines them or whether they simply occur as a result of normal business operations.
- *Processes have outcomes.*   Processes inherently impact the operation of a business at various levels in the organization. Processes have defined conditions triggering their initiation and defined or expected outputs.
- *Processes may occur within, outside, or between enterprises.*   Business processes define how people and other resources do work both within and between organizations.
- *A wide range of participants can carry out business processes.*   Individuals, organizational roles, or supporting IT business systems can carry out business processes. Work flows, therefore, are a kind of business process.
- *Processes may contain other processes.*   Since a process is a collection of activities, it's possible to represent any process as a type of activity that other processes can consume. In the case where a process is consumed by other processes, it is called a *subprocess.*
- *Processes may consist of automated activities and/or manual ones.*   A business process consists of activities that a person or a proxy for that person, namely an automated system, can perform.

In addition, when we talk about processes, we generally talk either about task-oriented processes, which represent the interactions between a user and a given unit of work, or about business-oriented processes, which represent high-level business requirements and the ways that various participants in an enterprise implement them.

Tasks in a process can be application-centric, when a system or software agent performs them automatically, or they can be human centric, when they involve manual tasks or human judgment and knowledge on top of automatic or system-based data. Furthermore, it's possible to limit the scope of a business process to a particular department in an enterprise, multiple divisions within an enterprise, or possibly many different internal and external organizations. Business processes might take a very long time to complete, in which case we call them long-lived, or they might complete very quickly, in which case they are short-lived.

Another way to understand business processes is to look at a number of examples that embody the various ways that organizations employ them. At a high level, procedures for requisitioning goods, purchasing supplies, assembling parts, designing products, supporting customers, and hiring employees are all business processes. At a low level, a process can be a well-defined set of steps that accomplish some business goal. For example, this 11-step list describes a formal process for a simple eCommerce purchase:

1. Customer browses online catalog.
2. Customer selects item and then places it in electronic shopping cart, if it is available.
3. Customer can then continue shopping or elect to check out and purchase items.
4. If customer elects to continue shopping, start at the first step.
5. If customer elects to check out, present payment form.
6. Charge customer's credit card.
7. Update store's financial accounting application.
8. Update store's inventory management application. If inventory falls below a certain level, notify distributor for replenishment.
9. Update sales database with the new purchase.
10. Store prepares product order and shipping statement.
11. Customer receives receipt and date for shipping.

This example shows a human interacting with a completely automated system—there is no need for human interaction by the company providing products to the customer. However, there are many processes in an organization that are either partially or completely human-based. For example, an insurance company might have a simple process in which agents fill in accident forms, which they then hand to a human claims processor who determines that accident claims under $2,000 require a claims adjuster's approval while claims over $2,000 require a supervisor's okay. The adjuster then determines if the claimant is at fault, and it is up to the underwriter to determine whether to cancel coverage or increase its cost.

Another reason companies formalize processes is to avoid ambiguities and difficulties in dealing with suppliers, partners, and customers. For example, consider a simple payment contract for goods. In an all-too-typical case, the buyer assumes that the seller will send an invoice after it receives the product it ordered. The seller, however, follows the practice that payment comes at the time of delivery and does not send an invoice. Thus, the goods arrive, and the buyer does not pay, waiting for an invoice. Meanwhile the seller becomes irked and initiates collection proceedings. A solution to this problem is the use of well-defined and communicated processes. These processes utilize standard documents, such as a purchase order, delivery agreement, and other such electronic or paper forms that contain the terms and conditions for doing business. As many firms have learned, trying to do business without specifying the *way of doing business* creates many problems.

However, companies are just as likely to err in the other direction. All too often, companies seek to enforce a single set of processes across their entire business, with the result being an all-too-rigid business as the end result. Although implementing well-defined, optimized processes is a sound business practice, today's companies need to be able to respond to change and leverage change. Instituting rigidly formal processes can amount to cement overshoes for even the most ostensibly efficient organization. Even looking for some happy medium solves nothing as well—after all, what company wants a mixture of uncontrolled activities and draconian processes? There's got to be a better way!

MISSING LINK IN THE IT CHAIN

Today's businesses struggle with a massive dilemma: Formalize your business processes to the level where everything is well defined, and you end up with a rigid, uncompetitive corporation that's unresponsive to change, or *don't* define your processes and end up with an uncontrollable mess that wastes money and pleases customers only by accident, if at all. Clearly, we need to identify some way out of this dilemma that will lead to our vision for the agile enterprise in a way that's both controllable and flexible. That path, like so many seemingly intractable problems, depends on IT. Yet companies have applied IT to the problem of business process for many years, so to understand where to go next, let's take a look at the progress we've already made.

Attempts at Automating Business Processes

For decades, technology has solved various different pieces of the business process puzzle. Indeed, hundreds of products on the market enable companies to translate their business processes into tasks that an IT system can implement. Such traditional solutions, alternatively known as business process management (BPM) or workflow tools, often present a flowchart-type visual interface or natural language business rules that enable slightly less technical businesspeople or their proxies in the IT organization to build a representation of the business process in a step-by-step fashion and then attach individual activities in a process to the company's operations.

However, this approach to business process development and creation often suffers because the person who is responsible for creating the representation of the process doesn't know all the details of the business process at hand in sufficient depth, is not up-to-date with the current state of how a business process is actually working in the company, and/or doesn't have knowledge of the whole process from end to end. As a result, most business process definition exercises often produce little more than "shelfware"—that is, they end up creating nothing more than writing on paper that represents either the business process as it used to be or the business process as it's supposed to be, but not the business process as it actually *is* or *will be*.

Jargon Watch: BPM

The acronym *BPM* can stand for two concepts that are relevant to the discussion of business process at hand: *business process management* and *business process modeling*. Business process management usually refers to a technology-enabled means for companies to gain visibility and control over long-lived, multistep processes that span a wide range of systems and people in one or more organizations. Of course, this definition of BPM doesn't say anything about how companies should actually accomplish such goals or what specific technologies or features someone can expect from BPM products.

BPM can also mean *business process modeling,* a set of practices or tasks that companies can perform to visually depict or describe all the aspects of a business process, including its flow, control and decision points, triggers and conditions for activity execution, the context in which an activity runs, and associated resources. A model is in fact just a representation of the process that allows companies to document, simulate, share, implement, evaluate, and continually improve their operations. Software vendors might in some instances provide business process management and business process–modeling capabilities in the same tool; in other cases, such capabilities may appear in different tools entirely.

Jargon Watch: Shelfware

Techies love making up catchy terms by combining parts of other words in geekily humorous ways. For example, they love taking the "-ware" suffix from the words *hardware* and *software* and putting it on other words, generating *wetware* (a human brain) or *vaporware* (software that doesn't really exist). Another example of this pattern is *shelfware*, which is written documentation for something that nobody actually implements—hence, all it does is sit on the shelf. Requirements documents, architectural plans, and business process models are three examples of documentation that all too often become shelfware.

Of course, not all process automation exercises result in shelfware. There are plenty of examples of processes that companies have successfully automated, such as manufacturing processes and purchasing processes, among others. However, those are some of the simpler processes to automate, because all the various conditions and exceptions are easy to understand. But most businesses are composed of tougher-to-automate cases. Reasons may include too many human workflow steps, or an excess of possible exceptions, too many judgment calls, or even an indeterminate order that the process steps must take. Sometimes the process is simply too darn complicated. Unfortunately, most business processes fall into one of these tough categories.

IT's Basic Limitation

The reason that IT-based solutions have been woefully inadequate for solving this wide range of process automation problems has to do with the way that software works. As anybody with even the slightest bit of programming experience can tell you, computer programs consist of machine-understandable instructions that the computer executes one at a time. Some programming instructions tell the computer to do some specific task; other ones tell the computer to evaluate some condition or perform some calculation and then jump somewhere else to execute its next task. But most often, the programming code sits around waiting for something to tell it when to start working. As a result, most computer applications are developed with the "do this, move to the next instruction, and then do that" school of thinking.

It's no wonder, then, that the easiest business processes to automate are the ones that most closely follow this step-by-step way of thinking. The eCommerce example in the last section is just such a process. Clearly, if you are able to take a process and write it down in this step-by-step manner, then it's relatively straightforward to get computers to automate that process for you, since you can simply write a program that follows the description or flow that you defined.

The challenges come, therefore, when processes have one of the many characteristics that make them difficult to automate—that is, when conditions are hard to evaluate, facts are not well known, or programs must deal with unpredictable change. That's when the description of the process and the process itself tend to diverge, and the process description becomes shelfware. What we need are better approaches to automating processes that don't lend themselves to they way that computers typically work.

Composition: A Key Piece of the Puzzle

A good example of a process that's difficult to automate is the procurement of parts and supplies for an automobile. A typical car today has tens of thousands of parts that come in various states of assembly from hundreds of suppliers. To make things more complicated, a typical automobile manufacturer must carry those parts for dozens of different models. Purchasing such parts is no simple shopping-list-at-the-supermarket exercise, to be sure. Automobile manufacturers implement complicated processes that must deal with all sorts of issues involved in procuring the simplest bolt to the most complicated fuel injection system. These processes may contain thousands of separate activities and are likely to change with significant frequency.

Now, let's say that corporate management calls for the automation of the parts procurement process. Your first activity might simply be to gather all the right people together in a room and start drawing out the process on a big whiteboard. A few problems you might run into are:

- The process has so many steps that you simply don't have the capability to identify all of them, let alone write them all down.
- As a result, you aren't able to gather sufficient detail to capture the essence of each step.
- Not all the right people are able (or willing) to participate in the process definition exercise, so the part of the process you needed them for ends up incomplete or inaccurate.
- By the time you get the exercise well under way, the business requirements for the part of the process you've already completed have changed. Even if you were able to finish, it wouldn't be a correct representation of the business process.

Now, let's say that instead of trying to tackle the entire process in one fell swoop, you assign a subprocess to each of several different teams. Clearly, breaking up a complicated process into smaller, simpler subprocesses has greater odds of success, since this time, at least, you have a chance at making some progress. Let's go through the previous list again:

- You have multiple teams working on different parts of the process, so you might have time to work through all the complexity by having smaller, more efficient teams.
- You may now be able to take the time to gather sufficient detail for each subprocess.
- Each team should contain the right people to define the subprocess at hand.
- As requirements change, only those teams affected by the subprocess need to be involved with the change, not the company as a whole.

Although this approach sounds promising, there are a number of pitfalls. First, the more subprocesses and separate teams there are, the greater the amount of complexity and cost involved in coordinating and managing these teams. Second, we now have to deal with the problem of coordinating across multiple subprocesses as well as trying to put all these subprocesses together to solve the overall business problem. How can you manage this new complexity while solving the original problem?

Putting subprocesses together into a single, larger process is called *composition*. Even if each subprocess solves a business problem, composing subprocesses together is still a challenge. If we assemble the subprocesses willy-nilly, then a business might omit some key operations or perform redundant steps. But more significantly, we still have the agility problem: How can the composed process respond to changing requirements? If we compose different subprocesses in a rigid and formal way, then the resulting composed process will be inflexible and rigid as well. Somehow, we need to build subprocesses in an agile way and compose them together in a way that maintains their agility.

Composing subprocesses into a larger process, therefore, can result in process definitions that still suffer from the shelfware problem. How can we possibly implement agile, flexible business processes unless they are actual representations of the business as it's currently running? How can we make sure that the more we compose business processes, the more they can respond to change and represent the current state of the business? We need an agile approach to business process automation that allows us to compose subprocesses into processes in an agile way that responds more in the way that people respond to change rather than a rigid structure.

WHO'S IN CONTROL OF IT ANYWAY?

All this time, we've been talking about IT as if it consisted of technology alone. Yet aren't people part of the IT picture? One easy way to answer that question is to look at a typical company's budget for IT. Although certainly there is money in the budget for computers, networks, application development, and the like, companies allocate most of it to pay for people. How can we address our core IT problems if we don't also take a look at the people part of the equation? As we address the core problems of IT, we also have to keep in mind the golden rule of business: "Those who have the gold rule." And so, we must address not only the problems of inefficiency and reluctance to change among the rank and file within an organization, but also the issues that come about when we want to change the behavior of those people who hold the gold.

Today's IT Organization

IT departments evolved gradually into the complex hierarchical organizations of today. In the early days, IT was an extension of the finance, manufacturing, or operations part of the business, depending on the industry. As IT grew into a strategic corporate asset, companies formed IT departments to focus on meeting emerging business needs.

With the emergence of the IT department came much of the hierarchical IT organization we have today, with the chief information officer or some similar title reporting directly to the chief executive officer, and departmental heads of IT, midlevel project managers, developers, network and database administrators, operations personnel, and support staff filling out the bottom rungs. As new projects emerged for companies to focus their IT efforts on, the IT organization increasingly grew larger and more regimented. New projects demanded new leadership and, consequently, larger budgets.

By the new millennium, many of the Fortune 1000 companies had IT departments that rivaled the size of many of their suppliers. Indeed, many companies in information-centric industries such as financial services soon had more people in their IT department than in any of their lines of business. Now, IT is critical to the competitive success and long-term viability of such industries, so it's no wonder they have large IT departments. However, with size comes inflexibility, and the more complexity an organization has, the greater the chance of inflexibility and chaos. Furthermore, this principle applies just as much to middle management as it does to middleware.

Silos of Control

One of the problems with the way that IT departments have developed over time is that in the most significant cases, new IT projects demanded new budgets and new management. Each new project—for example, a new customer relationship management project or enterprise resource project— ended up creating new departments within the IT organization that became their own "fiefdoms" with control, budget, and personnel resources of their own. Although having specialized groups within IT isn't a problem unto itself, each of these fiefdoms struggles to cooperate with others in the organization. Even worse, these different fiefdoms further limit a company's agility because they impose their own silos of control in the organization.

In the days where it was necessary to separate technology into isolated, monolithic blocks of functionality that required constant attention and baby-sitting to achieve the results that business required of IT, it made complete sense for such silos of IT control to exist. After all, IT itself was a bunch of silos, so why shouldn't executives manage IT in silos? However, as the post-1990s overspend hangover quickly set in, many senior managers realized that their IT departments had become bloated and resistant to change. As a result, it made sense for those managers to change not only their use of IT, but how they managed their IT organizations as well.

The problem with organizational change, of course, is that nobody wants to lose power. Once a person has responsibility, control, and budget

Jargon Watch: Silo

A *silo* is, yes, a tall, typically cylindrical structure that farmers use to store grain. In a similar fashion, the organizational metaphor that we mean here is of a structure that isolates its contents from outside influences. In an organization, then, a silo of control is a department or other division that maintains its own management hierarchy separate from other departments within the organization. A siloed organization therefore typically has several silos that struggle to communicate or otherwise interact with each other.

The other metaphor we're using for such an organizational structure is a *fiefdom,* a term borrowed from feudalism where the lord of the manor ruled his castle, lands, and serfs in a mostly autonomous fashion—in other words, as a silo of control. The days of feudalism are long over, so why do we have such a cultural hangover in our IT management?

for a certain project, he or she will seek to maintain that control and budget for as long as possible, even if the company as a whole would benefit from a leaner and more effective organization. Now, because we're talking about new technologies and IT approaches that can increase business agility, it's simple human nature that the people who hold the power, or the gold, in those silos will resist such change. Therefore, the only way for a company with a siloed IT organization to even hope to achieve business agility in the face of unpredictable change is to get rid of those IT silos.

Sounds straightforward, but such change is easier said than done. Remember reengineering? Reengineering, as you may remember, was a phenomenon of the 1980s and early 1990s that offered great promise of increased efficiency and customer focus by breaking down organizational silos and introducing a business process-based structure instead. In reality, however, reengineering was a limited success that came to be a euphemism for downsizing and of the susceptibility of management to fads in general. In retrospect, one of the main reasons why reengineering wasn't a greater success was because IT wasn't yet flexible enough to support the organization of business based on critical processes. Instead, the limitations of IT constrained the ability of business to change.

It turns out that the technical challenges to achieving business flexibility and agility are within reach and even somewhat simple, but the management and human challenges are substantial and complex. No longer can a company organize its IT department by application or system, because the future vision for IT is one in which companies build flexible, agile resources that they share among departments—and where business processes, not the underlying technology implementation, drive the resources.

The Secret Sauce: Loose Coupling

If you've made it this far in the book you may think that IT is nothing but trouble, and you might also be wondering if there's any hope at all for it. After all, we've been compounding complexity upon complexity for over 50 years now, and the resulting mess is a brittle, incomprehensible money pit. Maybe businesses should get rid of their IT departments and return to the good ol' days of rows of people with typewriters and adding machines.

Fortunately, the situation is really not that dire. The first part of the book laid out the problems with today's IT approaches; the rest, however, presents a way out of this mess through a new approach to the challenge of making IT work for the business. As we've been hinting, we frame these solutions into the context of Service Orientation, which presents a different way of addressing the relationship between business and IT. However, we're not ready to define Service Orientation yet, because we must first explain what a Service is. And to do that, we must explain the principle of *loose coupling*.

Loose coupling is the fundamental principle behind Service Orientation, so it's important that you understand it. It's a pretty heavy concept that has far-reaching business implications. To explain it, therefore, let's step back and tell a tale.

TALE OF DISTRIBUTED COMPUTING

Since the dawn of the information age, computers have had user interfaces. In the earliest days, these interfaces consisted of switches and blinking lights; later they evolved to paper tapes, punch cards, and the like. Eventually we had *terminals,* which were essentially screens and keyboards that users could interact with to send commands to the big computer in the back room and get the output back visually on the screen in front of them.

Before the development of the terminal, only a single user could interact with the machine at a time. Business users would have to submit their requirements to a specially trained operator, who would then feed those instructions into the machine and provide the results back to the user in a few hours or even days. This particularly burdensome and inefficient process separated the user from the power of computing. As companies sought to leverage their technology investments to a greater degree, they purchased terminals that allowed multiple users to interact with a single machine, all at the same time. This movement from single-user computing to multiple-user computing, enabled through technologies like time-sharing and terminals, was the first step toward distributing the power of computing throughout the organization.

The early, "dumb" terminals really did little else but facilitate the interaction between the smart user and the somewhat-smart machine. Every time you pressed a key, the terminal would send a special instruction back to the computer, and every time the computer wanted to send you some information, it would send the terminal a different instruction, which the terminal was just barely smart enough to turn into a letter or number it could display on the screen. Terminals were simply extensions of the big computer, and provided a way for companies to extend its power. You bought the terminals from the same vendor that supplied the computer, and the vendor determined all the special codes that terminals would use to communicate with the computer. In other words, the terminals and the computer were *tightly coupled* to each other, which meant that the same folks who built the computer had to build the terminals, and they also had to precisely define how the two communicated with each other. If another company wanted to build terminals, they would have to follow the rules and codes of the computer manufacturer precisely, or their terminals wouldn't work at all.

Fast forward 20 years or so to the *personal computer* (PC) era. By the mid-1980s, most businesspeople realized the power of personal computing and had PCs on their desks. Rather than having to share one machine with many users, users now had the power to use a single computer to run several applications like word processors, spreadsheets, and the like. By today's standards, these machines were quite slow and underpowered, but they were significantly better than the typewriters that had occupied the same desktop real estate a few years before.

More than just putting the power of computing closer to the hands of the business user, the PC signaled a shift in computing power from centralized systems to capabilities that companies *distributed* throughout their organizations (hence the term *distributed computing*). In spite of the fact that companies now distributed computing power throughout the organization, the central mainframes and associated applications and databases remained. To get the full value out of the PCs, therefore, companies had to find a way to connect them to the central computers by putting all the computers on a network.

At first, IT folks figured out how to use the PC as a terminal much like the dumb terminals they had been using to interact with the big system. However, users quickly realized that they could go one step further and take advantage of the fact that the PC is a computer in its own right and can actually do stuff with the information it gets from the central system, instead of just displaying it like the dumb terminal did. Basically, the PC quickly became more of an equal peer on the network, where people used it to access central *server* functionality through a *client* interface. Taking the client/server approach to distributed computing transformed IT, because the power of each PC augmented the capabilities of the central servers, and put enormous computing resources into the hands of businesspeople.

Nevertheless, client/server still had its drawbacks, many of which were due to the fact that it was still tightly coupled. To get the client software to be able to work with the server software, programmers had to control both ends of the communication. If they wanted to update the program on the server, they typically had to update the program on each client as well, which meant running around to everyone's office and installing the new software. Big headache!

Jargon Watch: Client/Server

From the name, you might think that client/server was about one client and one server, but in reality, the whole idea of client/server is that you have many servers, and several clients can access each one. The phrase *client/server* then refers to the overall organization of all such clients and servers, or an *architecture*, if you will, as we discuss in Chapter 6.

Web browsers are essentially clients, and Web servers are clearly servers, so in a broad sense, the Web is also client/server—but the narrower meaning of client/server refers to the smart, custom-programmed clients that speak to servers in a tightly coupled manner. Basically, programmers have developed the clients in the client/server interaction with a specific application in mind, whereas Web browsers are built to handle the variability and diversity of the World Wide Web. We make this distinction because the basic organization of the computers that make up today's Web sites—in other words, the architecture—is fundamentally different from how companies have traditionally approached client/server.

Now, client/server was tightly coupled, but as it happens, it wasn't as tightly coupled as the dumb terminals were. As part of the client/server trend, vendors established a standard language for accessing and updating the information in databases, as well as standard protocols for connecting to those databases. As long as the client and the server agreed on the language for accessing the databases and querying their information, then the programmers wouldn't have to teach both ends how to handle database connections and queries. In theory, it was good enough for programmers simply to follow the standards to make the client/server interactions happen.

Of course, theory and practice are not the same thing. Each database vendor had slightly different query languages, and each computer vendor had slightly different connection protocols. The devil is in the details, to be sure. So while client/server was a little less tightly coupled than terminals, for all practical purposes, it was still necessary for the same programmers to develop both ends of the communication.

Enter the Web

The Internet has been around since the late 1960s. The U.S. Government decided to open up the Internet to commercial use in the early 1990s, where before they had restricted its usesolely to government and academic purposes. At that point, the Internet was only a text-only medium, where *text* is the letters, numbers, and other characters that humans can see, understand, and type. But by the early 1990s, a researcher at a physics lab in Switzerland introduced a new technology called the World Wide Web, which allowed academics to exchange images as well as text-based information on the Internet.

With the Web came two new technologies: Web *browsers* that provided a simple interface to Web information and Web *servers* that enabled anybody to produce and distribute information on the Internet. Where client/server relied on standards for accessing databases, the Web went a few steps further. First, the Internet provided a standard way of going about networking, so now computers could find each other and communicate with each other following specific standards. The Web then added standard ways for sending, receiving, and displaying text and images, as well as standards for linking one Web page with another.

One of the keys that made the Web so easy to use and quick to proliferate was its dependence on text-based documents as a way to define the language for how to communicate and exchange information on the Internet. By this point, all computers could understand text-encoded information. The reliance on text made it easy for browsers to display Web pages. All of the formatting instructions—when to make a word bold, for example, or how to include images—were represented as text as well, so the browser simply had to read the text the Web server was sending it and do its best to display it. Any instructions the user might want to give to the server likewise appeared as text, so all the server had to do to understand what the user wanted was to interpret the text sent from the browser to the Web server.

The combination of this use of text and the small but potent set of standards for networking, transmission, and display of that text *loosely coupled* the browsers and the Web servers. Loose coupling means that as long as the programmer of each end of a distributed computing interchange agrees on some existing set of rules, each programmer is able to program and update his or her end of the exchange independently of the other. In other words, by agreeing on the standards of the Web, *any* browser could display *any* Web page from *any* Web server, regardless of the types of computers involved, which companies programmed the browser or Web server, or who assembled the Web page.

Now, theory and practice (not to mention human nature) being what they are, this loose coupling between browsers and Web servers isn't perfect. Unlike client/server, however, if there's some problem in a Web server browser, the Web still keeps on working. We all know, however, that some Web pages work in some browsers but not others. It's not supposed to be like that, of course, but that's the reality. Nevertheless, if you run into one of those pages that don't work on your machine, you can simply move on to some other page, and your computer (usually) keeps on working. In the client/server world, an incompatibility is far more likely to prevent the client from working at all.

The growth of the Web has exploded, in large part because it's so easy to use—not just for users of browsers, but also for the creators of Web pages. It seems that everybody and their dog has a Web site these days. That ease of use in turn depends on the loose coupling between browsers and Web servers, since it's that loose coupling that is at the core of the fundamentally forgiving nature of the Web.

So, what would the world be like if *every single interaction* with IT was as easy and forgiving as surfing the Web? What if *any* step in *any* business process could take advantage of loose coupling to the point that not only human-to-computer interactions had this easy, forgiving nature, but computer-to-computer interactions did as well? That's the power behind Service Orientation that we'll be exploring for the rest of this book.

POWER OF ABSTRACTION

We hope you buy the notion of loose coupling at this point. However, some of you may be thinking that there's some magic wand waving going on here.

How can the way that browsers access Web pages be so *simple,* after all, when IT is so frustratingly *complex?* In the last chapter we harped on how the increasing complexity of IT was swamping business, and the problem was only getting worse. Now we're going to make the case that there's a solution to this problem of increasing complexity—only we're not going to propose getting rid of much, if any, of that burgeoning IT infrastructure. So, what's the secret?

The secret lies in how IT has always dealt with complexity, ever since the days of the first digital computer (which was the code-breaking Colossus in England's Bletchley Park during World War II, by the way, for you history buffs out there). That secret is the concept of *abstraction.* In a general sense, the term *abstraction* means something that represents something else by simplifying or altering its appearance. For example, abstract art represents real things without looking much at all like them. In the world of IT, abstraction is a way to simplify the complexities of the technology with simple yet powerful representations.

Abstraction finds its roots in the very earliest software. The first programmable digital computers like Colossus dealt in the binary world of zeroes and ones—that is, *only* zeroes and ones. Programs were zeroes and ones. Output consisted of zeroes and ones. As a result, programming was very difficult and programs were quite difficult to understand, interpret, and correct. Today computers still work with zeroes and ones: creating them, moving them, and changing them into each other. At a fundamental level, that's *all* computers really do. Nowadays, of course, people hardly ever have to deal with this fundamental binary nature of computers directly.

The key to this ability to ignore all those zeroes and ones leverages the power of the computers themselves. Into the black-and-white world of the first days of computing came programs called *compilers* that let programmers work with English-like programming languages, such as COBOL. Fundamentally, compilers are programs that take the COBOL code, crunch it, and spit out the zero-and-one *object codes,* which are the codes that the computers actually understand. The first compiler writers had to write the first compilers by stringing zeroes and ones together—that is, by writing the object code manually—but as soon as they got that working, then programmers could use COBOL instead to generate object code automatically—even to improve the COBOL compiler itself—and then to write new compilers for new programming languages.

The COBOL compiler, therefore, *abstracted* the object code. COBOL statements were still computer commands, but the compiler had to turn them into the real commands that computers could actually understand. Humans could now work at a *level of abstraction* above where the computers worked, and the power of the computer itself enabled the translation between the human world of understanding and the computer's world of zeroes and ones.

There are two very important points to keep in mind about levels of abstraction. First, they do not remove complexity. Instead, they hide it from the user and simplify a user's interaction with complex technology. Second, levels of abstraction in the IT sense are not abstract in the conventional sense of being obscure or cerebral, as they arguably are in abstract art. On the contrary, IT abstractions are actually quite concrete, in the sense that COBOL was a real language you could read, write, and understand. Paradoxically, the binary object code underneath might be considered more abstract than the COBOL code in the sense that it's more obscure and cerebral (at least to the human), but that's not the sense we're using the word *abstraction* in. When we use the term *abstraction,* we mean an intentional simplification that computers can automatically resolve into the more complex, underlying representation.

The story of abstraction doesn't end with compilers, of course. Another important example of an abstraction is the graphical user interface (GUI), which provided a way to access underlying system resources through a visual environment. We've grown accustomed to dealing with icons, windows, menus, and the like populating our computer screen, and all of these things are abstractions. These GUI elements aren't *real,* in the sense that the computer doesn't understand them directly. Instead, it's smart enough to know how to translate them into the zeroes and ones it understands and then convert the digits it spits back out into the images you see on the screen.

Needless to say, dealing with windows and menus is *simple,* while the underlying technology is *complex.* That's the power of abstraction. At every step in the abstraction process, software allows people to work with relatively simple tools that access complex systems behind the scenes. That's the secret: the ability to layer one level on top of another, so that the tools people use get simpler as they also become more powerful. We'll leverage the power of abstraction to simplify the rats' nest of today's IT systems—not by replacing one complex technology with another, but by abstracting existing complexity to make it easier to comprehend and by improving its ability to respond to ongoing, unpredictable business change.

Abstractions and the Way We Think

It's human nature to think in terms of abstractions in many contexts, not just when we deal with IT. Much of the technology we use outside of computers is filled with abstractions, whether you're driving a car, using a household appliance, or getting surgery. It seems that our brains are wired to create and deal with abstractions as our primary approach to negotiating complexity in our day-to-day lives. The more complex things get, the more we crave simplicity, after all.

When we drive a car, we don't have to care about drive trains, steering columns, and master brake cylinders. Mechanics, however, must care about such things, even though such components are themselves abstractions that mask further underlying complexity. Automobile designers, in turn, must deal with this additional complexity that even mechanics can generally avoid.

So too with IT. When you as a knowledge worker are sitting in front of your computer, you may be working with a word processor or spreadsheet or what have you, and you don't have to care about GUIs or networks or compilers, let alone zeroes and ones. But if you're a network engineer or a programmer or the like, then it's your job to care about such things.

When everything is running smoothly, people are generally able to specialize in whatever layer of abstraction their work concerns. However, when something goes wrong, then people often must deal with underlying complexity. In the case of the automobile, this process is relatively straightforward: If you have a problem with your car, you might look under the hood, and if you have the aptitude, you might be able to fix the problem. If you don't, then it's time to call a mechanic.

In the case of IT, however, the process of resolving problems is much more of a dark art. Techies would like to think this occult aspect of solving IT problems is due to the fact that IT is more complex than systems like automobiles, but in fact, it's simply because the practice of IT engineering is less mature than auto engineering. In fact, new technologies and approaches are pushing IT to mature as an industry in much the same way that the auto industry matured past the point where every driver had to be a skilled mechanic. Be that as it may, today's IT people often have to wear multiple hats to get things working smoothly.

This ability to think at different levels of abstraction simultaneously therefore becomes one of the critical skills for all IT people as they become more senior in their position. Programmers routinely find themselves working with networks and operating systems, even though in theory these abstractions aren't their responsibility. Knowledge workers—business users who utilize IT resources as an active part of their day-to-day work—typically know a thing or two about getting their own computers to operate properly. On one hand, this ability to work on multiple levels of abstraction is essential to keeping things working, and a key part of how we're able to accomplish so much with the inflexible, complex IT that we have. On the other hand, it's better to leave fixing cars to the mechanics whenever possible, especially as the underlying systems become more complex.

As you've probably guessed at this point, Service Orientation is itself an abstraction. As we go through the concepts that form the basis for Service Orientation, it's important to keep in mind that they are abstractions—that is, to remember that they are technologies that rely on abstraction for both their power and their ability to mask complexity. But also keep in mind that such complexity still exists and that people will still need to work on multiple levels of abstraction on occasion to keep everything up and running smoothly.

ROLE OF OPEN STANDARDS

The Web was a successful abstraction in large part because it was a *standard*—that is, different computer vendors (mostly) agreed on what the Web was, so if you learned how to build Web sites or Web browsers, your skills worked on different vendors' computers. But have you ever wondered how certain standards have come to be? Let's leave the world of IT for a moment and look at standards more broadly.

Time for another tale: the establishment of standards for the width of railroad tracks. The width between the two rails, or gauge, of a standard railroad in the United States is exactly 4 feet 8.5 inches—a very strange number indeed. So, why do we use that width? Because that's the way that engineers built pre-railroad tramways in England (before those engineers subsequently went to the United States to build railroads there), and the folks who built the tramways in England used the same tools and methods that they used for building wagons, which used that wheel spacing. And why exactly were wagon wheels spaced in that odd dimension? Because that was the spacing of existing wheel ruts on many of the long-distance roads in England, and wheels of a different spacing would break on those ruts. This brings us to the final question of who built those old, rutted roads: the Romans. The Romans used that particular wheel width because that was the exact width of the back ends of two Imperial Roman war horses that they used in their chariots. So, when you wonder what horse's rear came up with a particular standard, in this case, you now have the answer!

What Is an Open Standard?

We depend on standards today in many ways in our daily lives. Standards govern the voltage coming out of our electric socket as well as the shape of the plug that goes into it. We need standards to help us make sure we put the right gasoline in our cars and figure out how far we've gone. In fact, standards are necessary for the development of any industry—without them, we are left with a chaos of different formats, sizes, and quality specifications for the products we use, leaving it up to the poor consumer to figure out how to put various things together. Indeed, standards are the key to reliability and predictability.

But what exactly is a standard? We'll answer this question in two parts. The first part concerns the nature of a standard itself. Standards are really about one thing: *getting agreement.* A standard represents a codified representation of an agreement on how to perform a process or implement a technology. Formal standards bodies, industry organizations, governmental bodies, consortia, or even individuals may define standards. Standards can be global and implemented across all industries, such as the Ethernet standard for computer networking, or they can be very specific to one particular application. For example, the U.S. legal system uses a standard language and process to conduct its daily business, while other legal systems use different languages and processes.

However, in the preceding cases, we are talking about de jure standards, which means that organizations come together to create them in advance and with conscious thought. More frequently, standards are de facto, implying that the simple act of reusing a technology, process, or language over and over again in an industry or geography has created the standard, without the conscious thought of a de jure standard. After all, that is how we ended up with the width of railroad tracks. De facto standards come about simply because people find them useful, and there is rarely a good reason to switch to another arbitrary format for doing the same thing. This is the most powerful lesson of standards: At the end of the day, they must accomplish something useful.

Companies with products or services to sell frequently propose and promote standards, and such standards are clearly self-serving efforts to promote the companies' particular approaches to implementing a given technology or process. Although those standards may serve the purposes of making such products easier to implement, they also make them harder to adopt across an industry, since competitors are loath to agree to follow the standards that their rivals have proposed.

As a result, there's a category of standard known as *open,* in that they aren't proprietary to a single company, and they're also available for public development and inspection. More specifically, we can define an open standard as one in which the developers of the standard put together all of its inner workings in full view of any individual or organization that cares to see it, and they create the standard so that many organizations can share it and continue to improve it, including ones that may compete with members of the body that created it. No single company or individual owns an open standard or is the sole authority for its creation or use.

Another good definition of openness comes not in the definition of the specification, but in the manner with which people use it. A product that follows a standard can interoperate with products from other vendors that also follow that standard. As a result, it's easier for users of such products to replace one product with a competing product. This advantage is primarily to the consumer, who has increased choice in technology suppliers. It might appear, however, that this replaceability is a disadvantage to the vendor. In fact, the opposite is true: Following open standards is actually an advantage for vendors in that they can make sure their solution fits well within the ecosystem of other products their customers purchase. Short-sighted vendors, predictably, often don't realize this point.

Problem with Standards

Of course, all this talk of standards veils the real issue at hand: *interoperability*. The whole point of developing a standard in the first place is to make sure that any two independent solutions will work with each other. Companies frequently tout the fact that their products are open and comply with standards, but in reality, no one really would want to use the product in an interoperable fashion with another in any case. For example, who cares if a garage door opener complies with a standard for its frequencies and codes if it is only meant to open *your* garage door? Furthermore, if a standard doesn't really need to be open in order for it to support your needs, then who cares who is developing the specification and how they're delivering it? Clearly, companies are now using the term *standard* flippantly instead of putting in the time and effort to improve the functionality in their products—after all, it's easier to create a new a standard than a new product.

But the problems with standards go beyond this shell game. Standards committee efforts fall into one of two camps, for the most part, which we'll call for simplicity the "least common denominator" (LCD) and the "kitchen sink." LCD specifications reflect only those elements that all parties manage to agree on. Sometimes this approach means that a specification with 60 elements gets whittled down to only 10, and then the result is the LCD that all parties can agree on. LCD approaches typically result in specifications that are too limited to meet any one particular company's needs, leading companies to customize them with proprietary add-ons, often defeating the purpose of having a standard in the first place.

In the kitchen-sink approach to the standards effort, however, the specification in question contains all the suggestions of all the parties, meaning that everyone has at least some of their suggestions included in the final result. The kitchen-sink approach results in a fat, bloated specification that is too large for everyone and not specific enough for anyone. Kitchen-sink approaches can also result in specifications that are too big for anyone to implement in their entirety. As a result, companies partially implement them on a selective basis, a fact that often puts companies at odds over which parts of the specification they will choose to implement.

Neither approach is ideal, and as a result, it's impossible to equate standards support with *excellence*. A standard is an agreement, and an agreement, at best, is a compromise. Furthermore, some people point to the futility of attempting to standardize certain things. Although it is fairly easy to standardize something as arbitrary as the voltage and frequency of electricity, it is a much harder, if not futile, effort to attempt to standardize complex processes or vocabularies. Every company has its own way of doing things and a specific vocabulary for how it refers to the most important parts of its business. Trying to get all companies to agree to the same processes or vocabulary for all their activities is a Herculean, if not Sisyphean, effort. It may indeed be possible to get agreement on the general methods and acceptable tolerances for creating and implementing processes, but no company will want to reduce its own competitive advantage to something that is standard and common across all its competitors.

Finally, another problem with standards is that there are just too many of them. It is very easy for a company to propose some specification for how to do things and then try to gather support from other firms to make it a standard. Many of these standards are not well defined and overlap with others that their competitors might be proposing simultaneously. All this standards activity causes confusion and a reluctance among the buyers of technology to adopt *any* of the standards, at least until the dust settles and one standard emerges as the victor. The problem is that in supporting one standard, a company may be inadvertently closing the doors on accepting another, conflicting standard.

There's an interesting postscript to the story about railroad gauges and horses' behinds. The Space Shuttle requires two solid rocket boosters (SRBs) to help it get into orbit. Morton-Thiokol manufactures the SRBs at a plant in Utah. Although the designers might have preferred to make the SRBs wider or longer, the railroad line from the factory had to run through a tunnel in the mountains, whose size depended on the width of the railroad tracks that went through them. As a result, the width of the tracks, and their legacy in the size of horses' behinds, had a direct impact on the design of the space shuttle SRBs. Lesson learned: Choose your standards wisely, as they will linger far longer than you might expect!

RUNNING IT LIKE A RAILROAD

There comes a time in the evolution of every marketplace when the benefits of cooperating in a standard manner outweigh the advantages of conducting business in a proprietary manner. Although in many situations there are clear economic incentives for vendors to lock in customers with proprietary solutions to customer problems, as a market evolves, competitors eventually offer sufficient selection and quality to afford users choice. At that point, competitors who cooperate on establishing standards can provide themselves with a competitive advantage over those vendors who continue to offer proprietary solutions, since customers no longer have to lock themselves in to a particular vendor. Basically, at some point in every industry there is enough agreement on what the products that customers buy must do; at that point, demand shifts from proprietary, vendor-specific solutions to standard approaches that all vendors agree to implement. The shift to leveraging standards is typically quite rapid when an industry reaches this tipping point, as market participants who do not participate are quickly left out in the cold.

It is not sufficient, however, for vendors alone to get together to decide on standards. After all, a need to sell new products motivates vendors, so why would they agree to anything that would limit their ability to introduce such new products to the market? At some point, customer requirements must offset self-centered vendor needs. A standard is just ink on paper or zeroes and ones in a file until vendors and customers can agree on how to do business in a standard way. The point here is that it is the *business,* not the *standard,* that is of critical importance: Only when buyers and sellers actually use the standards to conduct day-to-day business can they realize the competitive advantages of the standards. The significance of standards, however, far surpasses the ability of individual buyers and sellers to conduct business. Standards adoption, in fact, can transform industries, and often signifies the maturation of those industries as a whole.

Standards and the Maturation of Industries

There are many examples from history where the adoption of standards contributed to the maturation of that industry. Let's take once again, for example, the railroad business. Although horses' rumps ended up establishing the track gauge we use today, in the early days of the industry, several companies built out their own tracks using their own track gauges. Building out a proprietary system in this way made perfect business sense for such companies, as they each maneuvered for dominance in their industry. Whichever company ended up achieving such dominance would be able to dictate standards to whatever remained of their competition, with the dominant player being able to control not just the transportation service itself, but also the train car, track laying, and other related businesses.

In fact, the railroads were targets of the first antitrust legislation and lawsuits in the 1800s when they attempted to dominate everything from the railroad tracks to the ticketing systems. This dominance helped the companies solidify their control of the market, but it didn't offer customers the choice they craved. As vendors built out their infrastructure, customers began to feel the pinch, as long-distance travel required them not only to change trains, but to change train systems—tracks, stations, and the like, often many times on a single trip.

Proprietary solutions are also increasingly risky for the vendors, primarily because of the substantial capital expense they require to develop all the necessary infrastructure. The inherent inefficiency of proprietary solutions also contributes to the risk for each vendor. In England, for example, there were several different train companies serving the same popular train routes. Although there was an increased supply of trains for these routes, the overall demand reached its limit, and so the demand for each particular route decreased, increasing the expense per customer for every vendor in the market. Before long, nobody was able to make any money on those routes. So, multiple proprietary systems catering to a single market often lead to financial loss for the vendors in that space.

At some point, then, one or both of two developments naturally occur. First, a single vendor may come to dominate the industry, and it builds the power to either acquire or crush its competition. Such market domination leads to de facto standards, as the way Wal-Mart or Boeing or whoever decrees is the way to do business becomes the way everybody has to do business. The second possible development is when vendors get together and establish a set of de jure standards. Vendors take this "co-opetition" approach when they realize that they won't simply be able to stamp out competition through aggressive market behavior, and eventually customers get fed up with the plethora of proprietary solutions on the market.

It's important to point out that it's the customers who have the power at this point in the development of an industry. Customers—regardless of industry—always want better value: higher quality, increased choice, and lower prices. Once there are multiple competitors who are all offering sufficient quality in the marketplace, customers gravitate toward the less expensive alternatives. Vendors soon realize that by working together to establish standards, they can improve their business efficiency by lowering their own cost of production and thus offer their products and services at a lower price to their customers. Broad standards implementation improves business efficiency (think one set of tracks instead of several redundant sets, and the money that saved), which translates into both higher profits for vendors and lower costs for customers. Vendors who choose not to join such standards efforts become increasingly less competitive, until they must either participate or perish.

Inherent Limitations of Standards

Cooperative standards efforts, however, can go only so far, because every vendor must offer something to its customers that the competition cannot. Maybe it's a unique product, or a better—quality offering, or a less expensive option—in any case, each vendor must always offer something proprietary as a unique value proposition. The standards always reach a limit, since every vendor must offer some unique value proposition to the marketplace on top of simply implementing the standards. After all, everybody soon implements the standards, so there's no competitive differentiator for vendors who do nothing but implement standards in products.

Standard track gauges meant that each company's trains ran on everybody's tracks, so there was no longer any value in building tracks with a proprietary track gauge. Instead, the railroad companies had to compete on quality of service, the types of trains, the destinations they served, price, or other essentially proprietary offerings that enabled them to compete for their customers' business. It simply became uneconomical to compete on track gauges and vertical industry dominance alone.

Standards adoption increases *business agility* as well. If your trains run on all your competitors' tracks instead of just your own, you can both respond to changes in the business environment and leverage those changes for competitive advantage much more easily than if you had to build new tracks. It is the increase in business agility that interests us the most in this book, as the current state of IT has led not only to expensive solutions, but to brittle, inflexible approaches that impede business agility. It's important, therefore, to take a look at the business of distributed computing in the light of standards adoption to understand how we'll ever get IT that will provide the business agility companies crave today.

Standards, Agility, and IT

Fortunately, the world of distributed computing is currently undergoing the transition from proprietary approaches to standards-based approaches. Much of the technology in today's IT shops is still mostly proprietary, however, for the same reason that customers have always purchased proprietary solutions: That was the only way to get stuff that worked at all. As discussed earlier, proprietary solutions often fit the bill of the cheapest, most expedient solution to the business problems at hand, resulting in the inevitable rats' nest. The downside to these proprietary software packages predictably falls into the pattern discussed earlier: They are inefficient and inflexible. Companies often find themselves purchasing redundant solutions from different vendors to get the capabilities they require, just as a passenger might have had to switch stations to get on trains that ran on different gauge tracks.

Unfortunately, IT is fundamentally more complex than the railroad industry. Instead of tracks, we have networks, operating systems, applications, programming languages, and a whole laundry list of technologies that go into making distributed computing actually work. The good news is that standards efforts in IT have been going on for quite some time. After all, the secret of the Internet and the World Wide Web is their underlying standards that enable the loose coupling between browsers and Web servers, for example. Just as with the Web, standards increase the business agility of the companies using the technology by creating a certain level of interoperability across different vendors' products—in other words, the standard track gauge of the Internet.

Furthermore, companies absolutely require standards to become agile organizations. This need is quite clear if you imagine what your IT environment would look like if everything had a proprietary interface and a different technology implementation. The more things are similar, the easier it is to make changes and replace older technologies with newer ones. If every interface is different and proprietary, the more expensive it becomes to change over time. Agility favors standardization, and standardization enables flexibility. The key challenge businesses face today therefore is to find the right balance between standardization that provides flexibility and proprietary advantages that provide critical competitive differentiators.

The good news is that today's standards efforts have moved well beyond the basics of the Web to a much broader application across many aspects of distributed computing. We're going to go a step further and argue that we've actually reached the standards tipping point in IT, where vendors *must* support standards for interoperability or be left in the dust of their competition. This conclusion is very good news indeed—because it is the key to lowered costs, greater business efficiency, and, most important, greater business agility.

HOW TO THINK LOOSELY COUPLED

Let's take one more look at the railroad example. If you're a train buff, we're sure you're tickled, and if you're not, please bear with us—we'll be getting off this train soon. First, we have the horses' rear standard: Tracks should always be 4 feet 8.5 inches apart. So far, so good. Let's say your business is going to go out and lay some track, and to be sure, you want to follow the standard. Is it sufficient to know that the tracks must be 4 feet 8.5 inches apart?

The answer, of course, is not on your life! There's far more to laying track than simply getting the spacing correct—you have strength, grade, weather properties, and a whole list of other factors you need to follow to lay track that others would be willing to run their trains on. In other words, standards are only the starting point for true interoperability. In the real world, a standard is only a small part of the overall relationship among the parties that agree to that standard.

Instead of simply focusing on the standards themselves, then, let's concentrate on the parties and their relationships. Essentially, all such relationships boil down to the interactions between two parties, since we can express the relationships among larger groups of participants as the set of relationships between any two members of the group. For each interaction between these two parties, one *provides* something and the other *consumes* it. Before the provider can provide whatever the service is, however, the two parties must come to an agreement, or *contract,* that specifies the details of the service the provider is performing.

Supporting particular standards, then, is part of that contract, as are all the other aspects of the relationship between the parties (track grade, strength, etc.). And as with any good legal contract, the two parties are at "arm's length"—that is, they remain independent parties who don't get to mess around in each other's business, except as explicitly provided for in

---

Jargon Watch: Contract

In legal terms, a *contract* is "any promise or set of promises made by one party to another for the breach of which the law provides a remedy. The promise or promises may be express (either written or oral) or may be implied from circumstances." Although matters of law are always interesting, what we care about here is the contract between two automated IT systems. In this case, we care about a *software contract* that stipulates the set of promises that one system will make to the other, and the expectations of both parties. In IT, we implement a software contract through a *contracted interface,* which is an agreed-on language and vocabulary for defining, interpreting, and processing contracts.

the contract. Essentially, the contract loosely couples the relationship between the provider and the consumer of some agreed-on functionality or service.

It's important to note, however, that there are two different senses of *contract* in play here. First, there is the legal agreement between two business entities, say, the owner of the trains and the owner of the tracks. Second, there is the technical relationship between the equipment—the trains' requirements for the tracks that the tracks must meet. In order to simplify this technical relationship, we can use an *abstraction* that represents some simplification of how the trains and tracks work as well as the parties in the contract. In other words, we say that there is a contract between the tracks that provide the service and the trains that consume it.

Bear with us here, because this is a critical point. In the case of IT, when we talk about providers, consumers, and contracts, we're talking about *automated systems,* not about *people.* Now, discussing the relationships between business entities that provide and consume IT services is clearly important, don't get us wrong. In fact, Service Orientation extends the principles of how providers and consumers of services interact on a technical level beyond a discussion of the technology to the business level itself.

Jargon Watch: Provider and Consumer

There are always at least two parties involved in any interaction, one that offers some value and one that uses that value. A piece of software that exposes some piece of information or functionality for another piece of software to use is called a *provider,* and the software that wants to access or use that information or functionality is the *consumer.* Over time, a piece of software could easily be both a provider and a consumer, but for each individual interaction, that software takes on one role or the other.

We talk about providers and consumers as if they were people or businesses, and for good reason. Just as in all economic arrangements, there is a supply/demand relationship between providers and consumers. The more consumers there are, the greater demand there is for providers that can meet the needs of those consumers. The more providers there are, the more competition there is for useful features and functionality among providers. This supply/demand relationship is a healthy one that will help to govern the usability of the IT systems as a whole and make IT more responsive to business needs.

Providers, Consumers, and Contracts in IT

The reason we talk about providers, consumers, and contracts in IT is because we want the interactions between the providers and consumers of information and functionality to be loosely coupled. In order for loosely coupled interactions to work in IT, providers and consumers must have *contracted* interfaces. Just as legal contracts are documents that outline a set of enforceable rules and agreements written in a language that both parties can understand, in IT we need to define a contract that stipulates IT "rules of engagement" in a standardized manner that both the consumer and provider can understand. Such information should also appear in a document external to each participant that provides the information each participant needs to interact with the other.

A software contract is a document that specifies what a particular application or functional component expects of consumers and what those consuming applications can expect of it. The key here is that the people responsible for the provider and consumer define the contract in a way that is independent of how each piece of software chooses to implement it, giving us a stepping-stone toward loose coupling.

It's important to understand the relationship between contracts and loose coupling. Loose coupling mandates that two interacting parties should have as little information as possible necessary to govern their relationship. Furthermore, the entire reason why we want to loosely couple software is so that we can independently create and control each component of the IT environment. The way in which we choose to make loose coupling a reality is by implementing contracted interfaces on systems and by making sure that we enforce those contracted relationships while allowing each party to change *how* it implements the contract independently.

Loose Coupling and Common Knowledge

What makes something in the IT world coupled to something else is the level of *common knowledge* that the people controlling the two ends of such a distributed computing exchange. Some connections are very close and rigid, such as the connection between an axle and a tire on a car, while others are more peripheral, such as the effect of emissions on global warming. Yet other things don't seem to be connected at all, such as opening the window and changing the television channel. How do we know that one thing is connected to another? By making some change to one entity and observing if a change is made, or must be made, to the other entity. Moving the axle will necessarily move the wheel, and thus they are connected. But opening the window doesn't (or at least shouldn't!) have any impact on the current television channel.

Although some things are connected and others don't seem to be, there actually is a degree to which they are in fact connected to each other. Another way of putting the phrase *the degree to which things are connected to each other* is the concept of *coupling*. The more to which two things are dependent on each other, the more they are *tightly* coupled; the more that each discrete entity can change on its own without requiring a change from the other entity, the more *loosely* coupled they are. In a tightly coupled exchange, for example, the programmer responsible for creating the consumer must have detailed knowledge about the behavior of the provider, such as how to access each bit of functionality, the specific technology necessary to access the software, and the details of the data format that the provider offers.

In a loosely coupled exchange, however, the people controlling the two participants in the exchange have specific, *limited* knowledge about each other. That limited amount of information appears in the contract. In fact, companies engage in loosely coupled relationships with other companies all the time. Every business interaction between independent parties depends on a legal contract that defines the nature of how the two parties interact without stipulating how those parties will perform their tasks. This legal sense of *contract* enables the parties to go about their business and make changes to their internal processes independently of each other, while an enforceable set of rules continues to stipulate how they should interact with each other.

Contracts between providers and consumers of IT functionality work the same way. Even when the same company (or department) controls the provider and consumer in a particular interaction, it often still makes sense to put only enough detail in the contract to stipulate how systems interact at an arm's length, without going into detail as to how each party will perform its obligations. Loose coupling results from having contracted interfaces that make it much easier to update how each piece of software works independently of the others, since the contract specifies all the information about how each component must interact with other components. In other words, contracted interfaces provide increased flexibility.

Loose Coupling and Agility

The fundamental problem with traditional distributed computing architectures is that they are tightly coupled, which means that the architect must design each component system with the other systems in mind. As a result, making changes to one tightly coupled system often affects the whole architecture, requiring expensive and difficult reworking. Loose coupling, however, typically leads to greater business agility and flexibility.

Building loosely coupled systems enforces a kind of discipline on the creators of IT functionality, because they are not allowed to make assumptions about the system on the other end of the connection. Instead, they must work with an abstract representation of the remote system that the contract provides, where the specific properties of that system are left undetermined. As a result, developers must by necessity build more agile and flexible systems, because they do not have the luxury of controlling both ends of the communication between distributed systems.

Similarly, the nature of those interactions is a lot more reliable and robust, because the developer has no reason to believe the remote system will respond in any given time interval. Well-designed loosely coupled systems, therefore, should be both more robust and more flexible than tightly coupled components typically are. Consumers are agnostic with respect to whether the providers are available or working properly, and, therefore, they will be more likely to keep working under unexpected circumstances. As a result, loosely coupled, contracted systems are designed with unpredictable change in mind. The net result is that developers can make changes to their systems without breaking other systems in their environment.

The power and flexibility that contracted, loosely coupled systems can offer the enterprise are substantial. If an organization abstracts its IT infrastructure so that it presents its functionality in the form of loosely coupled systems that offer clear business value, then the consumers of those systems, regardless of their location, can access the functionality they need independent of the underlying technology that supports them. Furthermore, each system in the IT environment can change independently to meet unpredictable new business requirements without breaking the system as a whole.

SECRET OF THE BEST ICE SKATERS

To anyone who's been around the IT block a few times, the promise of loose coupling seems a bit pie-in-the-sky. "Let's get this straight," the cynic says. "I have some piece of software that I can write on my own, without having to know about any other software on the network. I can then go out onto the network and find some other piece of software that has the data or functionality I need, and then the software that I created can connect to it and access it, and I don't need to have any clue about how the other piece of software works. All I need to do is to follow some contract that's basically nothing more than a document." *Yeah, right, pull the other leg!* We're just so used to inflexible, tightly coupled IT systems that barely work that it's no wonder there are so many cynics out there.

In fact, you can think of loosely coupled distributed computing as being a lot like ice skating, or gymnastics, or any other capability that requires substantial skill and effort, all with the goal of making that effort disappear from view. In other words, the best ice skaters don't only skate well, they actually make skating look *easy*. The same is true of loosely coupled computing—when done properly, the cynic's implausible scenario actually does take place. Consumers can find and access providers without anybody having to program both of them to work together ahead of time. It just looks so easy! The secret is in hiding the complexity behind the façade of simplicity.

The fact of the matter is, there's really no magic here. Loose coupling is, in fact, quite difficult to achieve. If it were easy, after all, don't you think distributed computing would have been loosely coupled for years now, and all our systems would be as flexible and agile as we need them to be? There are a few reasons why we haven't been able to make our systems loosely coupled to this point. First, it's taken a while for systems to get as powerful as we needed them to be to make the development and exchange of contracts possible without bogging everything down. Second, and more important, it's taken a few decades for the IT industry to mature to the point that standards, best practices, and available products are now able to provide for the loose coupling that's so essential to the agility that businesses crave. Basically, IT has outgrown its adolescent years.

Metadata: The Secret Sauce

Of course, this book isn't going to teach you how to skate. Instead, we'd like to teach you enough about skating to appreciate the best skaters. After all, businesspeople don't need to know all the details about the inner workings of the technology. What they *do* need to understand, however, is how and when to apply technology solutions to business problems, and also how to select the appropriate technology in the first place—and above all else, how to avoid the wrong technology. It's not sufficient, therefore, for you as the reader of this book to simply take loose coupling at face value. It's important to peel back the abstraction just enough to get a good look at what goes into making loose coupling work—not so that you can necessarily make it work yourself, but rather to give you the tools to identify when someone else is doing it right—or not.

In the last section, we talked about how important software contracts are to loose coupling. Just as legal contracts make for solid business relationships, software contracts make for solid, loosely coupled distributed computing. Here's what goes into a contract, especially the kind that computers, rather than people, need to understand:

- Contracts should describe what a provider will give to any consumer that chooses to abide by the terms of the contract. The contract should define what functionality the provider provides, what data it will return, or typically some combination of the two.

- Contracts must have information both about the responsibility of the providers for providing their functionality and/or data as well as the expected responsibilities of the consumers of that information and what they will need to provide in return.
- Contracts also specify the rules of engagement between consumers and providers, known as *policies,* that govern who can access a provider, what security procedures the participants must follow, and any other rules that apply to the exchange.

What contracts *never* include are the data that providers and consumers actually exchange or any specifics about *how* a provider or a consumer will go about meeting the requirements of the contract. Instead, contracts consist solely of information about those specifics, which we call *metadata.* Metadata (the plural of *metadatum,* by the way, a word nobody ever uses) means *data about data.* For example, let's say some datum is the number *3.* Well, what exactly does that number represent? It could be a price, or a size, or the age of a person. That information about the data, namely the price, size, or age, is the metadata that surrounds or describes that datum. So when we talk about *age,* we are actually talking about *metadata.* The word *age* by itself isn't meaningful in a specific interaction, but it does have meaning in conjunction with the data it describes, since it helps us understand the meaning or context of those data.

Contracts, therefore, consist of metadata, because all the information in the contract refers to how the provider and consumer are to deal with the data they wish to exchange. Metadata may sound like a techie concept, and to be sure it is, but we're introducing it here because of its vital importance to loosely coupled distributed computing and, more broadly, to Service

---

Jargon Watch: Policy

What we mean by *policy* here pretty much follows the common usage: Policies are rules that some authority (say, corporate management) sets down for individuals or other resources to follow. A policy could be as broad as a corporate hiring policy or as specific as the rule that only managers of a particular level may access a specific application on the corporate network. Policies generally apply to people, but they can also apply to other resources, including software. For example, there might be a policy affecting software consumers that requires them to have the proper identification and pass certain security requirements to access a critical piece of information.

Orientation. The reason we bring up metadata at all is because metadata are the key to building agile IT interactions.

In essence, we want to move away from the typical way of making software work by *coding* its functionality into computer programs, instead moving toward *describing* how software should work with metadata. Essentially, if all we have to do to change how a complex, distributed application behaves is to change some of the metadata, then we no longer have to bring in the programmers and change the programming. Switching around the metadata takes *far* less time and effort than reprogramming, and is also far less dangerous—you're much less likely to break the application by changing metadata. Furthermore, metadata assist both computers as well as humans to understand the data that the metadata represent. You can think of metadata as a kind of lubricant that makes the various pieces of a complex IT situation move against each other more smoothly.

If you base loosely coupled interactions between various consumers and providers on contracts, and the policies that govern how people should use those consumers and providers are part of those contracts, then you're representing those policies as metadata as well. After all, a contract is nothing more than metadata that describe how parties will interact, and a policy is also metadata that describe the conditions under which those parties are entitled to engage in an interaction. As a result, it's possible for such a system to respond to changes in policies and contracts without the need for more tightly coupled, inflexible programming—essentially, change the policy, adjust the contract, and the consumers and providers simply follow the amended contract.

Although we still need software to make this vision of loosely coupled flexibility work, we need to change the way that we build that software in the first place. Computer programs by themselves won't make themselves agile; the way that we represent software functionality and data with contracts made out of metadata, in conjunction with the right management infrastructure, can help us build agile IT that avoids the rats' nest.

There's no magic in this vision of agile IT. In fact, getting the contracts, other metadata, and the management infrastructure working properly is still quite challenging, and many companies will struggle with those issues as they move to the vision of Service Orientation. Once you *do* get all the working parts running smoothly, however, then your ice skater will skate with the best of them—and make even complex distributed computing look easy.

HOW LOOSE IS YOUR COUPLING?

So far, we've essentially been touting the great advantages of loose coupling. If the inner workings of IT could interact in an agile and flexible way as if they were business partners engaging in some contractual business relationship, then they don't have to mess around in each other's business. They can remain separately controlled entities just like business partners, who sign a contract to specify a particular relationship but act entirely independently otherwise. Loose coupling, then, is simply a technical way to describe the independent, arm's-length relationship that software should inherit from the business world.

It's important, however, to place the discussion of loose coupling into the appropriate context. It may seem that we've pinned the success of flexible, agile IT entirely on the notion of loose coupling; therefore, you may be tempted to jump to either of two natural but false conclusions: (1) Because loose coupling is so good, then tight coupling must be bad; (2) there are only two levels of coupling, namely loose and tight, as if it were a black-and-white issue. Well, neither of these statements is entirely accurate.

As discussed earlier in this chapter, coupling is a concept that describes the level of common knowledge necessary by the programmers of a provider and a consumer in a distributed computing interaction. In a tightly coupled interaction, the programmer of one participant (say, the consumer, or client) must have detailed knowledge about the behavior and construction of the other participant (in this case, the provider, or server) in order to successfully complete the required interaction between the two systems.

Let's say, however, that the two participants don't need to have any information at all about each other or even know about each other's existence. In this case, we would call their interaction *fully decoupled*. If loose coupling is good, shouldn't full decoupling be better? Taking a look at what full decoupling means in practice should shed some light on this question. A fully decoupled interaction is one where the two parties in the interaction have no advance knowledge whatsoever about the structure or content of the interaction. They are basically operating without any contract whatsoever.

Without a contract, how is it possible for them to interact at all? Well, in computers, just as in life, some *event* takes place that causes one system to perform some task and then by necessity interact with another system somewhere else on the network. In some cases, we might think of these event-driven mechanisms as being fully decoupled in that one system can create some event and publish it on the network without providing any information or context about that event, and other pieces of software in the network would be able to figure out on their own how to process and understand that event.

However, it's important to point out that the term *decoupled* is actually a misnomer, because even in the most decoupled of event-driven interactions, recipients of events still have some information or common knowledge about those events. The consumers of events need to understand the

Jargon Watch: Event

The word *event,* of course, has a common meaning, and we'll start with that. An *ordinary event* is something that happens in the real world. In other words, an event is some change in the state of the universe. To extend that concept, an *ordinary business event* is a meaningful change in the state of the enterprise or of something relevant to the enterprise, such as a customer order, the arrival of a shipment at a loading dock, or the payment of a bill, for example.

A *software event* is a record of some ordinary or business event in software. Software events consist of data that describe the ordinary event, typically in the form of a message from one piece of software to another. There is also the notion of a *complex event,* which is an aggregation or correlation of two or more software events into another software event. Because software events always correspond to ordinary events, when we use the word *event,* we'll mean a software event, with the understanding that there's an ordinary event behind it.

data format as well as some metadata about the event, including its size, format, et cetera. However, these metadata are often ad hoc, in the sense that they come along with the event, rather than appearing in a separate contract. In other words, such interactions may be uncontracted, but they are not truly decoupled. Therefore, *full decoupling* really means "more loosely coupled than contracted interactions."

In between the extremes of tight coupling and full decoupling, then, are loosely coupled exchanges, where the two participants have specific but more limited knowledge about each other, namely as appears in the contract that provides the information each participant needs to interact with the other. As such, the concept of coupling is in reality a spectrum of levels. There's really no such thing as true tight coupling or full decoupling, but rather more or less loosely or tightly coupled in relation to some other distributed computing approach.

Software Contracts: No Panacea

In order to realize loose coupling, it's important to understand the relationship between the notion of contracts and loose coupling. Contracts, as you remember, are nothing more than agreements between independent parties on how they will interact, without specifying exactly how each party will perform its obligations under the contract. However, contracts by themselves are neither necessary nor sufficient to guarantee loose coupling. As we discussed earlier, open standards are vital to making loose coupling a reality; it's far easier to provide for loose coupling if the participants agree on contracts that they can understand because they follow open standards.

Proprietary contracts, however, can still offer a certain measure of loose coupling, but each participant must understand and code to the specific contract format ahead of time—in other words, they are still tightly coupled to the contract. In other words, each party must have a common understanding of the contract language in order to interact. As a result, distributed computing exchanges that proprietary contracts govern are less loosely coupled than those that standards-based contracts dictate.

However, even standards-based contracts often provide only a certain measure of loose coupling, because they don't always provide all the information that both participants actually require to interact. In a perfect world, we would include in the contract all the information necessary to guarantee a loosely coupled exchange, such as policy and other metadata, but in the real world, the participants either take some of the required information for granted or often simply overlook necessary information. In either case, such omissions or assumptions on the part of the consumers or providers tighten the coupling of the exchange.

Furthermore, the standards governing the creation and access of contracts aren't perfect either. These standards might include a number of ambiguities that encourage independent participants in an interaction to make different assumptions, leading to incompatibilities when they try to interact. Such incompatibilities mean that there is a coupling problem, even if all parties agree on the same set of standards. As time goes on, companies will remove many of the ambiguities, as well as create additional standards to help address some of these issues, but in the meantime, immature standards and improper assumptions about them threaten to tighten the coupling between providers and consumers.

Human Element

Humans have one thing that computers don't: wetware, the stuff between your ears. Humans have the incredible ability to understand information presented to us without any context. For example, I can say "May 25," and you'd know instantly that I'm probably referring to a date. But then again, the statement might in fact refer to a fragment of an address or the model number of a washing machine. Our wetware can narrow down the context to a few possibilities remarkably quickly and efficiently. Computers, however, are fundamentally as dumb as a post in this regard. They can't tell the difference between "May 25" and "Engelbert Humperdinck the Third." The software behind distributed computer systems as a rule simply isn't smart enough to make any sense out of an incoming message unless it has some sort of metadata about it to guide it.

As a case in point, let's say some piece of software produces an event that contains some financial information, perhaps formatted into something that looks to a human like a spreadsheet. In a very loosely coupled interaction, there may be no way for the consuming software to understand the contents of that fragment, but a human consumer may be able to recognize the fragment simply by looking at it and thinking "Hey, that looks like a spreadsheet. And hmmm, there are numbers in it. I wonder what would happen if I loaded it into my financial reporting system?" Furthermore, if a person sees the text "sales data," for example, it's a no-brainer for a human to assume the fragment contains sales data; a piece of software might never figure that out. However, this approach requires that human users be able to comprehend the information they see. If the information is represented in a language the humans don't understand, say, in Braille or Ancient Sumerian, then the information and its context are lost entirely.

Human comprehension, therefore, directly impacts how loosely or tightly coupled an interaction can be. The more we involve humans in the interpretation of data, the more loosely coupled that interaction can be. In the case of the World Wide Web, the goal was to display Web pages that humans could understand, and as such, loose coupling between browsers and Web servers was relatively straightforward, since browsers didn't need to understand the Web pages—they simply had to display the information so that humans could understand it. As a result, people can change their Web sites however they want, and other people are still able to understand them. If computers actually had to read Web pages for understanding, any change at all, even to the formatting of the information on the screen, would break the understanding between the providers and consumers of the information on the pages. When we talk about consumers as being pieces of software, however, an ugly question arises: Just how well must consumers *understand* the messages they send and receive?

The question of understanding depends on the *meaning* of such messages, a concept commonly known as *semantics*. The problem with trying to get computer systems to understand semantics is that it's very difficult (and some would say impossible) to include sufficient information about the meaning of a message such that a computer can understand it, regardless of its language or data format. For example, our international telephone system follows its own standards, and as a result, you can pick up your phone and call someone in China. Your phone and the phone on the other end of the call will be able to interact just fine—but if you don't speak Chinese and the other person doesn't speak your language, then you still won't be able to understand each other! Not only that, but adding some sort of Star Trekkian universal translator to the international phone system would be a far, far more difficult challenge than getting the phone system to work in the first place was.

The same problem plagues the world of distributed computing. A consumer and a provider may be able to interact just fine on a loosely coupled basis, but if they don't have a common understanding of the meaning of the messages they exchange, then it doesn't matter how loosely coupled they are—they may as well not be attempting to communicate at all. As a result, many companies seek to manually develop a common semantics for such interactions, typically with business partners. They'll spend time defining terms like *purchase order, invoice,* and the like, so that when one company sends such a document to the other, they can all agree on what the document means.

Since building a "universal translator" for business is still beyond our capabilities at this point, building agile IT boils down to a set of compromises. We now have the technology to build loosely coupled, agile approaches to IT, yet the struggles to automate the understanding of messages between providers and consumers remain. The hard work of business agility, therefore, often centers on making sure the parts of the business— human as well as IT—actually understand each other.

CHAPTER 6

Service Orientation: Light at the End of the Tunnel

At this point, you probably wonder what has taken us so long to define the terms *Service* and *Service Orientation,* the two main ideas of this book. The reason for our delay is that understanding these two ideas requires a significant adjustment in the way that we think about business and IT. We had to first discuss *business agility*—what it is, why companies need it, and the reasons that it's been out of reach all this time. Next we had to introduce the concept of *loosely coupled distributed computing* and explain why the primary limitation on companies' ability to be agile are their brittle, rats' nests of IT infrastructures. Even though this isn't a technology-focused book, we had to give you a sufficient conceptual background in the intricacies of loosely coupled IT so that we can intelligently talk about Services and the broader business concept of Service Orientation. Now that you are familiar with the darkness inside the tunnel, let's lead you to the light at its end.

WHAT'S A SERVICE, ANYWAY?

The word *service* is one of those vague terms with many different meanings depending on the context. In different situations, service is what you get in a restaurant or gas station, what you're in when you join the army, or what you endure in church. There is a common thread that winds its way through all of these meanings, however, and that is that the term *service* denotes actions or capabilities someone (or something) provides to another. Whether it is waiting tables, serving one's country, or preaching a sermon, there is always a provider of the service, a consumer of the service, and the actions that constitute the service itself. In much the same way, we're going to refer to the concept of software Services as IT functionality and capabilities that one computer system provides to another. In this case, we capitalize the word *Service* when we're talking about software Services to distinguish them from all the other meanings of the word *service*. Because we've already had the discussion about providers and consumers of data, software functionality, and contracted interfaces, when we talk about a Service, then, we mean *a contracted interface to software functionality*.

Let's take a closer look at this definition, and you'll see why we waited until Chapter 6 to put it down.

- Services are *interfaces* to software, not the underlying software itself. A Service interface simply defines the contractual obligations between consumers and providers. Sometimes people think of a Service as a piece of software that exposes a particular kind of interface, but those are the underlying bits of technology that we call *components*. It's possible, therefore, to expose components as Services.

- Services can be tightly coupled or loosely coupled (or anything in between, for that matter). It is entirely possible to define a Service interface that is rigid and inflexible to change, requiring change to both consumers and providers whenever some assumption changes; we also can define a loosely coupled Service that properly abstracts assumptions, so that it's more amenable to unpredictable change. We'll definitely be more interested in loosely coupled Services, but the fact remains that there are plenty of tightly coupled ones out there, and sometimes you want your Services to be tightly coupled. For an interface to be a Service, however, it must have a *contract*.

- We generally associate a Service with a provider, but, in fact, consumers have Service interfaces as well. After all, contracts are agreements that impose requirements on both parties in an exchange and typically provide metadata about consumers as well as providers.

- Services interact via *messages*. A message is simply a way of sending information from one party to another. Messages facilitate loose coupling, because they allow for a clean separation between providers and consumers. Because Services send and receive messages, you can think of a Service as an abstraction of the underlying software component that sits on the network somewhere and sends and/or receives messages as per its contract.

- Services may or may not have standards-based interfaces. However, because the adoption of standards makes it significantly easier to move to agile, flexible architectures that support unpredictable change, we're particularly interested in standards-based Service interfaces and standards-based messaging between Services. We call the standards that govern interactions among Services *Web Services* standards. Web Services specify a standard language for Service definition and interaction, but not all Services are Web Services, nor are Web Services necessarily loosely coupled.

Jargon Watch: Web Services

Few topics in the IT world since the dot-com bust have garnered as much hype and confusion as Web Services. Overblown, poorly named, and often misunderstood, Web Services have come to represent either a new approach to computing or little more than a way to simplify integration. Part of what has confused the market is that Web Services have very little to do with the World Wide Web.

Fundamentally, Web Services are standards-based, contracted interfaces to software functionality. It is the fact that the entire IT industry has settled on a particular set of open standards for distributed computing that makes Web Services special. Because of these standards, it's possible—in theory—to interact with a Web Service without knowing anything about that Service except for the interface it exposes. It is this loose coupling that accounts for the importance of Web Services.

If you remember nothing else about what a Service is, remember that it's an abstraction of some piece of software. The whole idea of Services is that you don't have to think of software as complex bits of code anymore. Instead, think of them only by their interface and what the interface is supposed to do for you as their contracts specify.

So What's the Big Idea?

You may be thinking at this point that we've pulled a bait-and-switch on you. We promised a business book, but we've been spending page after page talking about software Services and contracts and standards and abstractions, for Pete's sake. What gives?

Recall our discussion of eBusiness in Chapter 1—where an eBusiness is a company that incorporates IT into all aspects of its business. Easier said than done, of course, because of all the rats' nest issues that result from the increasing complexity of IT in today's organizations. Instead, for companies to *successfully* leverage IT resources throughout their business, they must have a different *way of thinking* about IT. The only way to achieve agility is for the business to consider IT resources to be loosely coupled Services available as the business requires. As a result, the emphasis shifts from the underlying systems and the components that make them work to the contracted interfaces that abstract where and how the Services perform their duties. That's what Service Orientation is all about.

Service Orientation, then, is a business approach that considers IT capabilities as agile resources the company can create, discover, combine, and access as needed. Through the power of the abstractions of loose coupling, standards, and metadata, we now have a road map for taking today's tightly coupled, proprietary IT rats' nests and transforming them into loosely coupled Services that enable Service Orientation.

It's vitally important, however, that we place Services into the business context. In the technical sense, a Service is a contracted interface, but in the business sense, a Service is a representation of a resource that is available to the business. In other words, Services are in the manager's toolbox alongside human resources (i.e., people) and physical resources (i.e., things).

How to build Services is not the focus of this book. But more important, dwelling on the implementation details would have led us to the same trap that other technology movements have succumbed to. Implementing a Service is an exercise that's for the techies and doesn't map the changing nature of business requirements to the capabilities of IT. What we really need to understand is *how* the business can and should use Services in the business, and *why*. Business agility, of course, is the fundamental goal of Service Orientation, but recall that business agility is a meta-requirement—the requirement that the business must be able to respond to future, unpredictable requirements. We must therefore break down this meta-requirement into the tactical business issues that companies are likely to face that Service Orientation is best able to solve—issues like reducing costs, meeting changing business needs, improving competitiveness, and complying with regulations.

SERVICES + LOOSE COUPLING = AGILITY

So far, we've defined a Service as a *contracted interface to software functionality*, but that technical definition clearly leaves a business-minded person flat. To bring us back up to the business world, we need a definition of a Service that has relevance to the *business* world. In that vein, we can define a Service as the output of a business resource, where some document external to the resource can sufficiently describe its capabilities. Of course, if you've been reading this book sequentially, you'll recognize that the document we're talking about is a contract—essentially, metadata that describe how to access and utilize the resource that the Service represents.

What you *won't* find in our business definition of a Service is any discussion of technology. We didn't say that the resource had to be built out of software, and, in fact, it may not be. It's possible, for example, for the Service to represent a business process, and that process might even involve human steps. We could even take this generalization to its extreme, where one company provides a Service to another entirely through manual, human means. As long as there's a contract that adequately specifies the Service, then it still falls under our business definition of a Service. We've actually taken the notion of abstraction from the world of computing (remember all those zeroes and ones?) and elevated it so that it can encompass both the worlds of IT and business.

Loose Coupling in Business

As explained in Chapter 5, contracts are the key to making loose coupling a reality, because the only way two participants in an exchange can interoperate effectively is if they have a preexisting agreement on what they are going to do and what their mutual expectations are of each other. As long as both parties stick to the contract, then it doesn't matter to either one what the other one does behind the scenes. It's only if one party, say the provider of a Service, violates the contract or, worse, if the contract is missing or incomplete that the consumer must dive into the details of what the provider is doing. Just as in business where a verbal agreement is often not worth the paper it's written on, so too in the IT world we need something in writing to clarify ambiguities, make terms explicit, and provide some means of enforcement in case one party goes back on their word.

We had been speaking in terms of technology, where providers and consumers were pieces of software, but here we're applying the exact same principles of loose coupling in the case where the participants are individuals or organizations. The clearest example of this principle is when the two interacting parties are independent entities. Clearly, most interactions between companies are loosely coupled in the sense that a business contract governs

Jargon Watch: CPFR

Collaborative planning, forecasting, and replenishment is a business process where trading partners use a combination of technology and a standard set of business processes for Internet-based collaboration on forecasts and plans for replenishing products.

CPFR enables trading partners to have visibility into one another's demand, order forecasts, and promotional forecasts through a process of shared brand and category plans, as well as an approach for identifying and resolving exceptions. CPFR is supposed to improve efficiencies across the extended supply chain, reducing inventories, improving service levels and increasing sales—when companies can get it to work properly!

the interactions between the parties, and the internal details of how one company meets the contract are none of the other company's business, unless there's a problem.

Now, it's important to point out that not all interactions between businesses are loosely coupled. A great example is Collaborative Planning, Forecasting, and Replenishment (CPFR). When two companies implement CPFR, a supplier works very closely with its customer's systems to ensure that the customer's inventory levels are at their optimal levels. CPFR, therefore, is tightly coupled at the business level.

Loosely coupled relationships also occur inside of organizations, although tightly coupled ones are more common than not, because companies tend to exert tight, central control over their processes. However, there are still many examples of interactions within organizations that lend themselves to loose coupling. For example, IT departments, help desks, and other service provider divisions within many organizations have what are essentially contracted interfaces for the rest of the company to follow. If your department contracts with your company's help desk for services, say, and you have no say in the internal workings of the help desk division, that's a sign you have a loosely coupled relationship with them.

Relationships between employers and their employees are also examples of tight coupling. Employees are tightly coupled to their organization, because the company that hires them has direct control over their behavior. Contractors, however, benefit from loosely coupled interactions in that a business only has the right to specify the work output and their obligations, but may not define how the contractors go about doing their work. In fact, the laws governing independent contractors essentially mandate loose coupling between the contractor and the hiring organization. Cross the legal line by dictating how the contractors must work, and now you must consider them employees.

It's important to note that we're not saying loosely coupled business relationships are good and tightly coupled ones are bad. Rather, we're simply pointing out the differences between the two. Each style of interaction serves its own purposes—the rule of thumb is to use the right approach for the job, rather than favoring one approach over the other in a general sense. In the help desk example, for instance, this one group serves several departments across the organization, and it makes sense to take advantage of as many economies of scale as possible. If each department controlled the help desk in a unique, micromanaged way, then the help desk wouldn't be nearly as efficient, and costs would skyrocket. As a result, the extra overhead of hammering out a contract to facilitate loose coupling is definitely worth it, because the organization can reuse the capabilities of the help desk much more efficiently with such a contract in place.

CPFR and other "just-in-time" manufacturing and distribution processes, however, are examples of business situations where companies sometimes require tight coupling. Some manufacturers, for example, have tight control over their suppliers so that they can manage their supply chain precisely. The most straightforward way to ensure this responsiveness is for the manufacturer to work closely with the supplier to ensure its internal processes are up to the task—a great example of tight coupling in action. In effect, although the supplier is a third party, the business manages the supplier as if it were an internal, tightly controlled resource.

However, even the tightest of business relationships often can benefit from loose coupling. It would be ideal for manufacturers, after all, if they could simply specify their particular speed and responsiveness requirements in their contracts with their suppliers and leave it up to the suppliers to meet those contracts without having to meddle in their suppliers' businesses. When a manufacturer/supplier ecosystem can reach this level of loose coupling, in fact, then all participants can be far more agile than in the tightly coupled scenario. For example, suppliers are free to adjust their internal processes without involving the manufacturer, as long as they can continue to meet the contract. Likewise, manufacturers have greater agility as well, because they no longer get bogged down by working so closely with suppliers. Instead, all they need to do is manage the contracts.

eBusiness Equation

Understanding levels of coupling between businesses or organizational departments is relatively straightforward—and also somewhat simplistic. However, we took the time to illustrate this point for a reason. The business concept of loose coupling is not an *analogy* to the technical concept. Rather, both concepts are different aspects of the *same* issue. In other words, every time we talk about the IT-centric concepts of Service, loose coupling, and contracts, we are simultaneously speaking of the business concepts as well. Basically, every Service is both an IT concept and a business concept at the same time.

We can make this claim only because Service Orientation means thinking of IT as a set of business resources, rather than separating business and IT into different concerns. Instead, we're talking about the full spectrum of resources available to the business, and IT resources are part of what a business needs to fulfill its requirements—and likewise, IT can't operate in a vacuum without business drivers. What makes Service Orientation unique is that, for the first time, we have a single, comprehensive approach for thinking of IT capabilities as business resources. And the secret to this approach is the fact that we are representing these capabilities as loosely coupled Services.

Indeed, this vision of Service Orientation brings us closer to the original vision of eBusiness as a company that includes IT in all aspects of its business. We're finally getting to answer the challenge of eBusiness in the sense that not only do such companies integrate IT into all business processes, but they do so to better meet the needs of the organization moving forward.

After all, loose coupling means being able to separate *what you do with your resources* from *how your resources work*. If you're in charge of a process (defining it, implementing it, managing it, or evolving it), you shouldn't have to worry about how the individual parts of that process work—or even if they're made up of software, human activities, or some combination of both. All you should have to worry about are the metadata for those subprocesses: the contracts that govern what they do. Any organization that can work with their processes in this way is far better able to respond to change and leverage change for competitive advantage than another company with inflexible, tightly coupled processes. In other words, if your business processes are truly Service Oriented, your company truly will be agile.

PROCESS THIS!

Business processes have always been an important, if understated, enterprise asset. How a company runs its business changes on a daily basis at various different levels in the organization—from high-level strategic changes to lower-level implementation details. As a result of these changes, enterprises constantly struggle to make their businesses more responsive to dynamic business needs by connecting business requirements to IT and human capabilities.

Many companies have learned that the way they conduct business is as important as the substance of their business. For much of the history of the modern corporation, especially since the rapid growth of the post-World War II period, global businesses expanded in size and scale without much regard to their formal business practices and methodologies. Since the Industrial Revolution, companies broke down work into constituent tasks as part of a doctrine of specialization of labor, as economic pioneers such as Adam Smith first espoused, as well as industrialists like Henry Ford and Andrew Carnegie.

This task-oriented, business function approach to work allowed companies to grow quickly by increasing task productivity and as a result brought about such radical innovations as mass production and the assembly line. Unfortunately, companies soon realized that as their products and service offerings grew, fragmenting work across the organization required an immense amount of communication, overhead, and organization in order to avoid extra costs, delays, and errors. The modern corporate bureaucracy was born.

As global markets became increasingly competitive in the 1970s and 1980s, it was clear to many companies that they had to begin to take the conduct of their work more seriously if they were to compete effectively on a global scale. One outgrowth of this desire to improve corporate competitiveness was the quality movement of the 1980s and early 1990s, which showed that the key to increasing quality, meeting customer needs, and improving profitability was to improve business practices, rather than just improving products or services.

W. Edwards Deming, one of the founders of the quality movement, showed that businesses could use statistics and other techniques to measure and improve business processes, in what he called *continuous process improvement*. Deming advocated that enterprises should forge closer relationships with their suppliers and customers in order to increase mutual value. He noted that many manufacturers routinely considered only the price of materials in selecting an appropriate supplier to work with, instead of looking at the longer-term implications on quality or on operational aspects such as shipping costs. The changes companies had to make in their business operations as a result of many of Deming's ideas, combined with other insights, formed many of the basic concepts of business process used today.

Deming also noted that most process improvements take place incrementally. Companies must respond to market pressures and opportunities, while also seeking to reduce their costs and increase the value they provide to their customers. These basic business needs form the main motivation for the creation, management, and execution of business processes. As a result, enterprises need a culture comprising both business and IT that encourages continuous process improvement.

As the importance of process emerged in the enterprise, companies realized that they must consider not only internal business practices and methodologies, but also their interactions with suppliers, customers, and partners. These requirements impacted the human resources in the enterprise as well as the emerging technological assets. In addition, as the dot-com boom led to a significant spending downturn, market and competitive pressures forced businesses to cut costs and do more with less. These pressures resulted in a significant desire to leverage existing technologies and relationships, while at the same time effecting process improvement—a very difficult challenge indeed.

Abstracting Process from Application Logic

However, automating business processes has historically been extraordinarily challenging for most enterprises, due to the inflexibility of their IT infrastructure. High-level business requirements must eventually filter down to actual activities connected to human-based tasks and IT-based systems. Yet when talking with IT and business managers, it is clear that many organizations consider today's IT infrastructure to be a bottleneck to operational efficiency. It is not that these systems do not work, but rather that they were not designed with change and flexibility in mind. Furthermore, many organizations record details of processes on paper (or electronically) as nothing more than reference documents. However, they maintain few of these documents so that they reflect day-to-day reality. As a consequence, this valuable knowledge often is outdated and unmanaged, and companies lose key process details as soon as the expert leaves the building. In essence, process definition has been disconnected from process implementation.

As a result, business requirements, process definitions, and IT implementations are all jumbled up together—applications are tightly coupled with process logic, disconnecting business process definition from IT implementations. Before we can attempt to get out of this morass by designing an approach that is capable of adequately handling business requirements, we must abstract four different parts of a business process:

1. High-level business requirements that result from senior management imperatives and overarching corporate goals
2. Processes that derive from translating requirements into a practical set of activities
3. Lines of control that connect individual tasks within a process
4. IT capabilities that discrete tasks or services represent and users or devices perform

Each added abstraction facilitates business agility imperatives by isolating the higher, business-oriented levels from implementation details. In essence, each abstraction serves to loosely couple the consumers of the functionality from the technology underlying the abstraction, facilitating agility by simplifying and reducing the cost of change.

So, given that abstraction can help us move from high-level business requirements to lower-level IT capabilities, it only makes sense to use Services to separate process definition from the underlying systems that implement individual activities in the process. Moving process into a separate Service-oriented layer considerably facilitates business agility for these reasons:

- A change in the process definition does not require a modification of underlying application functionality. The business now can rapidly change and redeploy processes as business requirements demand with minimal, if any, programming. Companies won't have to constantly rip into the technical plumbing each time they want to change or implement new business processes.
- Businesses can easily monitor, audit, and escalate critical business

process issues, because they have greater visibility into the overall process, rather than having the processes tangled up in the technology.

- Businesses can build processes by composing subprocesses, thus delegating business rules authority to different parts of the organization or to external organizations.
- Companies can implement a process using any Service that fulfills the basic requirements of that process's flow, allowing for variable implementations depending on the requirements of users.

However, although these ideas sound great in theory, how can we achieve flexible, agile processes when, in reality, we haven't been able to do so for the past few decades? Enterprises need an approach to building business processes where agility is its primary goal—in essence, a Service-oriented approach.

Service-Oriented Process

The power and flexibility that loosely coupled Services can offer the enterprise are substantial. If an organization abstracts its IT infrastructure so that it presents its functionality in the form of Services that represent how the business actually works, as opposed to tightly coupled systems that struggle to keep up with business change, then the consumers of those Services (whether they are at the same company or one of that company's business partners) can access those Services independent of the underlying technology that supports them. Furthermore, if Service consumers can change independently of the providers of those Services, then we can finally have the sort of agile, flexible IT infrastructure we've long wished for. If a process behaved like a Service, we'd have the best of all worlds: processes that reflect how the business truly operates and processes that are flexible enough to handle dynamic and unpredictable change without breaking or adding to the complex and costly rats' nest.

Remember that two of the fundamental tenets of business process are the notions of a process flow and the activities that comprise that flow. Somehow the notion of loosely coupled Services must be able to connect to the idea of processes, activities, and flows. However, a businesses made up of a grab bag of hundreds of miscellaneous Services doesn't promise to be particularly agile. What is more interesting is the aggregation or *composition* of multiple Services into coherent business processes. In order for this composition to occur, we need a way of composing Services into processes.

Clearly, in order to perform this composition, we need to apply business process techniques to Services. We need to combine the concepts of process and Service together so that we can compose individual Services into process flows that we can also describe as Services, so that we can include them in further compositions as we build more complex processes. We call this approach to business process *Service-Oriented Process*.

The Services that a process consumes might be local to an enterprise or available at a remote location. Furthermore, we might distribute processes that we expose as Services throughout the organization, allowing different groups to change and control their processes independently without breaking the consumers of those processes. In other words, the processes remain loosely coupled even as we compose them into increasingly more complex processes.

The secret to Service-Oriented Process is the Service contract and associated metadata. We describe Service-Oriented Processes as metadata that we publish and make accessible as if they were Services—because such processes *are* Services. As a result, it becomes impossible for a consumer to distinguish whether an invoked Service is actually a process. Users simply invoke the Service to accomplish some business goal or compose the Service into yet another process that they can in turn expose as a Service.

HOW SERVICE-ORIENTED PROCESS REPLACES TRADITIONAL INTEGRATION

Instead of thinking of the act of integrating IT systems as somehow connecting rats' nests of isolated systems and applications together, enterprises can now think of applications as processes that are compositions of Services that allow for ongoing change. Approaching complex IT systems from this perspective simplifies and clarifies many of the troublesome issues relating to distributed computing. Integration goes from being a troublesome chore that requires increasing layers of complicated and expensive technologies to a side effect of process execution. In fact, it's virtually impossible to create a Service-Oriented Process that does not provide the fundamental benefits of application and business integration. The mere act of composing a Service-Oriented Process meets most integration goals.

It's quite possible that a few years from now, companies won't be spending so much of their time and money on integration middleware anymore. Instead, every application that participates in a process will be responsible for providing the necessary integration. Enterprises then will be able to focus on more important aspects of their business: creating, managing, and evolving their business processes to meet ever-changing business needs.

After all, there's no doubting that today's IT environments are complex sets of systems, technologies, and distinct groups, each with its own goals and approaches for getting the necessary tasks of the business done. However, the more glue we've applied to tie systems together, the more we've glued ourselves into a rats' nest of systems that do more to prevent agility than enable it. So, rather than being an enabler of agility, traditional integration technologies and approaches tie organizations down.

Clearly, organizations must get their different systems to intercommunicate, but how can they do that without using all this brittle, inflexible integration middleware? The answer is to use Service-oriented approaches to building applications by composing Services into processes. However, to understand why this approach is better by far than the middleware approach to integration, we first must explain the cost of integration and how the various different approaches impact both cost and agility.

Understanding the Cost of Integration

An integration project is never a static or monolithic endeavor, and neither are its costs. The costs of a typical integration project go through four distinct phases: (1) the initial setup costs, (2) the cost of configuring and customizing the integration project, (3) ongoing maintenance costs, and (4) costs that occur when any of the elements of the integration project change. In the initial costs phase, companies spend money and time getting the technology or teams set up before they actually embark on the integration project. In the configuration and customization phase, the company implements the integration approach but hasn't yet deployed the system or seen any results. In the maintenance phase, the company has deployed the integration solution and is realizing benefit from the solution without making any additional changes. In the change phase, a company needs to make changes to the integration solution to reflect the inevitable, unpredictable changes in business requirements, technologies, policies, or any other significant business requirement change.

To understand the costs of integration, we need to compare three approaches to integration: custom integration, EAI (Enterprise Application Integration), and Service-Oriented approaches. The relative costs of these approaches are as shown in Exhibit 6.1.

First, lets take a look at the solid black curve, which represents the cost of custom, ad hoc integration. Custom integration involves dedicating current IT resources to the task of achieving some application goal that requires integrated results from multiple systems—essentially building custom code that directly ties together the systems in question. Such custom integration involves the smallest up-front cost of the three integration approaches, because the skills and tools necessary to complete the integration task are typically already in-house. However, as the project progresses, it consumes an increasing amount of developer time in proportion to the complexity of the integration task at hand.

During the maintenance phase, then, things start to get costly. Traditionally, companies spend most of their time and money maintaining existing

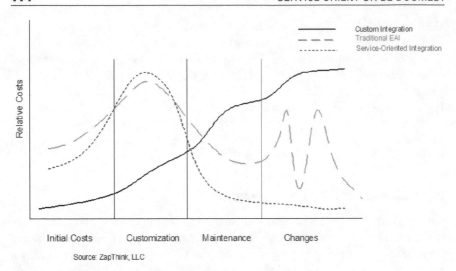

EXHIBIT 6.1   Relative Costs of Different Integration Approaches

integration projects and then dealing with the changes that occur in those systems as business requirements and technology change. However, it is those change costs that make the custom approach to integration a cost and complexity nightmare. Custom-coded systems are by definition tightly coupled and inflexible. Any change requires recoding of the systems and going through test, deployment, and maintenance phases all over again. Custom integration can work only with very small projects that do not change very frequently—basically, small, tightly coupled systems.

Fallacy of Enterprise Application Integration

The second approach to integration is the EAI middleware approach, as shown by the dashed green line in Exhibit 6.1. Traditional EAI solutions seek to solve many integration headaches by presenting technology-based solutions that efficiently manage and maintain connections among systems. In effect, most integration middleware serves to automate and centralize the integration tasks in the company, freeing it from doing custom integration on a point-to-point basis by centralizing all integration tasks.

Middleware has up-front setup costs that are much higher than custom integration, as shown in the first column of the graph. In a typical EAI solution, companies must spend anywhere from tens of thousands to millions of dollars on software licenses and hardware prior even to getting started on a particular integration project. However, the spending doesn't stop there. Typical EAI projects costs many times more than the initial costs and can easily dwarf the costs of custom integration projects.

What the proponents of EAI will tell you (and sell you) is that after you've built and customized the EAI system, the ongoing maintenance costs are very small, since centralized integration makes it easy to propagate any changes throughout the organization. As long as any major business assumptions don't change, then the costs of running an EAI solution over the long haul can be substantially lower than that of custom integration projects. However, such a change-free business scenario rarely, if ever, matches up to reality. As any company that has implemented an EAI solution will attest, the notion that a system will ever be in a steady state such that the company no longer has to spend money on integration is completely bogus.

Most large companies still spend over 70% of their IT budgets on keeping their middleware and everything it connects to up and running. The reason why EAI hasn't been the solution to the ongoing integration problem is because it simply applies more glue. Most companies are now realizing that EAI can become exorbitantly expensive when things do inevitably change. Then EAI system costs can spike, as shown in the fourth column of the graph. Because EAI pours concrete onto business processes, it tends to solidify existing processes rather than enabling an IT environment that allows companies to deal easily with change.

Do Standards-Based Interfaces Fix EAI?

One of the reasons why EAI approaches are so brittle and expensive is because they use proprietary technologies. Each EAI vendor controls the technology in its particular offering, reducing interoperability with other products and allowing the vendor to charge whatever it wants for upgrades and other software. This fact begs the question as to whether simply replacing proprietary interfaces with standards-based ones would solve the problems of EAI-based integration.

Although it is true that the use of standards-based technology lowers initial costs (because interoperability is simpler) and configuration costs (because companies aren't as locked into a particular vendor), simply replacing one kind of interface with another leaves the implementations just as tightly coupled and brittle as they were before. Instead of having to reconfigure hundreds of different proprietary interfaces when a system changes, techies now have to reprogram hundreds of standards-based ones. We call this problem the EAI standards shell game, where EAI vendors are simply moving the pea from proprietary to standards-based interfaces. This approach provides little if any loose coupling; nor does it address the fact that business requirements are constantly changing. In fact, all that vendors accomplish by adding open standards to proprietary EAI products is enabling their customers to pour standards-based concrete over existing business processes—but concrete all the same.

Enter Service Orientation

In the Service-oriented approach to integration, however, we're not simply leveraging open standards—in fact, we're not really integrating at all per se. Service-oriented integration is a side effect of building composite, loosely coupled, Service-oriented processes. We're composing processes out of Services and then exposing those processes as Services so other processes can consume them. There's no assumption that Services must be on the same system or even in the same country. Rather, the whole idea of Service-oriented integration is to compose Services regardless of their underlying technology. If we can compose Services together in an agile way such that changing business assumptions simply changes the *composition,* rather than the *implementation,* we can get away from having to spend money in times of change, let alone during routine maintenance.

It's important to note, however, that if you take a Service-oriented approach to integration, it is not sufficient simply to wrap existing systems with standards-based interfaces and call them Services. Rather, businesses must spend time analyzing their business processes and creating the *right* business Services, perhaps even requiring the composition of multiple Services to accomplish a single task. This loosely coupled composition enables the organization to support frequent changes in the underlying systems, as well as changes to business processes and underlying business assumptions, without the need to make interface changes that break the loose coupling of the Services.

The real win with Service-oriented integration, therefore, is in the dramatic reduction of cost at the maintenance and change phases of integration, as shown by the dotted line in Exhibit 6.1. The initial costs of moving to Service orientation are manageable, but not insignificant. It's the amount of time that it takes to build the *right* Services and develop the *right* contracts and metadata that accounts for the cost of this approach. So, what we now need is a way to move to Service orientation without swallowing a huge pill upfront. Fortunately, these are challenges we are well equipped to address.

CHAPTER 7

Is There an Architect in the House?

Now that we have all the raw materials that we need to build agile IT systems, what's the next step? If we simply think about building complicated systems by looking at their individual components, it would be like building a house with the materials we have lying around. Just because we have some wood, glass, nails, and bricks doesn't mean we know how to put them all together to build what we want. Sure, we might be able to build simple things like doghouses or maybe even a shed by just pulling together the various materials, but what if you wanted to build something more complex, such as a house or an office building? Well then, you'd better have a plan. A plan, however, will take you only so far. You also need the expertise and the discipline to follow the plan.

NEW DISCIPLINE OF ARCHITECTURE

The building construction analogy is a natural one, because the world of IT has borrowed the word *architecture* from that trade to refer to this combination of a plan and the discipline to follow it. Just as you would go to an architect to create a plan for your house or office building, so too would you go to an IT architect to help you design a solution to your specific business needs. An architect, after all, is concerned primarily with giving you what you want and helping you plan for ongoing change and growth. So too with IT, where an architect can help you plan whatever IT project you have in mind, as long as the project is important and complex enough to warrant having a formal plan.

In spite of the neat analogy between technology and building construction, the practice of IT architecture is still quite immature and broadly misunderstood in business. After all, we've had thousands of years to perfect the art of building houses, whereas IT is a relative neophyte. However, the immaturity of IT is just an excuse, because IT has become so complex that it's about time we've thought about how to manage the complexity. It's not just that businesspeople lack an understanding of IT architecture; even the folks in IT are often somewhat clueless as to what architecture is all about. It's as if carpenters and electricians and general contractors were content using their own expertise alone to build buildings without having an understanding of the necessity of following a plan that coordinates all of their efforts.

In fact, there's surprisingly little agreement on the actual definition of IT architecture. Of the many such definitions, one of the most coherent is the one the Institute of Electrical and Electronics Engineers (IEEE) created: IT architecture is *"the fundamental organization of a system embodied by its components, their relationships to each other and to the environment and the principles guiding its design and evolution."* We prefer this definition both for its precision and its brevity—everything you want from the definition of architecture is in there. Let's take a closer look:

- *The fundamental organization of a system* . . . Architecture essentially is the *organization* of a system, not the system itself. In other words, computers, networks, and software are not *part* of an architecture, but rather part of its *implementation,* just as windows, doors, floors, and chimneys themselves aren't part of a building's architecture, but rather part of the building.
- *. . . Embodied by its components and their relationships to each other* . . . An architecture consists of both the components of the system and their relationships. It's not just about the bricks, but how you connect them to one another to form a wall that matters.
- *. . . And to the environment* . . . This part of the definition is the most subtle and the most powerful. What is the environment of a computer? It's not the technologies and systems themselves, but above all else, it's the *user* and, more broadly, the *business.* When you think about the environment of IT, you have the users and everything that they're doing with the technology—in other words, the *business itself* is part of the architecture, just as the human who occupies the building is part of its architecture.
- *. . . And the principles guiding its design* . . . Not just the design of the system, mind you, but the principles guiding that design. In other words, *best practices* are a part of the architecture.
- *. . . And evolution.* The definition of architecture explicitly allows for, and even requires, change. To architect a system, you must include the principles for its evolution over time.

Put all of these parts of the definition together, and you have more than a plan—you also have *discipline.* By *discipline* we mean that architecture includes several tasks that architects may do well or poorly. If they do them well, then the resulting architecture will be good, yet if they do the tasks poorly, then the architecture will suffer. The architect therefore must have the discipline to do the tasks of architecture well.

In fact, doing architecture *well* is far more important than getting the definition of architecture right. Many techies apparently miss this point, if all the arguments over whether this or that practice constitutes this or that kind of architecture is any guide. We'll be talking about architecture extensively in this book, in particular, *Service-Oriented* Architecture. Sure, we'll define what we mean by that, but far more important to our discussion will be how to solve the business issues that were covered earlier in this book by applying architecture *well*.

Four Blind Men and the Architecture

Let's digress for a moment and examine the fable of the four blind men and the elephant. As you may remember, four blind men were asked to describe an elephant, and each one touched a different part of the animal. The one who touched the trunk thought the elephant was like a hose, another who grasped the trunk concluded it was a snake, the one who touched the leg thought the elephant was like a tree, and the fourth blind man, after discovering the elephant's side, concludes that it is like a wall.

Well, IT architecture is much like the elephant, and most people are much like the blind men who only see the architecture from one point of view. People who focus on computers, networks, and applications see architecture in terms of the organization and principles guiding those computers, networks, and applications. However, people who focus on writing software see architecture in terms of the organization of the applications and other software components. Likewise, if you're focused on business processes, then you'll likely see architecture as the design and organization of processes that occur throughout the organization. In addition, some people focus on the data that flow through the system, while others concentrate on the information a system provides and how people use it.

As with the blind men, all of these points of view have some aspect of the truth, yet none of them is complete. A sighted person would see the elephant has parts that look and function like a hose, tree, snake, and wall, but the elephant is not entirely like any of these. When it comes to architecture, it's important to have people who are experienced with viewing IT in different ways, but it's also important to have people with the big picture as well.

However, there are significant challenges in the division of responsibility between those people who see IT in its isolated bits and pieces and those people who are responsible for tying all the pieces together into a cohesive whole. IT can be so complex that it's vital to divide the responsibilities for its organization and evolution among different people who can each bring particular strengths to bear. Yet as with any diverse team, such architecture teams often struggle with maintaining adequate control over broad architectural initiatives. Likewise, isolated IT groups often end up digging themselves a deeper hole or building complicated rats' nests, because they have limited visibility into what's happening throughout the organization. Clearly, technology solves only part of these problems; issues of organizational control and management are often more of a challenge. As we'll discuss in Chapter 10, these human issues often dwarf the comparatively straightforward technical issues facing companies as they look to define and implement quality architectures.

Business of Architecture

Since the practice of IT architecture is relatively new, IT architects, regardless of their particular specialization, are a rare breed. It's difficult to learn what you need to know to be a good architect from a book, because good architects learn most of what they know from experience on the job. Furthermore, while most architects must have a firm grasp of the technical issues involved in implementing an architecture, they also need some understanding of the business as well. Just as when you decide to build your own house, you must work closely with an architect who can understand your vision, gather your requirements, put them into a plan, and see that the construction crew carries out the plan correctly, just so with IT architects—they must be able to work with users and understand users' requirements, and they must also be able to develop the plan and ensure that the technical team will follow it correctly.

What's more surprising is that most businesspeople have never interacted with an IT architect in their entire professional lives. The fact of the matter is, architects generally don't get sufficient respect or prominence in today's organizations. Many times their role is misunderstood or simply missing, and even organizations that have strong architects often isolate them into a group and deprive that group of sufficient authority to drive the architecture properly within their organizations. This lack of understanding, support, and experience with architecture is one of the primary contributing causes to the IT mess that so many companies have gotten themselves into. If businesses had a plan and the discipline to have followed it, they wouldn't be in the mess they are in now.

Simple enough, you might be thinking: All you have to do is fund and support your architects properly, and they'll get you out of the IT mess you're in today. Well, if it were actually as simple as that, fewer companies would have such a mess. The fact of the matter is, investing in architecture is a lot like going on a diet: It seems quite practical ahead of time, but when you see that double-fudge chocolate cake, all of a sudden it becomes enormously difficult. With architecture, companies often set out with good intentions, but then some urgent requirement for IT comes up, and the line of business is short on time and budget. As we discussed in Chapter 1, which usually ends up winning out: taking some extra time and money to get the architecture right, or finding the least expensive, most expedient way to meet today's business requirements? Well, one piece of cake won't do any harm, will it? Keep shortcutting yourself and your organization, and your diet—and architecture—will go out the window.

JUST HOW BIG IS THE BIG PICTURE?

The blind men may be happy touching the elephant and thinking about it in their own limited ways, but you want the person in charge of directing the elephant to be able to see the whole elephant and its environment as they truly are. When the elephant is your IT organization, it's critical that there is an architect or team of architects who are responsible for seeing the big picture across your organization. This special role in the organization deserves its own responsibilities, skills, and, yes, budget. We call this special kind of architect an *enterprise architect* and the big picture itself *enterprise architecture.*

Enterprise architecture is basically a discipline of IT architecture where we are concerned with IT in the context of the company as a whole—*both* IT and business. Let's apply the definition of architecture to enterprise architecture:

- *The fundamental organization of a system . . .* In this case, we're talking about a system that embodies the whole of the company, so the enterprise architect must work with the organization of the business as well as the technology.
- *. . . Embodied by its components and their relationships to each other . . .* The components we care about are not just the technology bits that run automated systems, but all the Services in the business, both IT and business Services, and their relationships between one another.
- *. . . And to the environment . . .* An enterprise architect knows that the environment of your company as a whole is the ecosystem your company plays in, including customers, suppliers, partners, and so on. Enterprise architecture doesn't stop at the edge of the enterprise; it continues outside the company. If your company serves consumers, then they are a part of your enterprise architecture as well.
- *. . . And the principles guiding its design and evolution.* And here's

the meat of what makes an enterprise architect. Enterprise architects have sufficient grasp of the business as a whole and its relationship to IT to understand and drive the principles guiding both its design as well as its evolution, especially in cases of unpredictable change.

As IT architecture broadly speaking is still relatively immature as a practice, enterprise architecture specifically is only now coming into its own as a discipline. To better understand what enterprise architecture is and how it fits into the grand scheme of an organization, let's take a look at one of the most popular models for understanding enterprise architecture and its role in the business: the *Zachman Framework,* created by John A. Zachman.

Zachman's key insight was to consider the problem of enterprise architecture in two dimensions. The first dimension is the various levels of abstraction that businesses rely on, including models of the technology in an enterprise, the systems that compose that technology, and the business that uses the systems. The second dimension consists of "W" questions: what, how, where, who, when, and why (how only ends in W, but you get the picture). For an enterprise, the *what* represents the information that flows through the organization and its extended enterprise; the *how* represents the functions and capabilities of the various parts of the organization, including the business processes; the *where* consists of the network that pulls together the information and functions, both in the technical sense and in the business sense of a network of business relationships; the *who* is the people or the organization itself; the *when* includes all scheduling and timing issues throughout the company; and the *why* represents the motivations of the business to take the actions it does—in other words, the business strategy. It is the sum total of all of these views that together comprises the enterprise architecture. Zachman represented these dimensions in a chart (see Exhibit 7.1).

Now, this book doesn't aim to cover all the detail in the exhibit. Instead, we're writing a book for business folks on how to handle their longstanding IT challenges. We're including the Zachman Framework to illustrate the breadth of responsibility that enterprise architects face in their day-to-day work. Enterprise architects use the framework as a guide for the models they must use to represent the elements of the architecture implementation. For example, let's look at the box at the bottom of the column under "Time," which represents the temporal context of the business, for example, the master schedule for the entire organization. The enterprise architect is responsible for using this model to drive the best practices for the business's scheduling efforts, in coordination with all of the other best practices represented by the other 29 models in the framework.

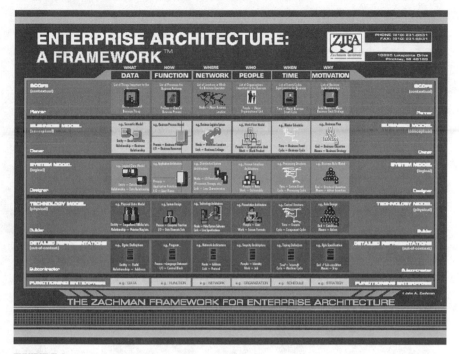

EXHIBIT 7.1. Zachman Framework

Sound complicated? Well, the Zachman Framework has a dirty little secret: Few if any enterprises are able to architect more than a small handful of the 30 models associated with the boxes in it. Instead, the framework represents a best case, providing guidance for enterprise architects to tackle different aspects of their organization as the business needs dictate. There is no one correct path through the Zachman Framework; instead, enterprise architects must find their own paths and implement those pieces that can have the most strategic impact on their businesses today. This iterative approach to enterprise architecture implementation is a best practice that we'll explore as we delve into how companies can move to Service Orientation.

Tag Team Enterprise Architecture

The Zachman Framework provides a lot of ground to cover, even for a simple enterprise—and whose enterprise is simple these days? Considering the complexity of the world's largest companies, it's clear that large organizations can't depend on just a single enterprise architect to manage their complexity. Rather, to have any hope of making progress with their architecture, most large enterprises require a team of enterprise architects. We'll talk more about how to build, manage, and empower such teams in Chapter 10, but we need to make t one other important point at this time to make the vision of enterprise architecture a reality.

Notice that the Zachman Framework covers the gamut from purely business models, such as business strategy, business locations, and the organizational hierarchy, all the way to deeply technical models, including detailed network, security, and data specifications. Although some enterprise architects are strong in both areas, most organizations build their enterprise architecture teams with both business-oriented architects and technically adept ones. As explained earlier, it's well past the time for the nerds to be sitting at their own tables, so both types of architect must have a good grasp of the other's area. However, the fact remains that in many companies, certain architects should focus on the business aspects of enterprise architecture, while others should handle the more technical aspects. The best teams will seek to combine architects of different specializations into a cohesive whole that can guide the company as the organization moves to an architecture that facilitates business agility.

An interesting implication of this division of resources is that there is a specific role for a business-oriented enterprise architect, or a *business architect* for short. Such business architects are responsible for the overall organization and planning of the operation of the business, including business processes to be sure, but also the organizational hierarchy, the schedule and timeline, and other parts of the business that the top two rows of the Zachman Framework represent. This business architect will serve an important role as companies struggle with the challenge of mapping their business requirements to IT capabilities.

Challenge of Architecture

If this section is making you just a bit incredulous, well, that's good to hear. The bar that the Zachman Framework sets for enterprises is very high. For most companies, the mere thought that there might be an individual or a group who is responsible not only for the overall corporate timeline, but also for tying the timeline to IT issues, business process, and more seems like a fairy tale. It's ludicrous to assume that many organizations have the wherewithal to create such plans and then have the discipline to implement them. Furthermore, many companies don't have a place in their organizational hierarchy, let alone budgets, to give architects the authority and control they need to be effective. After all, to many companies, enterprise architects look simply like another layer of middle management—something we learned to rue just a few chapters back. The challenge is not simply making enterprise architecture a reality, but finding its just, and peaceful, place in the organization as a critical agent of change.

So, we're at an impasse: Enterprise architecture is a significant challenge that is seemingly out of reach for many companies, yet this same challenge represents the path they must take in order to get out of the death spiral of IT complexity. It's as if we're showing you the way up a mountain, but then we're telling you to take the one that goes straight up a cliff.

Fortunately, this impasse is transitory. Service Orientation represents an organizing principle that can help guide organizations through the labyrinth of enterprise architecture. Zachman laid out the overall map but didn't provide a guide for prioritizing your route through the framework or a way for determining which parts of the framework are more important to you than others. After all, companies are all different and thus have different strengths and priorities that would affect their best approach to enterprise architecture.

As the next section explains in detail, Service Orientation offers organizations an agile approach to tackling these tough enterprise architecture issues across both business and IT. Service-Oriented Architecture, in particular, offers enterprise architects a particular architectural road map that tells them where to start, what's important, and which way to go. As you might expect, given the thrust of this book up to this point, flexibility is built into Service Orientation. The Service-Oriented approach to the Zachman Framework therefore thinks of it as a guide rather than a straitjacket. After all, the whole idea is to develop techniques for organizing IT and people's relationship to it so that the organization can respond to change and leverage change for competitive advantage.

PUTTING ALL THE PIECES TOGETHER

In this section, then, we finally bring together the two strands we have been spinning throughout this chapter: *Service Orientation* and *enterprise architecture.* At first glance, the concept of Service Orientation seems to be more business-oriented, while enterprise architecture leans more toward technology—but in reality, both concepts bridge IT and business. Indeed, in many cases these concepts are spun from the other perspective, with some peddling Service Orientation as solely a technical concept while others push the notion of enterprise architecture as a business concept devoid of technical underpinnings. As with every complicated concept, the reality lies between these extremes. More than anything else, Service Orientation is a way of looking at the relationship between business and IT. Enterprise architecture, however, is a set of best practices—a discipline, if you will—for building businesses that leverage IT resources. We're solidly grounding both of these concepts, however, in both business and IT.

To make Service Orientation a reality, therefore, businesses require an enterprise architecture oriented toward Services. Such an architecture cannot rely entirely on either business or technical concepts alone. With an enterprise architecture grounded in Service Orientation, we're looking for a broad set of rules and practices that govern the design and evolution of organizations that leverage business resources as Services. We call that set of rules and practices *Service-Oriented Architecture (SOA)*.

Service-Oriented Architecture as Enterprise Architecture

To tackle the elephant that is Service Orientation, it's important that you don't take the blind man's approach. Instead, think of SOA as enterprise architecture, the broad view that ties together all the different elements of the business-IT relationship. It's the role of the Service-oriented architect (an enterprise architect who practices SOA, naturally) to take this big-picture view of the business-IT relationship and to drive the process of creating the overall plan for the architecture. The Service-oriented architect must then work with other architects in their organization, as well as individuals in a variety of other roles, to flesh out the architecture. You can think of these other people as the blind men who only have one view of the elephant each; the Service-oriented architect is the one person who can see the elephant for the complete whole that it is.

The first step in any SOA project, predictably, is to identify the requirements of the business. With SOA, however, the primary business requirement is the meta-requirement of building an architecture that responds to unpredictable change—in essence, an agile architecture. Nevertheless, the architect must first be aware of specific business requirements on IT—for example, some new business capabilities, new products, new business relationships, or new budgetary constraints. Regardless of these business needs, however, the Service-oriented architect must realize that these requirements are never the end of the story, but rather the beginning.

SOA projects, after all, are not your typical IT projects. Typical IT projects begin with a fixed set of business requirements, and the architect or someone else on the team sits down with the business stakeholders (the people with the requirements) and distills a set of *use cases* for those requirements The technical team then takes those use cases and uses them to drive the IT implementation that supposedly will meet the business requirements that the stakeholders laid out. In essence, the typical IT project starts with the assumption that the business has fixed requirements, and it's the role of IT to translate those requirements into some stable implementation that the business can use on an ongoing basis.

Jargon Watch: Use Cases

A *use case* is a simplified representation of a particular business requirement applied to a particular actor, where the word *actor* means someone or something that takes action in an IT environment (often a person, but frequently another piece of software). People familiar with the concept typically represent a use case by drawing a stick figure to represent the actor and then arrows representing what the actor should be able to do.

As a simple example of a use case, let's consider withdrawing money from an ATM. The actor would be the bank customer, and the use case would show the customer putting in the card, entering the PIN, clicking the "withdraw funds" button, entering an amount, clicking "OK," and then taking the money, receipt, and card.

Use cases typically map linear sequences, as in this example, one for each actor and activity the system should support. In the case of SOA, however, use cases work at a higher level of abstraction, since the point to the SOA is to respond to unexpected requirements, not just expected ones.

Use cases for SOA projects, however, are a different kettle of fish entirely. Instead of laying out specific "I want the system to behave this way" kinds of requirements, SOA use cases describe how various users may wish to leverage the Services that will be at their disposal—Services the architect must then identify, design, and schedule. And so, rather than assuming a set of fixed requirements ahead of time, Service-oriented architects must expect requirements to change. The resulting solution then must not just meet the transitory requirements of the business, but also must be able to meet future requirements as necessary.

In SOA, therefore, a use case ties business requirements to the technology implementation in a dynamic, fundamentally Service-oriented way that takes into account both the meta-requirement of agility and the loose coupling of the Services. From these use cases, then, the architect can begin to flesh out the overall design of the architecture.

View Model of SOA

Typically, Service-oriented architects need specialists to help them with various parts of the architecture. After all, since SOA is enterprise architecture,

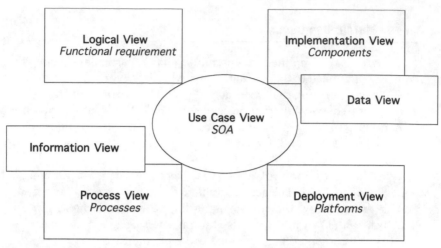

EXHIBIT 7.2   View Model of SOA

it covers the overall interaction between business and IT, which for most large companies is a truly daunting task. It's helpful, therefore, to have an approach for dividing up the responsibilities on the architecture team.

This approach follows the wisdom of the old quip: How do you eat an elephant? One bite at a time, of course! Only this time, the elephant is the enterprise architecture and the bites are the various views that different specialists on the architecture team take. We can then assemble each of these views into the View Model of SOA, as shown in Exhibit 7.2.

We illustrate the View Model of SOA as six rectangles and one oval. Starting at the four corners of the View Model are the four main views that various members of the architecture team should take. At the upper left, we have the *Logical View,* which represents the functional requirements for the architecture—in other words, what the architecture implementation is supposed to *do.* We call this a Logical View because it represents the logic of how the business runs. Business users take the Logical View, because it represents the business perspective of the architecture. In this view, Services represent abstracted capabilities the business can leverage as needed.

Individuals responsible for understanding, planning, and managing the organization's business processes take the *Process View.* Often the business will put some line-of-business user or business process architect on the architecture team because that person knows how the business works, mostly through a familiarity with its processes and constituent activities. These process-oriented folks are experts in taking business requirements and fleshing out the details of the processes that will meet those requirements. This view understands that Services are the raw material for processes and helps users represent processes as Services to the business.

The *Implementation View* is most familiar to the techies, in particular, programmers and technical architects who create and assemble software. These experts focus on components that underlie the various Services and processes—the chunks of software (either custom-written or off-the-shelf) that offer some kind of functionality. People who take the Implementation View are responsible for exposing components as Services, so they see Services as contracted interfaces to software functionality.

The *Deployment View* concerns the run-time systems and platforms that in turn underlie the implementations and help the software do its job. Included among the platforms are the network, servers and other hardware, as well as operating systems and other software infrastructure. We often fit middleware into the Deployment View, although the more business logic and process control sits in the middleware, the more we might put middleware into the Implementation View or even the Process View. Systems architects and network architects typically take the Deployment View. In this view, Services represent metadata that the systems must manage and support.

In addition to these views are two additional ones that we're going to break out from some of the views we've just discussed. The *Data View* relates to the Implementation View, but focuses, predictably, on the data in the organization. You'll find data architects taking this view, because they are more concerned with how businesses represent data than with how to implement systems that consume the data. And finally, the *Information View* relates most closely to the Process View, because it concerns how the organization creates, moves, manages, and uses information, which is different from simply storing and moving data, because information represents how people use data to guide decisions and processes. It's no surprise that information architects typically take this view. Both these views see Services as windows into the information that the company uses.

Most important of all the views is the oval that represents the whole elephant—the view the Service-oriented architect must take to keep the overall SOA project on track. We call this view the *Use Case View,* because in SOA, use cases connect business requirements through the Services to the underlying implementation. The sighted individual sitting on top of the elephant takes this view to help guide the organization in the direction it needs to go, even though the blind men below are walking along with the elephant.

Putting the Elephant Back Together

It's important to remember that everybody on the architecture team, regardless of which view each takes, has an equally valid perspective on the

overall architecture. We want the views to guide the thought of each participant, but not to go so far as to restrict the thinking of the team. In other
words, it's perfectly fine for team members to look through the eyes of the
others and try to see the overall architecture from the other points of view.
The Service-oriented architect, as the leader of the team, must be particularly adept at seeing the architecture from all perspectives, because it's that
person's responsibility to maintain the overall plan and course of the project.

To understand how to apply the View Model to SOA, it's critical to
place Services in the proper context. Services act as the crux of the architecture—the central clearinghouse that at once represents business requirements to IT and IT capabilities to the business. The practice of SOA,
therefore, predictably centers on the Services themselves: how to specify the
right ones, how to build them, when to use them, and how to compose them
into processes.

WHERE ARE THE ARCHITECTS?

If you've been paying attention, one of the things that the movement to agile
IT requires is a new set of roles and responsibilities in the organization.
After all, we've taken the time to berate today's IT departments for being
responsible for the rats' nests that are the cause of today's inflexibility, and
we've also chastised the business folks for making expedient, shortsighted
decisions that only make the problem worse. So, are we just sour-faced
naysayers who have nothing positive to say about IT and its leadership, or
is there a way out of this puzzle? Is there anyone in the organization who
can hope to get the vision of Service Orientation right, or is this all a hopeless struggle?

Fortunately, there is hope, and it comes in the form of enterprise architecture. In the early part of this chapter, we discussed the role of architecture
and the new importance that it has in today's IT organizations. So, if there's
a need for architecture, then it figures that there's a need for *architects*. After
all, if that's the role of the person doing architecture for building houses,
then it makes sense we need someone in the corresponding role for designing complex IT environments.

Enterprise Architect's Roles and Responsibilities

Although we have plenty of good definitions of architecture, it's harder to
find such a clear definition of what exactly architects are and what their role
in the organization is. In fact, there are many different types of architects in
organizations today who serve many, often vastly different, roles. What
we're looking for in this book, however, is an enterprise architect who is

able to merge the worlds of business and IT in order to make Service Orientation a reality. Such an architect should be able to perform these functions in the organization:

- *The Great Communicator.* As part of the definition of architecture includes the environment of IT, namely the business and its extended enterprise, a key duty of the architect is the ability to keep one leg firmly planted in the business and its requirements so that IT can always be responsive to the business, and not vice versa. An architect can translate ill-defined, abstract, or incomplete business requirements into a set of Service definitions or a model for how to define those Services in spite of ongoing, unpredictable change. In effect, the architect serves to intermediate the worlds of IT and business in much the same way that the human resources department isolates the business users from having to know all the intricacies and complexities of hiring and firing employees. In much the same way that we seek to simplify the IT world by abstracting its complexity, the architect helps to create an abstraction of the IT organization to the business user and provides a corresponding abstraction of the business to the IT organization. Having a good architect in place will prevent the rest of IT from speaking directly to the business organization, which is in fact a good thing.

- *The Simplifier.* Businesses are complex entities. IT is likewise a complex assortment of disparate technologies. There's simply no way that any one individual in the company can have an adequate understanding of all the intricacies of both the business and IT worlds. Thus, the enterprise architect has a key role in distilling the complexity of the business world into a set of more easily understood Service definitions, processes, and associated metadata. Likewise, the architect needs to simplify the complicated morass of IT technologies and infrastructure into a set of reusable Services and contracts that define the obligation of IT to meet ongoing, changing business requirements.

- *The Evolutionist.* A good architect realizes that nothing ever stays the same. Thus, architects are responsible for not just meeting today's requirements using today's technologies, but managing change as well. Architects need to be able to implement technologies and approaches that help them encapsulate changing requirements into metadata as well as maintain the evolving set of Services in the company. The business organization is clearly not responsible for maintaining these Services, as they change over time, but neither is the IT organization responsible for maintaining changing business requirements. You can think of business and IT users simply as the parties that engage in a contractual relationship with the architect as the role that helps define the terms of the contract and make sure that both parties abide by the terms they've agreed to.

- **Champion of Thrift.** There's sufficient technology in the organization to meet much of the business's ongoing requirements. However, most companies simply don't have enough understanding of architecture to make efficient use of existing investments. We can't count on business users to think strategically about IT agility; if it were up to them, they'd simply continue their practice of making decisions based on the most expedient, cost-effective solution to their problems of the day. Likewise, we can't depend on the IT rank and file to focus on thrift; most developers and operational folks within IT would much rather implement the latest technologies and cutting-edge infrastructure than work with the hulking system that's been chugging along for the past decade. It thus falls on the shoulders of the enterprise architect be the champion of thrift and extend the value of existing IT investments. Such architects must be able to find ways to reduce the need to invest in unnecessary technology and allow companies to build systems that can evolve with changing needs.

- **The Pragmatist.** Good architects must be more than great communicators, simplifiers, and economic magicians—they must also be able to make realistic, stepwise improvements to the business use of IT. Business users and individuals within IT each see the elephant through their own perspectives; the architect, however, must be able to see the elephant for what it is, maintaining a pragmatic mental picture for how the organization can evolve iteratively while still maintaining a single, cohesive vision of the organization's architecture.

- **Master of Best Practices.** Rather than focusing simply on using the latest, greatest technologies or delving into the latest acronym or business fad, the architect is responsible for developing the best practices for architecture for the organization. Good architects will have the opportunity to not only define a business's overall approach to architecture for the years, and perhaps decades, to come, but might even have an impact on the IT industry as a whole.

Who Should Be an Architect?

For enterprises to be successful with their SOA projects, it is absolutely critical that they have one or more people serving the role of enterprise architect—or Service-oriented architect, if you will—who are able to create and manage the big picture of enterprise SOA. These enterprise architects often have very different titles and diverse responsibilities from one organization to another, and often don't even agree on what enterprise architecture is. Some enterprise architects are very technical; others are more IT managers than hard-core techies. Many companies also have enterprise architecture teams or committees that serve the role of the enterprise architect, rather than a single person. In addition, some enterprise architects are at the level of senior developers; others can be vice presidents who report directly to the chief information officer. Therefore, finding the enterprise architects in an organization can be difficult, whether you're inside the organization or outside looking in.

Although the new breed of architects has somewhat different responsibilities from IT or business peers, these individuals must have the same broad understanding of both business requirements and technology implementation. Depending on the focus of the practice they belong to, they may require deep vertical industry knowledge. But in all instances, architects must have significant understanding of how to meet continually changing business requirements through business processes consisting of composable, loosely coupled Services.

It is certainly possible for those who have traditionally been in the IT role to become architects, but they must be able to think in terms of architecture and be able to fulfill the functions we described earlier in a credible way. Likewise, it is also possible for someone who has spent an entire career in the world of business to be able to gain enough IT knowledge to become a credible architect. Unfortunately, experience has shown that there are simply not enough people in IT or business capable of thinking in terms of in the agile, flexible, Service-oriented way that the business requires.

Architect Talent Crunch

Companies are now realizing that implementing SOA means far more than a simple reorganization of application resources. After all, implementing Service Orientation is not simply about taking existing systems, wrapping them in standards-based interfaces, and connecting them together in the sort of tightly coupled, inflexible manner that contributes more to the rats' nest problem. The broad, business-based movement to Service Orientation should lead to the ability of companies to undertake broad reorganizations of their business based on how they leverage IT assets across the enterprise. As a result, architects need to also be versed in helping their organization handle the broad human change issues necessary to transform their business.

Unfortunately, there are far too few Service-oriented architects to go around. The pending shortage of these architects puts the Service Orientation build-out most at risk. After all, where will all these skilled architects come from? Companies aren't simply looking for bodies they can train, because one of the key requirements for credible architecture is real-world expertise in how to build Service-oriented systems. Rather than looking to develop the necessary skills from scratch in their existing IT talent pool, enterprises are going to seek the help of third-party service organizations that have been building Service Orientation talent over the past few years.

For many consulting firms with a business-only focus, however, Service Orientation remains mostly an alien concept. These firms may understand in general how IT impacts business, but they have no concept of how Service Orientation will significantly alter the business landscape. As a result, there is a serious lack of consulting firms that can make Service Orientation a reality for most organizations. In addition, even though consulting firms large and small are building SOA teams, the number of consultants they are training or putting into early SOA engagements is far less than the number that enterprises will require in the coming years. There will be movement between small and large firms, as well as recruiting from industry, but there will also be a trend among consultants to leave their firms and work directly for enterprises.

As a result, a talent squeeze will drive up the rates of the more experienced consultants and drive down the quality of the average consultant, as large numbers of inexperienced and poorly trained consultants chase the rapidly growing, newly available opportunities. Just as with the dot-com build-out, the shortage of consultants may seriously impact companies' ability to execute the business transformation they require and may degrade the overall quality of SOA implementations.

Therefore, architects will be in the catbird seat for the next few years and perhaps even decades. Enterprises that have SOA-savvy personnel should nurture, grow, and encourage them, because the lucrative offers for their talent will be coming soon. Whatever you do, don't let the Service-oriented architect talent squeeze jeopardize your motivation and desire to implement agile, flexible IT.

WHITHER THE IT DEPARTMENT?

There are few recurring themes in our discussion of the movement to Service Orientation. First, companies will be able to make increasing use of the IT investments they have already made. Second, organizations will be able to keep pace with ongoing change through adjustments to contracts or other metadata, without requiring the implementation of new systems or code. Finally, companies are able to meet new requirements through the composition of existing Services into business processes that disparate business users in the organization own and manage, freeing them from requiring IT to control the systems. Given these themes, does the business of the future even need an IT department at all, or will the IT department shrivel into a shadow of itself, simply supporting existing systems and meeting contractual requirements for Services?

Mythical Business Analyst

Vendors of software and hardware products have long pitched the ability for nontechnical people in the organization to be able to use their products. In fact, a long time ago, the term *business analyst* referred to the people in the organization who interacted with various bits of technology without needing the technical acumen that true techies have to develop software applications or administer systems. Over time, however, the role of the business analyst has evolved and diversified. Today's business analyst can have a critical role in building the Service-oriented applications of the future.

In some organizations, the business analyst analyzes how the business operates and specifies solutions to business problems. However, that role sounds very generic, and indeed many people in IT would define their roles similarly, as would many enterprise architects. We'd like to propose a more limited definition of the term, where a business analyst is really a *business* user who is responsible for specifying the needs of a particular business division. You can find business analysts in sales, marketing, customer service, human resources, business planning, manufacturing, or anywhere else in the organization. A business analyst is typically the primary business liaison to various IT departments and is responsible for configuring the systems to do what the business requires.

Clearly, the business analyst doesn't replace or substitute for the architect. Business analysts can make some decisions and changes on their own, but they don't have the responsibilities, capabilities, or focus on the long-term direction of the company that architects should have. Architecture isn't simply about putting processes together or configuring existing applications. Rather, architects must come up with the plan to start with and make sure that the business and IT users are engaged in contractual relationships that contribute to greater business agility and flexibility over time. Business analysts surely are important people in this relationship, because they might be responsible for fulfilling the business-side terms of the contractual relationship, but they aren't responsible for the architecture of the company as a whole.

Likewise, the role of developers, administrators, and operational staff in IT doesn't go away simply because business analysts can evolve and manage processes simply and directly. Business analysts may be users who are able to combine and recombine Services as necessary to met ongoing and unpredictable change, but someone still has to build the Services in the first place. Over time, a company will need to create fewer new Services to meet ongoing business requirements, but business users always will require a set of Services that simply don't exist. The organization will still need developers and other technical personnel to create and support these new Services.

Furthermore, someone has to make sure that IT is living up to the terms of the contracts between business and IT. Architects are responsible for creating the contractual relationships, and business analysts are just one party to the contract. Of course, IT is responsible for meeting its side of the agreement. Developers, administrators, and operational staff have to make sure that systems are up and running, loose coupling is actually in effect, and legacy systems can fulfill their role in the architecture.

The Shrinking IT Department

Although there's no doubt that companies will need to maintain substantial IT departments for the foreseeable future, it's clear that the size of those IT departments is shrinking and will continue to shrink over time. In the past it might have been necessary to have a virtual army of IT development and

Jargon Watch: Outsourcing and Offshoring

Outsourcing became a political issue during the 2004 U.S. presidential elections. It seemed that nobody liked the idea that a company might turn to some third party to get critical work done. It turns out that there was in fact confusion between two related but very different terms: outsourcing and offshoring.

Outsourcing is simply the contracting with a third party to complete some task or set of tasks. Outsourcing is different from simple subcontracting in that the third party is free to use whatever approaches and methodologies it wishes wish to perform a task as long as it fulfills the terms of the contractual relationships with clients. In essence, outsourcing is a loosely coupled business relationship.

People often confuse outsourcing with *offshoring,* whose value proposition is that labor is cheaper outside an industrialized country. Offshoring means sending some task to another country because it's cheaper there. It's clear that offshoring and outsourcing overlap, but aren't the same thing. Companies often offshore tasks to another division of their organization in another geography, and companies often outsource tasks to a third party from the same country.

administration staff to manage the rats' nest of tightly coupled systems; one goal of Service Orientation is clearly to reduce that unsightly mess. If there will be fewer systems and less complexity, companies shouldn't need to keep their hordes of IT staff around in the numbers they're accustomed to.

Not only is the reduction of the IT rats' nest contributing to a decrease in IT staffing, so too is the movement to outsource those tasks that are considered to be commoditized, repetitive, or even menial in the organization. Companies have long seen outsourcing as a way to reduce their costs by shifting the responsibilities for development and maintenance to a third party. In the past decade, companies have outsourced hundreds of thousands of IT jobs to third parties that are able to complete those tasks at much greater economies of scale.

Of course, because individuals are very resistant to change, we can expect people to resist the movement to Service Orientation—especially if their jobs are in jeopardy. Rather than looking at Service Orientation as a benefit, these people will resist even the most basic hints of agile, IT architectures. We implore these people to see the writing on the wall and become architects. Don't be part of the problem, be part of the solution!

CHAPTER 8

How to Think Service Oriented

By now you've realized that Service Orientation requires at least as much change in the organization of our IT departments as in the implementation of technology. After all, changing the technology we use is much easier than changing the way we think. Companies are used to implementing the latest and greatest technologies, but are loath to change the structure of their IT departments. Yet the movement to Service Orientation requires more than simply implementing new techniques and methodologies—it also requires a change in the very way we think of IT. In this chapter, we'll help you rearrange your thinking in a way that's Service oriented and, in the process, move your organization that much closer to the goal of agility in the face of unpredictable business change.

WHEN NOT TO USE SERVICE-ORIENTED ARCHITECTURE

The first step in changing your thinking about how companies use IT is understanding when *not* to change your thinking. You'd think that with this book's laserlike focus on the benefits of Service Orientation, we'd be of the opinion that SOA was good for all users, systems, and situations. As a matter of fact, SOA is particularly valuable in certain circumstances—namely, in heterogeneous IT environments that are subject to frequent change. However, in many situations—if your IT environment isn't heterogeneous, for example, or isn't expecting much in the way of change—then maybe an SOA isn't right for you.

In these cases, the advantages and benefits you can receive by building and running an SOA implementation—greater business agility, empowering business users, squeezing more value out of IT, reducing the cost of integration—actually may be outweighed by the cons of SOA, including its greater performance overhead, the increased need for architectural discipline, and the requirement that companies change how they consume and produce IT assets. Here, then, are four situations where you might not want to use SOA:

1. When you have a homogeneous IT environment
2. When true real-time performance is critical
3. When things don't change
4. When tight coupling is a pro, not a con

When You Have a Homogeneous IT Environment

If you are an organization that uses the technologies of a single vendor, it's possible that the additional overhead of SOA would not be cost-effective for you. This situation is particularly true if your IT infrastructure has a narrow purpose, say, running a Web site. If you have a small number of servers, an SOA may not add sufficient value to your IT investment. Most small companies, for example, have a small, homogeneous network. For these companies as well as for larger companies that have staked their claim in a single-vendor technology implementation, the overhead, complexities, and organizational change that SOA mandates often are an impractical addition to an otherwise simple infrastructure.

Homogeneity, however, works on different levels: hardware, software infrastructure, applications, and data. Heterogeneous hardware environments may not benefit from SOA unless you also have a heterogeneous mix of applications and middleware. After all, one of the benefits of SOA is to abstract rats' nests of middleware.If there isn't enough middleware to gum up the works, then SOA might be overkill. But on the flip side, if you have a homogeneous software infrastructure, a heterogeneous mix of applications may necessitate a Service-oriented approach to exposing application functionality.

Counterpoint: When You Would Like to Expose External Services   Even if your internal IT operations are all in order and quite homogeneous, you still may have to deal with external third parties. In such cases, SOA resolves issues of flexibility and visibility across multiple firms, even when individual companies have homogeneous IT environments.

When True Real-time Performance Is Critical

I don't know about you, but I'm glad the antilock braking system in my car isn't based on SOA. In fact, embedded systems like those found in cars and specialty equipment often require responses in the millisecond range or faster. As SOA relies on loose coupling between Service consumers and providers, SOA is not well suited to situations that require strictly enforced response times. Basically, tight coupling has its benefits: The more you know about the other party, the more you can impose control and requirements on that party. When complete control is critical, it's better to depend on a tightly coupled system than one that can allow for dynamic change. When a life depends on speed, I'd rather go with a tightly coupled architecture any day.

Counterpoint: There's "Real-Time" and Then There's "Right-Time" The business desire to move to "real-time" interactions means something quite

---

Jargon Watch: Real-time

Real-time is one of those terms that gives jargon a bad name. First, it has too many different meanings, and second, it's become little more than a clichéd marketing slogan for many companies. Let's unravel this mess and make sense out of the term.

The core idea of real-time is something that happens right away, as opposed to something you have to wait for. For example, you expect a Web page to load right away, while a bank may process your deposit overnight or even over a couple of days. So far, so good—except *right away* is a relative term. Sometimes we mean in less than a second, or maybe less than 30 seconds, or maybe we mean faster than overnight. It really all depends on the situation and the business requirement at hand—and the patience of the participants.

This cliché reaches the utmost in cliché-ness in the phrase *real-time enterprise*. A real-time enterprise is ostensibly one that responds to customer needs *right away*, but in reality, it can respond to customer needs fast enough to keep most of their customers happy, or, at the very least, it can respond faster than the competition (even if that's not even close to right away). The most practical sense of *real-time enterprise* is a company that avoids arbitrary forces slowing down its ability to react to customer desires or, more broadly, to any business change. IT, of course, is an endless source of such arbitrary forces, so building an IT infrastructure that responds efficiently to change is critically important for any real-time enterprise. For our purposes, *real-time* refers to satisfying a contractual agreement on how long some action should take.

different when you're talking about an embedded system versus a real-time enterprise. If an enterprise can get some critical business intelligence in 30 seconds rather than having to wait overnight, that's real-time enough for most companies. And if an occasional query takes an hour, that's usually okay too. In fact, SOA is an excellent approach for companies looking for ways to speed up onerous batch processing without having to throw away their legacy applications. In these cases, we're not talking about real-time as much as right time. When SOAs can provide business value at the right time, they are the most valuable.

When Things Don't Change

This is the "if it works, don't mess with it" situation. If your requirements for that dusty old legacy system in the corner aren't expected to change, then why bother messing with it? In fact, this principle applies to companies and networks of all sizes. How many of you have a perfectly good computer that's more than five years old? If it's meeting your needs, then who says you have to chuck it?

In many organizations, there exists a wide range of systems that are likely to be just as good now at doing what they did five years ago—as long as you don't mess with them. We're not just talking about the computers themselves here, but also the applications running on those computers. If there are few reasons to change the application, reorganizing these dinosaurs to fit SOA might not return sufficient value to make the effort worthwhile.

Counterpoint: SOAs Can Unlock Business Value in Even the Most Crotchety Old Systems   This counterpoint probably won't apply to that ancient Macintosh hiding in a closet somewhere, but many companies can benefit by Service-enabling enterprise legacy systems, if only to wring more value out of them. Even the oldest system in use can continue to offer value to the organization as things change. In some cases, Service enablement means installing new software on the old box, but not necessarily. The goal is to expose Service interfaces on those dinosaurs and then make them participate in business processes that consume those Services in new ways.

When Tight Coupling Is a Pro, Not a Con

Loose coupling is great for enabling communications between applications in a distributed computing environment and for making it easier to change the elements of such an environment. After all, if you don't have to know anything about the system at the other end of the line, then communication and change are both simple and straightforward. When you build an application that will reside on a single computer, however, loosely coupling the components of that application from each other introduces needless overhead. Indeed, the developer controls all those components at once, so what does it matter that one component needs to have an intimate understanding of the workings of another?

Counterpoint: Moore's Law Takes Care of Performance Challenges, So What's the Real Downside to Loose Coupling? Performance has rarely been an impediment to the adoption of any single technology for very long. Moore's Law does a nice job of resolving computing challenges that were intractable only a few years earlier. Even the smallest of today's computers can match what only a supercomputer could have handled only a decade or so in the past. Why not use Service-oriented development approaches for all your applications if performance is the only issue?

The truth is that we can. Most applications can benefit from loose coupling, even if the benefits are slight, because it's cheaper to throw more hardware at the problem than to rebuild the system every time something changes. In addition, an increasing number of hardware products accelerate SOA implementations, and there's also every indication that computers will keep getting faster and hard drives will keep getting bigger. The advantages tight coupling has over loose coupling are rapidly diminishing as the days go by.

KEEPING UP WITH THE COMPETITION

Now that we know when *not* to use SOA, let's talk about many of the various reasons you *should* be Service oriented. One of the reasons why business agility is so critical to today's companies is that business markets never stay still. Indeed, it is the nature of business to seek every possible competitive edge, whether new technologies and approaches, more aggressive pricing and marketing, or enhancing the customer experience and value proposition. Therefore, it is clear that companies that can respond more quickly to change or, even better yet, can introduce change in their particular markets will have a sustainable edge over those that can't. We've been harping on this idea that Service Orientation can address the key challenges of agility, especially with regard to the role that IT plays, for most of this book. Here are some actual examples of what real companies have done to implement SOA to solve their particular business agility and competitive challenges.

Case Study: Large Telecommunications Company

Telecommunications is a great example of an industry that undergoes continual and dramatic change. Since the invention of the telephone, a constant stream of new products and technologies has been roiling the telecom markets. Modern telecom firms sell a wide range of products including mobile services, data networking, video and entertainment services, and various pay-per-use or monthly subscription services. Each new service impacts a significant part of the organization, requiring new support infrastructure, technical staff to get the new systems up and running for customers, changes to billing and payment, as well as the technology infrastructure to support the new offerings. Thus, the company that can best offer new services at the lowest cost while maintaining flexibility is often the company that is most successful in the telecommunications market.

It is no wonder, then, that one large U.S.-based telecommunications firm used Service-oriented approaches to optimize the way it used its IT systems. In particular, this firm recently went through a merger with another large telecommunications company and needed to integrate the other company's products and services quickly. After the acquisition, the newly merged company realized that over 50% of its IT systems were redundant—that is, the merged companies had multiple instances of the same functionality throughout their systems. On average, they had developed each individual piece of IT functionality 5 to 25 times, including one they had deployed 45 different times! All this unnecessary redundancy meant unnecessary cost and complexity. Given that each acquired firm's IT was a rats' nest of systems, all this unnecessary IT meant significant inflexibility. The folks quickly realized that SOA was a way out of their complexity problems.

The company first kicked off an SOA initiative in early 2003, and it went live in late 2004. The main focus of the SOA effort was to transform 250 business transactions, such as verifying customer credit histories and looking up customer information, into 57 Service-oriented applications that could handle over 200 transactions as a group. After going through a relatively speedy transition from tightly coupled applications to loosely coupled Services, the company had a core set of reusable, shared Services that it could compose to meet new business requirements.

The results were staggering. The firm slashed its overall IT budget by a full 50%. The set of standards-based Services could handle over 3 million transactions per day and helped the company roll out a new set of product offerings in a time frame that seemed overly ambitious just a few years prior. For this telecommunications firm, the movement to SOA enabled the business agility it needed to stay competitive and reduce IT cost and complexity in the face of ongoing, unpredictable change.

Case Study: Large Insurance Company

Telecoms aren't the only companies facing ongoing change and competitive pressure. Even the seemingly stodgy insurance industry is susceptible to continually changing markets that force companies to rethink how they do business. One of the largest investment and insurance companies in the United States faced such a challenge, which led it to adopt SOA. The particular insurance firm in question is a leading provider of investment products, life insurance and group and employee benefits, automobile and homeowners' products, and business insurance. Largely as a result of this broad product offering, it has a wide array of disparate, heterogeneous IT systems.

The IT organization within the company's property and casualty division developed an in-house tool in the mid-1990s that allowed the firm's agents to broadcast requests for quotations to multiple carriers and get a response in a standard format. The system then took the response messages, authenticated the agent who sent them, transformed them, and then routed them to the appropriate system in the firm to handle the particular requests. The original version of this tool was a tightly coupled solution that exhibited several weaknesses, in particular the fact that it was expensive to maintain and manage as the document formats changed.

When it was clear that it was time to update the tool as new technologies became available, moving the initiative to a Service-oriented approach made sense to the insurance company, because it was looking to solve internal integration problems, including the interaction between heterogeneous back-end systems and the agency portal that supported the agency channel. In particular, the firm adopted a system where a centralized set of Services would evaluate incoming documents and then make rules-based decisions about which internal systems should handle those requests. This new, Service-oriented system replaced the previously tightly coupled approach by allowing business users at the insurance company to change the way they processed incoming documents without having to involve the IT department. Thus, the key benefit that SOA provided this company was to shift the control of the business process from the hands of the IT staff to that of the line of business.

In addition, the solution that the insurance company put in place did not require substantial, risky changes to enterprise systems, IT procedures, or customer behavior. It was able to solve an otherwise knotty problem of many-to-many integration in a straightforward way with an SOA implementation, and as a result the company now is well positioned to build on that solution as it continues with its SOA rollout.

Case Study: Loyalty Program Company

The two previous SOA case studies concerned large enterprises. However, there are plenty of examples of midsize companies that have implemented small but significant projects in a Service oriented way to solve substantial problems for the business. One particular case in point is an airline loyalty ("frequent flyer miles") program. Loyalty rewards present a challenging problem for companies that offer them. These firms want to reward customers by giving them credits they can redeem for additional services without any charge. However, companies must accrue those loyalty benefits as a liability on their books, because their customers can redeem them at any time. This liability motivates companies that offer such rewards to get customers to redeem their credits as quickly as possible, preferably with services or products that don't cost the company much in the way of additional expense. Furthermore, loyalty programs are expensive to maintain and market, and as such represent an ongoing cost to the business that doesn't necessarily return the desired benefit.

To solve these problems, this loyalty program company offers consolidated services that offload the responsibility of maintaining such programs from firms that want to offer the benefits, while also providing a range of methods for redeeming credits—well beyond air travel. The challenge this company faces is that it must integrate with an increasing number of suppliers that wish to offer benefits, each with its own back-end systems, representing a significant point-to-point integration challenge. Furthermore, the loyalty program company must keep up with the large number of customer communication channels, including call centers, Web sites, and direct mail. Finally, these firms operate on a slim margin, making money by arbitraging credits and benefits.

The company decided to implement a Service-oriented solution to its IT challenges, and do so at break-neck speed in order to reduce its overall risk and increase its time to market. The chief executive officer's mandate was twofold: Create new reward redemption opportunities for members, and be first to market with online methods to purchase credits and redeem rewards. In addition, the company had a mandate to build its partner (customer) base, interact in real time with suppliers, and protect members' privacy. On top of those mandates, the company also wanted to reduce development and implementation costs, minimize impact on and use of enterprise systems, and increase visibility into transactions.

The loyalty program company decided to implement a simple set of Services that suppliers could access through standards-based interfaces. These Services were easily accessible via the Internet, so that new suppliers could connect simply and inexpensively. The Services extended the company's existing back-end infrastructure, requiring no new coding to implement the Services. But more significantly, the project went from proof of concept to production in 38 days from start to finish. The results were staggering: The company could now add a new partner for rewards redemption in a matter of hours, rather than days or weeks. The company is now able to grow its nonair redemption by more than 500% from 2004 to 2007. The system will save even more money in the future as the company uses its Services for a wide range of new programs and activities. Most important, SOA gave the company the agility it needed to offer value in an industry where margins are slim.

SERVICE ORIENTATION FOR BIG FISH

Large enterprises in particular certainly have a lot to gain by moving to agile architectures. Indeed, when you hear people talking about significant IT projects, they like to talk about the largest of large companies. Often we talk about these large companies as if they were one large constituency—the Fortune 500 or Global 1000, for example. Indeed, these companies are a significant force in IT. As a group, they are responsible for more than 50% of all IT spending worldwide, and for many major software categories, such as mainframe, customer relationship management (CRM), and enterprise resources planning (ERP), they represent an even greater percentage of overall spending. What does this sort of organization need from SOA, and is Service Orientation more than just another fad that software vendors and consulting firms foist upon this unsuspecting but heavily spending crowd?

Cutting Out the Fat

One of the mantras of the post-dot-com boom-n'-crash decade is that companies must continue to cut the cost of IT and lower their overall spending. Companies are now stuck in the single-minded thinking that such spending now must decrease year over year, posing a challenge to organizations that must not only maintain existing IT systems, but also implement new technologies and approaches, such as the kind that SOA represents. How can such firms ever hope to continue to innovate if all they are doing is reducing their spending year after year? Fortunately, SOA presents the interesting paradox: Even though architecture requires new spending, it leads to the reduction of other IT spending to a much greater degree.

In particular, SOA enables the elimination of needless, tightly coupled middleware. As companies solve their integration challenges architecturally, there will be less need to use the bulky, inflexible, and far-too-costly Enterprise Application Integration (EAI) and other middleware they now have in place. As such, the cost of architecture is significantly less than the tens or even hundreds of millions of dollars that most firms are spending annually on this inflexible glue. This cost reduction from SOA is more than simply the elimination of software licenses. The more middleware that companies can get rid of, the fewer hardware systems, consulting services, and even internal staff are needed to manage the remaining complexity.

SOA also promises the elimination of redundancy through increased reuse of IT assets. Companies have spent hundreds of millions of dollars implementing the same basic projects over and over for different purposes. For example, most companies implemented their first customer databases a few decades ago, but they are still implementing the same sort of application functionality to this day in their CRM, ERP, portal, and Web-based systems. When will all this redundant and unnecessary spending end? Only when we can get true reusability of Services. SOA enables companies to build Services once and reuse them multiple times to solve different challenges as they arise.

SOA for Mergers and Acquisitions

One of the things that big fish companies like to do, even more than slimming down and optimizing their resources, is swallow smaller fish. Merger and acquisition (M&A) activity drives most industries. In particular, the financial services market, especially banking, equities, and insurance, not to mention telecommunications, grows through acquisition. After all, there are only so many people out there who need a phone or a bank account or a department store, and once you've saturated your market, the only way to grow is by buying out your competitors. As such, the larger the company gets and the more mature the market, the more that a company will have M&A as part of the way it does business.

An M&A activity is exactly what it sounds like: taking two large, separate organizations and then smooshing them together to form one, larger company. We hope that, in this smooshing process, nothing breaks, and that's where IT is frequently more the challenge than the solution. Integration challenges pose a significant headache in getting two formerly separate companies to work together as a single entity. After all, each company made its own technology decisions for different and sometimes opposing business reasons. When a merger occurs, not only do we need to deal with one company's rats' nest, but now we must deal with two.

M&A is an inherently messy business, but it's one that companies want to get over with as quickly as possible. Although it might have taken months, if not years, to hammer out the business arrangement that led to the merger in the first place, once it happens, executives are eager to get on with running the new, combined business. Anything that slows down the integration of the two companies adds significant risk. For this reason, acquisitive companies typically look to dump or untangle the rats' nests that come with the acquisition.

Service Orientation offers companies that are acquiring other businesses a significant advantage in that they are able to rapidly and easily absorb the other company's technologies and infrastructure with little impact to their own. If a company has built an architecture to deal with unpredictable change, then an M&A falls into the bucket of that sort of change. When the company it is acquiring is a tangled mess of IT systems, extending the SOA to deal with the new division's IT issues presents a straightforward approach for integrating the two companies' IT shops.

Merging two companies into a single entity requires two broad sets of activities: combining the complementary capabilities of the two companies together into a unified whole, and identifying and removing the redundancies that result from parallel efforts at each company. SOA helps with both tasks. If the company can represent the IT capabilities of both companies as Services, then the business can adjust existing processes and build new processes by composing the new Services with the old. Furthermore, if the combined IT team identifies redundant capabilities, then it can streamline the underlying, redundant technology without impacting the consumers of the functionality.

On the flip side, when companies that are looking to sell out have SOA in place, then acquiring them will be inherently less risky, making them even more valuable to the acquiring company, even if the acquirer has a rats' nest itself. The benefits to the acquiree include greater valuation, faster time-to-market for the new combined entity, and, even more important, no interruption in the business of their existing clientele. In addition to making the post acquisition process smoother, the fact that the acquired company is Service-oriented means that it can make use of the new owner's capabilities much earlier in the transition.

Addressing Cultural Issues of Mergers

Combining the technologies of two companies is one thing; combining the cultures is something else entirely. Culture clashes can lead to internal political upheavals, mass defections, and, worst of all, decreased attention to the customers' needs. In many instances, companies bungle M&A to the point that the customers of the acquired company leave as a result of mishandled customer service, screwed-up service delivery, and apprehension about how the new company will treat them. If an acquiring company can guarantee its current level of service, maintain the same overall governance, and maintain its customers' trust, then the transition will be seen not only as positive in the minds of existing customers, but perhaps a reason to do even more business with the new combined entity.

Service Orientation can help with the cultural issues of M&A as well as the technical ones. When the merger leads to additional lines of business, a company that thinks in a Service-oriented way will consider each line of business as both a Service provider and Service consumer, able to interact with different parts of the organization on a contractual basis. As long as the company focuses on these contracts, one line of business need not concern itself with how another line of business handles its internal operations. Just as Services act to separate dissimilar technologies so that they can work together in a loosely coupled fashion, so too can taking a Service-oriented approach to the business help to resolve dissimilar cultures.

Big fish will become ever larger due to the natural forces that made them big in the first place. However, these large companies must not necessarily suffer as a result of their size. Leveraging the benefits of SOA to act and become more nimble and make the process of getting even larger will justify the move to SOA. Even more powerful than leveraging agile *architecture,* however, is in leveraging agile *business.* Remember, Service Orientation is a broader approach than IT. If companies can think Service oriented, then they will be better able to respond to all different kinds of change, even mergers and acquisitions.

SERVICE ORIENTATION FOR SMALL FISH

There are plenty more fish in the sea than just the big ones that gobble up smaller fish and come to dominate the ponds they swim in. Indeed, the vast majority of businesses out there are of small and medium size. Although large firms lead IT by virtue of their spending power, small and medium-size firms dominate by their sheer numbers. In fact, most large businesses deal with scores of smaller ones as part of their day-to-day activities. It is also true that small businesses are different from their larger peers in that their problems are of a smaller scale, more external in nature, and require significantly lower IT investment.

Furthermore, even divisions of large companies share many characteristics with small businesses, so paying attention to the small end of the Services implementation scale pays off for all organizations looking to leverage the power of Service Orientation. The short-term promise of Service Orientation applies to organizations where the integration cost and complexity is high because their IT infrastructure is heterogeneous—that is, consisting of a wide range of disparate technologies that are difficult to get to interoperate. Certainly a heterogeneous IT environment is the norm in companies of any significant size, but the smaller a company gets, the more homogeneous its IT infrastructure tends to become. You might think, therefore, that Service Orientation offers little to the small or medium-size company that has, until now, simplified its IT universe by standardizing on homogeneous environment. Look more closely, however, and the benefits of Service Orientation to these smaller companies become clear.

It's Still About Integration

At its core, every business shares the same elements: products or services it sells, customers that buy those products or services, suppliers that provide the components of a product or service, and the operations that make producing, buying, and selling possible. For large enterprises, each of these operations can be extremely complex, involving hundreds or thousands of different systems, individuals, and processes. To get the business running properly, all those internal systems must work together, resulting in the tremendous need to simplify internal integration.

However, the smaller that a business is, the more external its integration issues become. Rather than dealing with internal heterogeneous infrastructures, small businesses must integrate with their suppliers, customers, outsourced vendors, and partners. In some industries, such as insurance, healthcare, and government, external integration is the primary integration issue, because there are a large number of disparate, disconnected parties to integrate. For such companies, Service Orientation can make just as a significant dent in reducing the cost and complexity of external integration as it can with internal integration for larger companies. The challenge these small businesses face is that they must be able to implement and consume Services across enterprise boundaries while staying within their small-company IT budgets.

Nevertheless, simplifying integration is not the be-all and end-all for enterprises looking to implement Services. After all, the promise of business agility is just as intoxicating for small businesses as it is for large ones. Small businesses thrive because they are nimble and agile enough to make business decisions on the fly. However, small businesses that depend on technology, like their larger peers, can be also bog down if their IT infrastructures are not capable of rapidly changing in response to business requirements. Therefore, technology-centric small businesses have much to gain by following the principles of Service Orientation, principles that allow them to outsource critical aspects of their operations and make changes to their businesses with minimal IT impact.

Consuming External Services

The most obvious approach small companies can take to leverage the power of Service Orientation is to consume Services that external parties provide. This consumption takes the ability of an individual to access some company's Web site one step further. While you're already familiar, say, with going to a shipper's Web site to track a package, what if a piece of software you were running did that for you automatically? A small company's accounting system might query a sales tax Service, or maybe a customer management application might use an address verification Service. Industry-specific examples abound as well. Insurance agents' own software can access critical Services that the insurance carriers provide. Doctors' offices' account management software can process insurance claims via Services. The list goes on and on.

On one hand, many of these capabilities have been available via a browser interface for a while now, and the move to Service Orientation can automate that process. On the other hand, some interactions between a small company's computer and a large company's systems have been around for years as well. Take electronic insurance claims submission, for example, which has been available since the early 1990s, first via modem and later over the Internet. The problem with these older approaches is that they were all tightly coupled—that is, the insurance company had to provide software to the doctors' offices, and every time the larger company wanted to change the functionality, it had to update all of the practices' applications. With Service Orientation, however, it's possible to update the Service without breaking the consumers of that Service—after all, that's the power of loose coupling. The old way of submitting electronic claims just got a whole lot easier, and more agile.

Embedding Services into External Business Processes

Small businesses have lots to gain, not just by consuming Services but also by exposing certain core business operations as Services. Although business models for selling access to Services online are still emerging, companies can realize significant benefit by providing Service interfaces to products and services they already sell. For example, manufacturing companies can expose their inventory and shipping processes as Services so that their customers can gain better visibility into ordering and fulfillment. The benefit to a small business: making it easier to embed their Services into customers' business processes can increase sales, customer satisfaction, and competitive advantage. In fact, companies that embed their supplier's operations into their own will find it harder to replace them—not because of the technology, but rather because of their usefulness to the organization.

All businesses offer products and/or services for sale. However, most companies don't define themselves simply as the products or services they carry, but rather the impact that their offerings have on their customer—in other words, their value proposition. Incorporating these products or services into the other company's business process increases their value. For example, FedEx is not just an overnight package carrier; it provides global logistics and communications Services for its customers, partners, and other third parties. FedEx strives to be part of each company's purchasing or logistics process in order to deliver a differentiated value proposition.

However, traditional forms of integration do not support this value proposition. Most companies implement integration as an arm's-length activity that isolates their own business processes from their customers' or partners' processes. When these companies consider implementing SOA, they only see limited value: that of reducing the cost of that arm's-length integration. But companies don't really want integration at arm's length; they want to embed their products or services into their customer's business processes. Such embedding is where the true transformational value proposition of Service Orientation lies for smaller companies, and it is an important way that small businesses can significantly impact their larger brethren.

Rise of Service Marketplaces and Smart Consumers

As Service Orientation moves past the emerging technology stage and becomes widely available, we see a few important trends developing that impact small companies in particular (as well as large companies, for that matter). First, there is already a movement toward Service marketplaces—companies that act as brokers for Services that various other companies provide. A small business can use one of these Service marketplaces as a one-stop shop for Services. In the long run, the small business's software will be able to access such marketplaces automatically to find the capabilities needed.

The second trend is in the maturation of Service consumers—pieces of software that routinely find and access Services, which can be either internal or external to the organization that's running the consumer software. Think about how a browser can access internal portals and external Web sites; which sites the user goes to is limited only by the user's imagination. Now, instead of a browser, think about any piece of software being able to access Services in the same way—it could be your accounting package, your spreadsheet, or any industry-specific application you might have running on your own computer. Even for the smallest of companies, the notion of *application* moves beyond a single program on a single machine to a collection of Services scattered around the world, available as needed. That's the power of Service Orientation for small fish.

SOA TO STAY OUT OF JAIL

The corporate climate isn't particularly favorable to public companies these days, large or small. The visions of young executives cashing in on their stock options and threatening to put traditional brick-and-mortar businesses out of commission have given way to images of corporate failure, such as Enron and MCI, and executives such as Martha Stewart and Bernard Ebbers trading in their yachts for handcuffs. Implicit trust in corporations and their management is a thing of the past; accounting firm fraud and the intentional misleading of stockholders is the dreadful reality of the present. Stocks have taken a tumble and shareholders are taking it out on the executives. "Lie to us, and you go to jail" is the new rallying cry of today's shareholders. No matter that those same exaggerations of earnings and revenues benefited shareholders in the go-go days of the late 1990s. It is now hangover time, and blaming others sure looks better than blaming yourself for poor investing practices.

In today's harsh corporate environment, being an executive, or even a board member, of a public company is not for the faint of heart. A whole raft of new laws and rules meant to protect the public, provide transparency in corporate management, facilitate government regulation, and smooth the interactions between businesses and their stakeholders will impact businesses for decades to come. These laws, with fancy names like Sarbanes-Oxley, the PATRIOT Act, Basel II, the California Privacy Act, Graham-Leach-Bliley, and HIPAA require that firms take full responsibility for their actions. The penalty for transgressions? Sometimes executives go to jail.

In this tough business climate of heightened competition, complex regulations, and constant change, management must be able to set guidelines for the company and then have sufficient visibility and control to ensure that people are following those guidelines. Information technology is at once the most important asset for providing these capabilities to executive management, while at the same time it impedes the very visibility and control IT promises to provide through the complexity, opacity, and inflexibility of the typical enterprise IT environment. If we are to make SOA a viable reality for most firms, it must provide agility without compromising the visibility and control companies require of their IT infrastructures.

Governance: Managing the Behavior of IT

Corporate governance describes this visibility and control that companies require, both for regulatory compliance and long-term competitiveness. IT governance is that part of corporate governance that applies to IT. IT governance in particular describes how people entrusted with the authority over some aspect of the business will consider IT in their supervision, monitoring, control, and direction of that business entity. How the various lines of business apply IT will have an impact on whether the company will be able to attain the vision, mission, or strategic goals that company management has set for it. IT governance specifies who has the rights to make decisions regarding IT, what decisions they can make, and an accountability framework that encourages the IT usage behavior corporate management seeks to exhibit. IT governance is not about making specific IT decisions (management does that), but rather determines which individuals and roles with the company systematically make and contribute to those decisions.

IT governance involves four basic capabilities:

1. The ability of an organization to define IT-focused business practices, technical standards, and repeatable processes for accomplishing organizational goals
2. A governing body that provides compliance tools to those individuals responsible for complying with IT requirements and policies
3. Tracking, monitoring, and enforcement capabilities that enable the organization's management to ensure compliance or take action should the company not be in compliance with the stated requirements and policies
4. Making all activities within the enterprise available for analysis and active involvement in the evolution of policies as well as conformance processes

IT governance is the most critical area of corporate governance in today's competitive enterprise—both the governance of IT and the use of IT for corporate-wide governance. However, how can executives rely on their IT rats' nests to offer the governance they require? The answer lies in architecture, because architecture provides the framework for the IT infrastructure and its use within the organization. Unfortunately, however, many organizations are struggling with their enterprise architecture, just as they are faced with IT governance challenges.

SOA in particular requires proper governance, because SOA mandates a connection between business requirements and IT capabilities through the power of abstraction, loose coupling, and composition. In order to make the business goals a reality, companies require governance to make sure they build and compose the *right* Services in the *right* way. Providing these capabilities for SOA initiatives is particularly critical for the success of those initiatives. Without such governance capabilities, any SOA initiative will likely succumb to the "silo effect," where different groups within IT handle issues of management in separate ways, thus preventing the organization from effectively building reusable Services or implementing any cross-departmental policy or security requirements.

SOA Governance

For companies with siloed IT shops and rigid delineations between IT and business, IT governance can be problematic, because of the numerous difficulties facing the people responsible for driving IT governance. In many such cases, the business and IT users are often at odds with each other. In enterprises that have adopted SOA, however, the cross-functional nature of SOA improves this situation. The enterprise architect has broad responsibility for both IT and business across organizational silos. Therefore, IT governance within the context of SOA—what we're calling *SOA governance*—promises to augment the IT governance process while mitigating its risks and facilitating the dialogue between business and IT users. SOA governance aims to provide the visibility and control necessary for IT governance while increasing the business agility today's organizations require. Likewise, SOA provides an enterprise the ability to govern other aspects of their business as well.

The IT governance process begins with setting objectives for the enterprise's IT efforts. Traditional IT governance processes then distribute these objectives to each department within IT, for example, applications, networking, and operations. SOA governance, however, introduces the notion of *domain ownership*. The owner of each Service domain must handle such issues as Service management, business logic encapsulation, location independence, and the data format issues associated with its Services. When the people in charge of some product area want access to a Service from a domain, they make a request to the owners of the domain, and the two groups determine the relationship between their respective spheres of influence, creating a Service-level agreement between them. Such relationships and agreements also exist between domains.

There is a common misconception that SOA governance is governance

Jargon Watch: Service Domains

Service domains are managed sets of Services sharing some common business context. In many cases these sets of Services are business Services, such as customer information, order processing, or product analysis. The people responsible for each domain maintain the applications that support its Services and maintain the interfaces to its Services for other domains.

The reason that companies need to worry about Service domains in the first place is because they will be sharing Services across different departments within the organization. As a result, the departments alone will struggle with issues of funding, control, and maintenance of those shared Services. Taking the Service domain approach provides a business-centric solution to this siloed IT problem set.

of an SOA, as if SOA were one more IT asset in need of governance in the organization. That belief, however, indicates a fundamental misunderstanding of the role of SOA. Fundamentally, SOA is enterprise architecture—when an enterprise adopts SOA, it should approach the organization of all of its IT assets from a Service-oriented perspective. As such, Service Orientation provides a broad organizing principle for all aspects of IT in the company—including IT governance. That's why we say SOA governance is IT governance in the context of SOA, rather than governance of SOA.

Furthermore, SOA requires a reorganization of IT personnel and the users of IT into domains. The need for governance highlights the importance of such reengineering, but is not its cause. On the contrary, the need to break down silos and organize a company's efforts based on the core needs of the business is as old as the term *reengineering* suggests. SOA allows the enterprise to organize IT functionality into Services that meet the needs of the business, finally enabling companies to achieve the long-desired business goals of breaking down silos and focusing on the needs of the business and the customer.

SOA Governance: Mandatory

For most organizations today, corporate governance remains a significant part of ensuring their long-term business success, and IT governance is a key part of the broader corporate governance. As a result, IT governance will become progressively more pervasive as a means for providing the compliance infrastructure necessary to satisfy emerging regulations and reduce overall liability. An architectural approach like SOA is necessary to improve the alignment of technology with business goals and manage risk within the organization.

Specifically, SOA primarily provides a way to significantly reduce risk by providing increased operations visibility. Governance, compliance, and general risk reduction offer a different quantifiable benefit than increased business agility. Compliance and governance lead to a reduction of liability, while business agility offers an increase in business opportunity. All are important, but they speak to different parts of the corporate psyche. Just how much is compliance worth? The answer lies in how much noncompliance will cost a company.

Senior management can no longer ignore IT governance and compliance issues. Enterprise architecture provides an effective framework for addressing statutory and corporate governance requirements by improving planning, providing the ability to prove compliance, increasing executive management's visibility and control, and offering a better understanding of the value of technology investments.

Nevertheless, few companies have enterprise SOA implementations today. Thus, SOA governance is for many companies a future-looking initiative. It makes sense for companies to consider SOA governance in their overall IT governance plans, even if their SOA is not yet of enterprise scope.

Companies should be proactive about SOA governance for two reasons:

1. Setting up their initial SOA initiatives with the visibility and control necessary for governance gets them started in the right direction. After all, there's no reason for even the earliest SOA projects to fall outside the governance process.

2. The earlier a company begins to implement SOA governance, the sooner it will be able to apply the agility and flexibility of SOA to its broader IT governance problems.

SOA FOR USER EMPOWERMENT

Big fish, small fish, it doesn't matter—when you get right down to it, regardless of their size, companies are made up of *people*. In all our discussions of business and technology, sometimes it's easy to lose sight of this basic fact. Customers and suppliers consist of people as well, regardless of whether they are in a business or simply consumers of goods and services. And remember, we are *all* this familiar kind of consumer, when you come right down to it.

It makes sense, then, to think about how Service Orientation affects us all as individuals—at work, at home, or wherever. Remember when we discussed the Charlie Chaplin movie *Modern Times* in Chapter 4, where poor Charlie found himself enmeshed in the gears of an uncaring business machine. Now we have the notion of Service-Oriented Process—business process in the control of businesspeople. We've retired Charlie's big gears and replaced them with tools he can control. How do we make sure that we aren't simply replacing a person stuck in one machine of business with a person stuck in another?

Not everybody in a company is either in IT or responsible for building, managing, or evolving business processes. In fact, most workers are more like Charlie, trying their best to get their various jobs done with the tools at hand. Many people, in fact, find themselves participating in one or more processes yet have no control over the processes themselves. For these people, the move to Service Orientation has subtle but powerful effects. The tools they use in their daily lives to get their jobs done—such as spreadsheets, portals, business applications of one sort or another, whatever—can now participate in Service-Oriented Processes. These dedicated applications that focused solely on knowledge worker productivity are now potent

Service consumers that can empower the ordinary line-of-business individual to become a business process professional. As a result, these familiar tools now have new power to leverage the flexibility of composite applications built from Service-Oriented Processes.

Empowering the Rank and File

To drive this point home, let's take a look at an example. Carla, say, is a call-center representative for a bank. She takes calls from banking customers and accesses various systems on her computer to help address each customer's question or concern. In the world of tightly coupled, inflexible, monolithic IT systems that existed before Service Orientation, Carla's day-to-day work involved several different applications—a mainframe emulation program that provided core account data, a CRM application that provided customer history and support information, a portal for tracking corporate information and human resources material, and a spreadsheet application that enabled her to track her daily activity and view information from her manager. And of course, she also had her telephone, which was a sophisticated call-center model with many functions.

Every day she would perform what techies sarcastically call "swivel chair integration": While on calls, she would have to jump from one application to another, sometimes copying and pasting information to perform integration manually using her own experience and intuition to guide how to get information from one system to another. In spite of her best efforts, Carla occasionally made mistakes that she or another call-center rep would later have to fix. And although her boss has repeatedly told her that an important part of her job is advising customers about products they might be interested in, she always had a difficult time understanding which products were right for each customer. Simply put, the systems she used each existed in their own universe, requiring the poor human operator to piece the business process together, resulting in inefficiency, lost productivity, low quality, and a high error rate.

After her bank implemented SOA, however, Carla's daily life became dramatically simpler. The bank implemented a single composite application that leveraged all her existing applications, but combined them to offer the same capabilities she had formerly achieved through swivel-chair integration. Leveraging Service-Oriented Process, she's able to use a single Service to access all the information and functionality she needs to support her customers. She is able to spend less time on each call, and the information about her customer is at her fingertips. She's now able to identify at a glance which products the bank offers would be of the most interest to the customer, leading to increased sales for the bank and a bigger bonus for her.

Furthermore, as various business changes work their way to Carla's in box, she's able to make adjustments quickly and efficiently. Maybe it's a new marketing campaign, followed by a regulatory change, or maybe a new product the bank wants to promote. The Service-oriented tools are so powerful, flexible, and easy to use that Carla can take advantage of them to do her job in the face of whatever change her boss can throw at her.

It's important to note that we didn't mention specifically what kind of tool Carla is using to do her work now, because it doesn't matter. Maybe it's a spreadsheet, or a browser-based portal, or even a telephone-based application. The point is that regardless of what tool is appropriate for a particular situation, it's now powerful enough to leverage composite Services that pull together various IT functions and data from different systems into whatever arrangement makes the most sense for the user. In other words, from Carla's perspective, IT resources are nothing more than business resources she can leverage as needed in her work. Through the power of loosely coupled, composable Services, Service Orientation has empowered her, and she needs no knowledge of the technology behind the scenes that makes it all happen.

Consumers and Their Consumers

Service Orientation empowers users outside the company walls as well. For this example, let's take a look at Kevin, who uses technology from the comfort of his home as he consumes goods and services. Today Kevin is an online auction fanatic who spends a considerable amount of time at his favorite auction site looking for collectibles to purchase or listing items to sell. Let's look a few years into the future, however, as various Service-oriented online auction tools become widely available. Today Kevin uses a variety of tools to enable his auction addiction—a browser, naturally, for accessing the auctions; a spreadsheet for tracking his sales and purchases; a word processor for composing auction listings and communicating with the buyers and sellers he interacts with; and the home finance program he uses for all his home finances, including his auction efforts.

Each of these applications that Kevin uses on a regular basis is fundamentally separate from the others; they don't talk to each other in any meaningful way. But with the emergence of Service-oriented tools, Kevin is now able to compose the auction, finance, sales tracking, and customer information together to make the auction process significantly less time consuming and thus more profitable. For example, Kevin's spreadsheet is now able to access an auction results Service from the online auctioneer. His home finance program uses a Service for calculating sales tax and shipping. And each of the applications he uses communicates with the others through the power of Service Orientation.

Now, it's possible, of course, for applications to communicate with each other today without the use of loosely coupled Services; communicating with an online resource is nothing new either. What Service Orientation brings to the party is the agility benefit—when the provider of a Service makes some change, Kevin's Service consumer applications are able to adjust to the change automatically. And on the flip side, Kevin is able to recompose the Services at his fingertips to do all sorts of new things without having to get any of his technology providers to change their offerings.

Let's say that Kevin quits his day job and decides to make a living through online auctions. He may simply keep buying and selling items—after all, many people do make their living that way—but Kevin has some better ideas. He leverages the fact that the online auctioneer offers several Web Services as well as the fact that other companies offer such Services. Using the applications on his home computer (which is now the core of a small business), he's able to craft a value-added business on top of the auction Services. He strings together various Services into a new process that offers some unique value proposition to his growing base of customers.

Kevin is also able to use his personal applications as Service providers—to communicate not only on his own home network, but also with outside parties if he wishes. For example, Kevin might join a group of like-minded online auction aficionados, not just for conversation, but also to provide valuable capabilities to each other via the power of Services. As the number and power of Services available on the Internet explodes, the sky's the limit as to what kinds of business opportunities ordinary people like Kevin might be able to come up with.

Carla and Kevin both significantly enhanced their productivity and their control of business processes by consuming various Web Services and by composing existing Services into new processes that they can in turn expose to others. And if Kevin and Carla can do it, so can anybody else—whether in a large company or a small business or anywhere in between. Service Orientation essentially opens up an entire new marketplace based entirely on Services.

SOA FOR VALUE CHAINS

Enterprises of all sizes have long sought to automate business-to-business (B2B) interactions in a reliable and secure manner. The chain of interaction, or *value chain*, from the suppliers of components to the assembly of those components into finished goods to the end customer is a complex web of interactions. Each manufacturer of finished goods has relationships with dozens or hundreds of suppliers, each of which in turn have relationships with dozens or hundreds of manufacturing customers. These interrelationships have enabled increasing sophistication in the way that companies buy and sell raw materials and sell their products on the market. The increasing globalization of business has resulted in suppliers existing anywhere in the world, covering many different countries, languages, and time zones. This globalization has added challenges and pressures in the effort to optimize supply chains, increasing the value proposition of agile, flexible IT systems based on SOA.

The increasing automation of portions of the supply chain allows suppliers and consumers to gain increasing levels of awareness of the efficiencies in the supply chain process and greater security and reliability in the interactions between partners. Companies track their products, via their

Jargon Watch: Supply, Demand, and Value Chains

Is thunder the sound of lightning, or is lightning what thunder looks like? It all depends on how you look at it. So it is with the notion of supply chains and demand chains. A *supply chain* is the set of companies and their products and services that form the component parts of a finished product. Supply chains connect the raw materials to the finished item through every step of the manufacturing and assembly process. A *demand chain,* in contrast, is the set of companies (or consumers) that connect a finished product with the final consumer of that product.

Sometimes it's clear where a supply chain ends and a demand chain begins. Take automobiles, for example. The supply chain begins with iron ore, rubber trees, petroleum, and the rest of the raw materials that go into each car, and ends when the finished auto rolls off the assembly line. The demand chain begins with shipping the cars to the dealer and ends with the consumers who purchase them. However, in other cases, the distinction between supply and demand chains depends entirely on which way you look at the situation, much like thunder and lightning. Take, for example, an assembly robot that the auto manufacturer uses in the factory. The robot rolls off its own assembly line, placing the last link in its supply chain—but its demand chain is a part of the car manufacturer's supply chain.

Hence the need for the term *value chain,* which recognizes that supply chains connect to demand chains and that the distinction between one and the other can be vague and fundamentally unimportant. Value chains, therefore, connect raw materials to the consumers of finished goods and services, and include all the participants along the way.

stock-keeping units (SKUs), from the time they roll off production lines at numerous suppliers to the time they arrive at end-user locations. This increase in automation allows the supply chain to move from a simple linear set of steps to a complicated web of interactions among different companies scattered throughout the globe. The key to making this web work is the use of automated, audited B2B interactions that are reliable and secure in order to reduce the need to track the movements of goods and services manually on paper.

Business-to-Business in the Past: Electronic Data Interchange

Many large firms will tell you that they've been accomplishing the goals of reliable, secure, guaranteed interactions between companies for decades, in the form of *Electronic Data Interchange* (EDI). EDI is an aging data format and networking specification for B2B integration that dates back to the 1970s. Although EDI has gained widespread acceptance over the years, it is a rigid and tightly coupled technology that uses arcane document formats and aging networking technology to enable point-to-point interactions between disparate enterprises. In addition, even though EDI provides a rigid format for how companies exchange information, the large degree of variability among different applications of EDI leads to significant ambiguity when implementing the standard. Users must resolve these ambiguities in a tedious, manual manner, which can be quite cumbersome to companies that must deal with dozens, hundreds, or even thousands of trading partners.

Nevertheless, EDI gained significant traction within a wide range of industries, because it not only simplified interactions with third parties, but also addressed the critical security and reliability needs of end users. Through the use of the *Value-Added Network* (VAN), a pre-Internet way of connecting companies with each other, companies could interact using EDI-formatted messages with large numbers of suppliers and partners without having to worry about handling security and reliability on a point-to-point basis with each trading partner. The VANs emerged as a means to provide basic connectivity between supply chain participants in the form of store-and-forward mailboxes that provided protocol conversion, security, and guaranteed delivery.

However, the EDI VANs left a sour taste in the mouths of many companies due to their steep implementation costs, monthly line charges, and per-transaction fees that racked up as the number of interactions increased. A key problem of traditional EDI VANs is that their cost structure made them prohibitively expensive to implement for the majority of businesses, especially as the Internet blossomed. Only the largest of suppliers could afford the costly setup fees associated with complex EDI software tools and the exorbitant per-transaction fees. As a result of these high costs, many small and medium-size firms simply could not afford to participate in the electronic, automated supply chains of their larger trading partners. Without their participation, the value of these electronic trading networks were dubious indeed—companies simply could not replace their paper-based processes with electronic ones, because they still had to support the small firms that could not afford to connect electronically.

Then the Internet and the Web came along, with the hopes of speedily bringing about the demise of EDI and the VAN. The Internet as a ubiquitous communications network promised not only to simplify dealing with multiple systems, but also to reduce the cost of connecting to various business endpoints. Yet, while providing the communication backbone for enabling B2B integration, the Internet itself is insufficient to handle the integration needs of most companies. For one thing, the Internet has no inherent security or reliability that matches the functionality of the EDI VAN to guarantee secure, reliable interactions between partners.

SOA Fills the Gap for Internet B2B

Today standards-based interfaces and document formats are fast becoming the lingua franca of disparate, heterogeneous information on the network, and Web Services represent a new, open standards-based approach to getting systems to integrate with each other. Rather than planning in advance how a specific application will tie into another application, Service Orientation advocates the concept that developers can now think about how a specific application exposes itself as Services to any application that cares to speak to it. The use of standards-based Services allows arbitrary applications to communicate with each other without concern as to the other system's internal implementation. Thus, it is no surprise that enterprises and IT vendors alike are latching on to SOA as the primary means for solving B2B integration issues.

The business benefits of Service-oriented B2B integration over the previous, tightly coupled approaches of EDI are clear:

- Enterprises can *reduce their cost of integration* because they have agreed on the interfaces between their systems and businesses in advance—reducing the dependency on complex, expensive, and/or custom integration approaches.
- Enterprises can *reduce the total cost of ownership of their heterogeneous systems* since standards-based, interoperable systems give businesses more choice of vendors and the flexibility to solve their specific business needs.

- Enterprises can *realize a significantly expanded market opportunity* since rather than relying on partners and suppliers to implement specific, proprietary technology approaches, vendors can provide solutions that will work in their customers' environments, allowing them to reach partners that may have been inaccessible in the past.
- Enterprises can *reduce their time to market* because they can increasingly depend on critical architectural and infrastructural elements to exist in their partners' IT environments and rely on the interoperability of those elements to reduce their need to develop time-intensive, expensive, and proprietary solutions.

Companies are finding that SOA provides not just a framework for dealing with their short-term B2B integration challenges, but also gives them a way to increase their competitiveness in all industries, particularly where margins are slim.

Case Study: Retail Industry

A large consumer goods company with over 50,000 employees and operations in over 30 countries delivers product information electronically via a Web site to its wholesalers and retail chains. The Web site includes eCommerce capabilities as well as a rich, online product catalog. However, despite the rich capabilities of this eCommerce application, changes to application functionality required extensive reprogramming. As a result, responding to continuous business changes was increasingly more complex and costly.

The developer team sought to solve this agility problem by exposing the product catalog as externally available Services, which internal users as well as partners could utilize to enter product information directly through a loosely coupled, standards-based interface. By providing a standard, abstract interface to product catalog information, the developers were freed from having to write the queries manually.

The firm realized a number of key benefits by implementing secured, externally available Services, including:

- *Faster time to market.* Through the use of Services, the firm is are able to update, change, and distribute product information more rapidly, improving accuracy as well as accelerating the process for inputting new product information into the product catalog. It is also able to reuse the Services across a wide variety of platforms to accelerate future application development.
- *Reduced application development and maintenance cost.* Exposing the catalog functionality as a Service freed the development team to

focus on more strategic value-added projects rather than manually coding product information into a database.

As this example illustrates, SOA and Service Orientation in general are not pie-in-the-sky ideas that sound good but have little reality behind them. On the contrary, companies are making enormous progress implementing Service-oriented approaches today-to reduce the cost of integration, both internally and externally; to improve their competitiveness; to increase their visibility and control in their organizations; and to create new business opportunities that were not feasible before. Service Orientation is within reach. The greatest challenge you face is in *thinking* Service oriented. Service Orientation, after all, affects how both business and technology work, and how they work together. It's not a quick fix, by any means, but it's not impossible, either.

CHAPTER 9

Okay, So Where Do We Start?

It's a good sign you've made it this far in this book, because by now you're probably convinced of the benefits of SOA in the narrow sense, as well as how Service Orientation can be applied more broadly in the organization. But if you work in a large company, you probably feel like a very small cog in a very big wheel—and that wheel either turns in many directions at once or turns *very* slowly. One problem with Service Orientation, after all, is that it is requires change throughout the enterprise, in the same way that SOA as enterprise architecture affects all aspects of the business. Sure, there are enormous benefits to be gained by moving to SOA, and there's no question that whatever rats' nest of technology you have today will continue to plague your organization until you finally take action. What steps can you take today to do something about it?

Many of the firms that understand the concept of Service Orientation are left with burning questions about how to take the theoretical concept of SOA and put it into practice: "Okay, so where do we start? I get this whole SOA thing, but what do I do when I come into the office *tomorrow?*" If you're wondering the same thing, then wait no longer. All will be revealed in this chapter.

IDENTIFYING THE PROBLEM

The last thing you want to do is boil the ocean. If your company is like most organizations, IT has a wide range of challenges facing it—competitive pressures, inefficient spending, regulatory requirements, you name it. Service Orientation can help with all of these problems—but not all at the same time. You must first identify what hot-button issue is important enough to target with your first SOA initiative.

The specific issue that should be the focus of your attention is different for every company, because it all depends on your organization, your industry, as well as the internal politics regarding the interaction between lines of business (LOB) and IT within your company. We have seen some patterns appear, but these may not apply to you. For example, many people in the banking industry have the challenge of creating a single view of the customer, and many large banks have to deal with multiple divisions brought on board through acquisitions, which only makes creating the single customer view that much more difficult. As a result, many banks focus their SOA efforts on building a set of shared Services that increase their visibility into customer data, reduce the redundancy of application functionality, and eliminate errors associated with accessing data across such disparate divisions. Another case in point is the insurance industry, which looks to support their channel of independent agents. Many large insurance firms are moving to SOA to better serve this constituency and reduce the cost of working with this highly distributed channel.

Taking the Solution Approach

It's important to keep in mind that since this book focuses on Service Orientation as a solution to the long-lived problems of IT, our discussion of how to tackle individual problems with Service-oriented solutions must be prescriptive. However, the last thing we'd want to do is set down one specific problem-solving strategy and expect to apply it to every problem that plagues IT. SOA is no silver bullet, after all. Rather, the right way to make SOA work for you is to start with a particular business problem and then identify whether taking a Service-oriented approach will solve that problem.

Taking this problem-first perspective can be difficult, especially for IT personnel. Techies predictably tend to focus on the technology, and they're more likely to think "Here's a hammer, let's go find some nails" instead of "We need to build a house, let's figure out which tools to use." It might seem that in all this discussion about SOA, we are writing a book about a set of tools. But don't be fooled—although Service Orientation does provide a practical set of tools, the point to this whole exercise isn't simply to apply technology for technology's sake. It's to solve a particular set of business problems.

You may therefore have two motives behind your SOA plan, one more tactical and the other more strategic. Your tactical motive should always be to solve an urgent and important business problem. You never have to look for these, because their sheer urgency moves them to the center of attention. Your more strategic motive, however, may be to champion Service Orientation, because of its power to make your company better able to deal with problems in general. The roadblock most organizations face is that the strategic benefit that SOA represents far too often takes the back burner to the shorter-term firefighting activities.

Formulating an SOA Strategy

This pattern of two motives for implementing SOA has been repeated time and again, across industries and geographies. Unfortunately, most business-people aren't in the position today to recommend SOA as the best approach for solving a particular business problem, because SOA is still an emerging, mostly unproven concept. In addition, because SOA is complex, technical, and still emerging, champions of SOA are mostly IT folks or sometimes the occasional business manager who is quite technical. It's natural, therefore, for these individuals to take the dual motive approach—solve a business problem and, as an ulterior motive, introduce SOA into their organizations.

This "SOA as ulterior motive" ploy, then, drives the format of the SOA strategy for many organizations. Clearly, if you want to slip SOA in the back door, as it were, you're not going to propose some grandiose, expensive, enterprisewide rollout of SOA. Instead, it makes more sense to start small and build gradually. The best idea is to begin with a small but significant project that solves a specific, limited problem and also builds acceptance for Service Orientation among management as well as SOA capabilities among the architecture and implementation teams.

Once this small project has gained acceptance, companies should quickly follow up with a broader SOA initiative as the second step. Sometimes these intermediate SOA initiatives are internal to one department, but ideally, they are cross-departmental. It is best to implement cross-departmental SOA initiatives at this phase, because they afford an organization the opportunity to build shared Services that different departments can leverage—and in so doing, force the enterprise to work out many of the organizational issues surrounding shared Services.

Only after several cross-departmental initiatives have taken hold might working on an enterprisewide SOA initiative be a good idea. But that doesn't mean you shouldn't be thinking in terms of the entire enterprise from the very beginning, even at the initial project stage. From the earliest SOA pilot project, enterprises should have a long-term architectural plan for their organization. The last thing you want is to foster localized SOA initiatives that go off in different directions or create redundant Services. Doing so will bring us right back to the days of the rats' nest, giving you nothing but a siloed organization for your efforts, only now the silos will be incompatible architectural visions!

Having a master plan, therefore, is essential for keeping a gradual SOA strategy from heading off into the weeds. It's important, however, for this master architectural plan to have the right amount of detail—not too little, but also not too much. Too little detail, and the ambiguities will plague your SOA rollout with incompatibilities and/or redundant efforts. Too much detail, and you risk "analysis paralysis"—spending too much time trying to hammer out the plan before you jump into the water and begin implementing SOA. Keep in mind that you'll be continually updating and improving the plan as you learn the lessons that only rolling up your sleeves and implementing an architecture can teach you. If you try to get the plan right before getting your hands dirty, you'll never be able to get it right at all.

CHOOSING YOUR BATTLES

As we mentioned briefly, one of the best ways to take your first step into the daunting challenge of implementing SOA is to implement a pilot project. Pilot projects are great ways to try out new approaches as challenging and complex as SOA. They lower the risk of moving to a new architecture, while at the same time they build acceptance for the new approach and solving some business problem in the process. However, it's possible to choose the wrong pilot project, and it's also depressingly easy to really foul one up. It is time, therefore, to take a closer look at what makes for a good SOA pilot and how to learn from the mistakes other people have made and avoid SOA pilot pitfalls.

Let's further define a pilot project by contrasting it with the related *proof of concept*. Both pilot projects and proofs of concept are trial projects that seek to evaluate some new technology or approach and determine whether a company should invest further to expand the project. The difference between a pilot project and proof of concept lies in the intent of the trial. A proof of concept should indicate whether the concept is worthy of future efforts, but in and of itself it does not solve any critical business problems. A pilot project, however, goes one step further, yielding a working result that, although limited in scope, actually addresses a real business problem. Pilot projects often yield limited results, but those results should actually provide a real return on investment to the business. Proofs of concept, however, are generally intended to illustrate a concept that requires further buy-in, from business or technology management, to be able to be applied to a real business scenario.

There are many reasons why a company would want to undertake an SOA pilot project, including:

- To build acceptance for SOA within the organization
- As a means to work through some of the more challenging aspects of architecture and planning its constituent Services

- To bring the technical team up to speed on the intricacies of SOA
- To develop and fine-tune methodologies and approaches for implementing SOA
- To evaluate various commercial products that purport to help with SOA rollouts

Pilot projects are a great way to reduce the risks involved in moving to a new architecture. After all, today's perennially constrained IT budgets don't allow for high-risk projects. Therefore, it's vitally important to build acceptance for SOA with the powers-that-be, particularly because architectures don't have features-only implementations do. As a result, the best SOA pilot projects solve some real business problem, and do so cost-effectively. The best way to build acceptance for your new approach is to solve a problem on a shoestring budget. Furthermore, the SOA pilot serves as a low-risk first step in the ongoing process of implementing SOA.

This desire to implement a specific project that solves a particular business problem, however, can lead to trouble, if you focus too much on the new functionality and not enough on the architecture. Remember, the whole point of the SOA pilot is to pilot SOA, which means *architecture,* not simply new software. And that's the primary SOA pilot pitfall—putting together a project that purports to be an SOA pilot, but in reality doesn't adequately pilot the architecture. Or, even worse, is simply the old architecture warmed over with new, standard-based interfaces.

SOA Pilot Pitfalls

Unfortunately, people still confuse architecture, and especially SOA, with other concepts, such as standards-based interfaces. In particular, people confuse SOA with Web Services. SOA, after all, is software architecture—a set of best practices to follow, or a discipline. Web Services are little more than standards-based software interfaces, so piloting SOA is very different from piloting Web Services. Implementing standards-based interfaces is a near-trivial exercise in taking the systems that you already have and adding some new technology with little need for a consideration of architecture. SOA pilots, however, are mostly exercises in architectural planning, modeling, and organization.

It's possible to implement SOA without Web Services, and it's also quite straightforward to build Web Services without SOA. Just about any SOA project today, however, will include Web Services, because standards can simplify loose coupling dramatically. However, utilizing standards-based interfaces by themselves is by no means sufficient to guarantee that you're moving the organization closer to the goals of Service Orientation. As a result, companies that fall into the SOA pilot pitfall have pilot projects that are ostensibly SOA pilots, but in reality are piloting only Web Services.

It's possible to succumb to this pitfall even if you have a crystal clear understanding of the distinction between Web Services and SOA. Such pilot projects often begin with the best intentions of truly piloting the architecture, but the pilot team ends up focusing on building the Services, and they neglect the architectural work necessary to run the new architectural approach through its paces. After all, developing architectural best practices is hard! Figuring out how to build the *right* Services, all the while assuring loose coupling through contracted interfaces, is not for the faint of heart.

It's not fair to blame the IT staff for this shortsightedness, however. Sometimes an enterprise's neglect of architecture results from a constrained budget, micromanaging executives, or a technical team that lacks an adequately skilled and experienced architect. It's important, therefore, for your SOA pilot to have adequate funding as well as architectural leadership both skilled enough to put together the architecture pilot and experienced enough to manage the team and play interference with senior management.

SOA Pilot Essentials

To drive home the differences between an SOA pilot and other sorts of pilot projects, let's take a look at what your SOA pilot should have:

- *An architectural plan.* SOA is enterprise architecture that provides a comprehensive, high-level plan for how the business interacts with IT. Specifically, SOA should help a company build IT that can respond to unpredictable change. An SOA pilot, therefore, must take some subset of this enterprisewide plan and put it through its paces.
- *A specific scope.* Implementing SOA includes identifying the right Services to build. The best way to accomplish that identification is to start with existing or desired business processes and decompose them to identify areas of redundancy that might lend themselves to reusable Services. For your pilot, you must decide which business processes are within the scope of the project. Too few and you won't have much of an SOA exercise; too many and the value of the pilot decreases. Also, it's imperative that companies don't try to tackle too big a business process at once. It's best to start with a simple yet important business process that can enable your SOA pilot to show a rapid, verifiable return.
- *Clear acceptance criteria.* Every pilot must be able to answer these questions: How will you know when your pilot is complete, and how do you determine whether it was successful or not? More broadly, how can you best leverage the SOA pilot to teach you the lessons you set out

to learn? You should have an explicit finish line for your project with specific acceptance criteria that enable you to score your results. Finished doesn't mean done—it just means that the pilot has met its goal. In all likelihood, the pilot is just the starting point for all future SOA endeavors in the enterprise.

Understanding which acceptance criteria you should have is especially important for avoiding SOA pilot pitfalls, because these criteria act as specific goals your team can focus on as it plans and executes the pilot. Acceptance criteria will vary from company to company and project to project, because there are so many different reasons for companies to undertake SOA projects. Here are three common acceptance criteria that may make sense for your SOA pilot:

1. *A complete architectural design.* By *complete,* we mean within the scope of the pilot project. Such a design should include not only the broad plan you started with, but details about Service contracts and other elements of a working SOA implementation. You may even have the requirement that this design should be adequate as a starting point for a follow-on SOA project.
2. *Reusable business Services.* Services are necessary but not sufficient for SOA. Your acceptance criteria might contain a target level of reusability for the Services you build, including the number of Services and the number of consumers per Service.
3. *Governance criteria.* You want an SOA pilot that you can build future SOA projects on top of, not a one-time, ad hoc SOA project that has little promise for the future. A full-blown SOA project should include a governance infrastructure that handles identities, policies, and rules for the ongoing management and evolution of the SOA implementation. Your pilot may lay out a framework for this governance infrastructure. If it does, you should have acceptance criteria that define success for such a framework. Governance is a way of making sure that you will be able to leverage your SOA pilot for future successful projects.

If you're an IT manager, the best thing you can do to avoid SOA pilot pitfalls is to put a seasoned architect in charge of the pilot project. Never forget that SOA is architecture—you can't buy it from a vendor, and you can't build it with programming code. Architecture is a set of best practices that guide your implementations, regardless of the technologies you choose to implement them. No one but an architect will have the expertise to drive the architectural parts of the SOA pilot.

In practice, however, SOA pilots rarely if ever consist entirely of architecture. To achieve the goals of the pilot, you must put SOA into practice with a working implementation. Never mistake the implementation, however, for the architecture. If you do, you'll be joining all the other failures in the SOA pilot pitfall.

TOP-DOWN PLANNING AND BOTTOM-UP PLANNING

Earlier in this chapter, we pointed out that you should take your SOA rollout one step at a time, moving from a pilot project to limited SOA implementations, eventually working your way up to an enterprisewide SOA rollout. We also pointed out that you need a high-level plan that can guide the whole initiative, so that your step-by-step efforts don't end up working against your primary goal of proving that SOA not only *can* solve problems in your enterprise, but actually *will* solve problems. It's important to understand how to balance the long-term plan with the tactical steps you should take to make SOA a success.

When we break down the best way to build SOA, we're able to flesh out two intertwining approaches, which we call *top-down* and *bottom-up*. In the top-down approach, the architects get involved with the project by putting together a long-term architectural design. Because SOA is enterprise architecture, this design should include elements from each of the seven different views in the View Model of SOA: logical, process, information, implementation, data, deployment, and use case. It's important to have the right level of detail in this plan, as too much detail can slow down the project and too little can lead to poor architecture.

Once the high-level plan is complete, the next step in the top-down approach is *process decomposition,* which seeks to break up current business processes into subprocesses with an eye to identifying the right Services to build. Once you've identified the right Services to build, you can proceed to detail the contracts for those Services. The contracts, in turn, drive the development of the components that underlie the Services. We discuss process decomposition further later in this chapter in the section "Closer Look at Process Decomposition."

In contrast, the bottom-up approach begins by looking at your current IT resources and building them up so that they solve an increasingly wider range of business problems. The bottom-up approach to Service definition is simple to understand and describe, which might explain why it is a particularly popular approach with techies in the organization. Identify those applications that you should expose as Services. Once you've created those Services, you can compose them into business processes.

The problem is that neither of these approaches is sufficient on its own. Your approach to SOA should be both top-down (through process decomposition) and bottom-up (exposing existing functionality as Services and composing them into processes). If you take only a top-down approach, you're likely to recommend building Services that are technically difficult or complex to implement. Taking solely a bottom-up approach can yield Services you don't need or, even worse, Services that don't fulfill the requirements of the business. For your pilot project, it's important to identify those IT resources you wish to include in your Service-building activities. However, don't simply build Services based on the capabilities you already have; think about the Services you *need* in order to make your pilot a success.

Top-Down/Bottom-Up Catch-22

It might seem like we've worked our way into a Catch-22: How do you know which IT resources you should use to build Services until you decompose your processes? How can you be sure a business process is a good target for decomposition until you identify the appropriate IT resources that will go into Service-orienting it? The answer is that you don't need to have this knowledge on the first day of the project. The point of the project is not to start with a completely well-understood problem and directly implement a complete solution, but rather to discover the available information and go from there. What's more important than the knowledge you'll have on day one is the *methodology* you follow that enables you to dive into the process decomposition and Service definition activities, only to circle back, improve the plan, and revisit the processes and Services. We call such a methodology *iterative*.

Jargon Watch: Methodology

A *methodology* is a set of rules for achieving a desired result. *Methodology* is the application of methods to a class of problems that all have something in common. A great way of thinking about a methodology is as a recipe. Just as in a cookbook, where a recipe lists ingredients and steps to take to achieve some dish, IT uses methodologies to guide its projects.

Because all IT projects are complex and run into unexpected turbulence of various sorts, it's important that your methodology not be too rigid. Just as a recipe doesn't make you a good cook, a methodology won't give your team the expertise it needs to do a good job. Rather, the methodology is a guide that provides guidance and some measure of repeatability to your IT projects.

An approach is iterative if you leave tasks in incomplete or unfinished form, so that you can circle back later and work on them some more. We call each of these loops an *iteration*. Each iteration should make progress on all the stuff you've been working on, tackle something new, and often complete something you've been hammering out for a while. In this way your project makes progress on each iteration. It's a good idea to take an iterative approach whenever the project you're working on faces unknowns that you won't be able to resolve until you get into the project. Indeed, an iterative methodology that keeps the company continuously working on and improving its Services is the only way that SOA will ever meet the business's changing needs.

Think about it: If you're able to create a complete, detailed plan of action before building anything, and the plan never changes once you get into the implementation, then an iterative approach is probably not warranted. However, virtually all IT projects are impossible to plan completely up front, and SOA initiatives are no exception. In fact, having an iterative methodology for your SOA project is critical: Without it, you'll build the wrong Services, fail to stay within the scope of the project, or create enormous rework for your team. Don't assume that you'll be able to define the right Services in advance or have the right systems already in place to implement those Services. You must expect to evolve your Services continually. Start small, but iterate quickly toward Services that show a real business return.

Taking an Iterative Approach

In the case of your SOA rollout, the first iteration will include a sketchy high-level plan, a first pass at process decomposition, and a quick inventory of existing IT resources. The second iteration will revisit each element of the project and improve on it, based on what you learned before. Therefore, the second version of the plan will include more detailed Service contracts and business processes that utilize the Services, leading to a clearer picture of which IT resources you'll want to use. At some point, the plan will become relatively well developed and stable to the point that it can be evolved continuously without having to start from scratch. Each iteration will add more detail into Service definitions, contract specifications, process compositions, and the rest of the nuts and bolts of putting together an SOA implementation.

Taking an iterative approach solves two problems. First, it allows you to make progress on the complicated task of Service Orientation by giving you a road map for your project even when you're sketchy on a lot of the details ahead of time. Second, iterative methodologies reduce many of the risks inherent in an IT project. You're far less likely to end up with something that either doesn't work or simply doesn't meet business requirements if you start small, iterate rapidly, and evaluate the project status on an ongoing basis. Fundamentally, iterative methodologies let you deal with unpredictable change—changing requirements, changing IT capabilities, and a changing skill level on the team. As business agility is about dealing with unpredictable change, it should come as no surprise that all SOA projects should be iterative. After all, you can't build something flexible out of a box of rigid parts.

You should recognize the "ulterior motive" format for your SOA strategy as being iterative in nature as well. In fact, it makes sense to nest your iterations: Your pilot project should be iterative, as should your departmental and enterprise rollouts individually, but you should also think of the overall arch of your long-term SOA strategy as being iterative in nature. Furthermore, there's really no such thing as being "done" with your SOA initiative. SOA implementations are always in a state of flux, because they deal with changing business situations so well. As a result, iteration should become a way of life for your organization—not just to launch projects in the first place, but over the long-term lifetime of each initiative.

CLOSER LOOK AT PROCESS DECOMPOSITION

Most business processes are sufficiently complex that it is not particularly easy to understand them in one step. Rather, we must somehow take the more complex activity and chop it up into smaller pieces that we can combine to solve the overall problem. In addition to being able simply to understand the problem better when we've divided it into smaller parts, most IT systems require us to cut up large business problems into pieces that they can understand. No computer system can understand when a person says "Send this invoice to my customer." Rather, we must define that process as a set of specific instructions or tasks that a computer must execute to translate the business requirement into specific activities.

In order to take the next step of the SOA pilot project, then, first we have to take the high-level business requirements and encode them into Service-Oriented Processes that allow the business to make changes to the processes as a whole without having to rip and replace business logic that the systems must understand. The top-down approach to SOA, therefore, breaks down existing business processes in order to identify the appropriate Services to build, a technique we call *process decomposition*. Once we've fully decomposed existing processes, we'll be able to identify the best Services to build in order to maximize the reuse of those Services. At that point, we'll be able to compose those Services once again into business processes, only this time, they will be Service-Oriented Processes.

The best place to begin the process decomposition exercise is to identify the existing processes that are most appropriate for decomposition. For an SOA pilot project, you should base this selection on a measure of risk versus reward. In other words, choose business processes that should be simple to decompose and yet will yield the best results. As you move toward a broader SOA implementation, however, you should select processes that fall into a natural group, where what you're looking for are potential areas of redundancy. So, for example, if you have three procurement processes that all take advantage of the same order entry and inventory systems, then there is likely to be some considerable overlap in the processes. Therefore, there's no need to encode the same Services repeatedly. This exercise suggests areas of redundancy you'll be able to simplify. It's also important to select the right number of processes—enough to solve a tangible business problem, but too many, and your project faces the risk of taking too long and being overly complex. Remember, your approach should be iterative; you'll always be able to go back and add more processes later.

The next step in the process decomposition exercise is to adequately describe the processes so that a computer system, rather than simply a person, can understand them. In many cases, this step is the most difficult for organizations, as it first requires sufficient understanding of the details of specific business processes and the individuals who have that understanding are spread throughout the organization. Finding these individuals, enlisting their help, and getting them to work with the team to describe the processes is no small challenge. The result of this particular activity should be a reasonably detailed, step-by-step definition of each process. Your challenge is to include enough detail to identify subprocesses without getting bogged down into too much detail. Once again, the best, lowest risk approach to describing existing processes is iterative. Begin with a high-level description, then go back and break it up into subprocesses, and repeat. You'll know you're done when you can identify common subprocesses across most or all of the processes you're describing.

Look for the Services

At this point, we can align our top-down process decomposition exercise with our bottom-up Service exposure activities. Because we now have a good listing of the activities that compose our processes, we can look in the organization to see if we already have the right Services in place to meet those new process requirements. Logically, you'll be looking for Services you already have available as well as Services you'll need to build or buy from a third party. You can locate these Services either by talking to the various folks in your IT department or, even better, by using technologies that store metadata about Services. Regardless of how you find the Service resource, ideally you will find the information you need to decide whether it fits the bill as is, or if you need to create a new contract for it to meet the needs of the processes you're trying to compose.

However, in many cases (especially when your SOA initiative is still in its early stages), you will not already have existing Services that can provide the functionality or data you require. In this situation, you should first start by defining the contract for what the Service should do, so that you can build it from scratch, repurpose an existing Service, or buy it from a third party. At this point, we must distinguish between two basic kinds of Services. The first kind of Services we're talking about in this section are what we like to call *atomic Services*. An atomic Service is a contracted interface to some underlying component, data, or other working software. The other kind of Service is a *composed Service*, which is an abstraction of a collection of Services composed together to form a more complex Service—and such composed Services are, in fact, often business processes in their own right. The difference between atomic and composed Services is really just a philosophical one, because Service consumers should never know if the Service they are consuming is atomic or composite. The only time this differentiation matters is when you're trying to build the Service from scratch.

We generally associate atomic Services with specific, technical functions, while composed Services are more business oriented—but this pattern isn't a hard-and-fast rule. Indeed, the difference between atomic and composed Services is really just a technical detail, because Service consumers should never know if the Service they are consuming is atomic or composite. The only time this differentiation matters is when you're trying to build the Service from scratch.

You may be specifying either atomic Services or composed Services at this point. It's often unclear when a particular Service is an atomic Service or a composed Service. When you're decomposing processes, however, identifying Services is part of the exercise, and you may find yourself defining both new atomic and new composed Services—again, in an iterative fashion. Over time, however, the process decomposition exercise will result in mostly composed Services, especially as an increasing number of such Services are already in existence.

Remember that Services can have multiple contracts, so the data and functionality a Service provides to one process doesn't have to be exactly the same as what it provides to another process. In fact, it is this flexibility that you were looking for when you decided to implement SOA. Therefore, two processes might share for example an "update customer record" Service, even though they put different information into the customer record or the same information in a different format. The composed Services you identify, therefore, should have specific business value while at the same time have flexible technical capabilities.

In addition, as you build Service-Oriented Processes, you're actually building Services because, in SOA, processes are exposed and consumed as Services. You may find that the Service you've identified is actually a process in its own right, and that's fine. In fact, you don't have to worry about whether the Services are processes. Your goal is to decompose your existing processes into Services (which may also be processes) so that you can recompose the processes in a Service-oriented way, ideally sharing several Services across different processes. A Lego block metaphor comes in handy here, because you can visualize the component Services as interchangeable parts that you can compose into many different kinds of Service-Oriented Processes, similar to the way a child builds things out of Legos.

Who Is Responsible for Process Decomposition?

The team you need to put together to have a successful process decomposition exercise should be a mixture of different people. Clearly at the highest levels of the business process, an actual LOB executive must be involved, because only management is responsible for business processes at the highest level. However, as the process decomposition activity forces us to think in increasing detail, we have to involve lower levels of management in the organization, because the senior-level folks typically don't have the process knowledge to know specifically how certain things are done. As far as they are concerned, the process becomes a "black box" without needing their knowledge of specifics.

We can't expect most lower-level business folks or IT personnel to be responsible for decomposing processes either. The LOB rank and file can help with aspects of the exercise but rarely have enough of the big picture to understand the whole process. IT managers and developers are in charge of only their specific functions and don't have the knowledge necessary to understand a whole business process from end to end either; nor are they capable of explaining how different processes are related to each other.

It's important, therefore to have a *business process architect* on the team. Such architects rarely have the title "business process architect," however. Often they are business analysts or other specialists within the LOB. Identifying the appropriate person can be a challenge but is critical to the exercise. You should also have the enterprise architect on the team. The enterprise architect should be the facilitator who works with the different levels of management in the organization as well as business process architects and business analysts, to appropriately decompose a business process. The enterprise architect is the glue that holds all the various levels of process knowledge together so that the team can follow the high-level plan that reflects the business processes as they currently are in the organization and as they will change over time.

As processes by their nature are continuously changing, and as process decomposition requires an iterative approach, enterprise architects will spend much of their time evolving the Services in their organization by working with all levels of the business to make sure that as business processes change, so too do the Service definitions, and as IT implementations change, so too do the compositions of Services. Ideally, the organization will reach a state where it needs very few new Services, but even in those cases, the architect will have to continue to tweak Service contracts, manage Service and process compositions, and make sure that the Services the company produces facilitate an environment of agility.

FIND YOUR CHAMPION

Because of this environment of agility, SOA projects are fundamentally different from most other IT projects from the business perspective. Because one of the fundamental goals of SOA is to build reusable Services that consumers across the organization and beyond can access, it often doesn't make sense for a single department or LOB to drive SOA projects on its own, without involvement from any other group in the organization. In the early pilot phases of an SOA rollout, individual departments might tackle SOA implementations successfully, as limited SOA projects are generally more likely to succeed than cross-departmental or enterprisewide initiatives. However, the issue of fragmented SOA initiatives rears its ugly head as discussions about reusing Services across departments begin in earnest.

Reusable Services sound good on paper, of course—there's no questioning the cost savings and agility benefits from streamlining redundant, inefficient applications across the organization by representing software functionality as loosely coupled Services. When people begin to consider the nontechnical issues of how to pay for, control, and manage the Services, however, SOA projects risk losing their way and may find themselves bogged down in issues no architecture or technology expertise can resolve. After all, when faced with change, it is human nature to look for ways the new approach won't work, rather than pulling together as a team to figure out how to make it successful.

Fortunately, there is hope for cross-departmental and enterprisewide SOA initiatives. Many companies facing the move to SOA have risen above the squabbling to drive cross-departmental SOA implementations that should lead eventually to successful enterprisewide SOA rollouts. These successful companies all have one thing in common: an effective *champion* who leads the charge for SOA.

Who Is the SOA Champion?

A champion is usually an individual, or sometimes a small team, who understands the benefits of SOA, can communicate those benefits to both business and technical audiences, and is committed to bringing SOA to the organization. The champion essentially plays the role of an evangelist who must use the power of persuasion to get all involved parties on the same page with respect to the goals of the SOA initiative, the funding and management issues, and the long-term SOA plan.

SOA champions are often managers or executives, but not always. They can be either business oriented or technical, although they must have a reasonable understanding of both. They often do not have a budget for architectural initiatives or even a direct purchasing responsibility for the software or services that go into an SOA initiative, but they must have some influential role over the SOA buyers: the managers who pay for SOA initiatives out of their own budgets.

SOA buyers can include a range of managers in both IT and business, including those in charge of application development, network operations, or security, or even managers responsible for implementing corporate policy. However, these managers are unlikely to be SOA champions, because of their relatively narrow focus or limited ability to be charismatic about an architectural initiative. The only SOA buyer who is also likely to be the SOA champion is the rare enterprise architect who has his or her own budget and implementation mandate—an emerging role for many companies.

However, the SOA champion need not be the person who is driving the overall SOA effort, or even the buyer or the buyer's boss. Indeed, SOA champions might in fact fill other roles in the organization. The role they play also impacts how they must go about their champion duties:

- *The chief information officer.* Having the chief information officer (CIO) as the SOA champion in the organization is the best situation to be in, because CIOs have both business and technology responsibility as well as the power and budget to make things happen. The downside to having the CIO as champion is that these executives have a lot on their plates, and generally they won't be able to devote large amounts of time to championing SOA. In practice, however, it is unusual for the CIO to be the champion for SOA in the enterprise because good CIOs tend to be risk averse. They usually will not champion any cause that they don't already understand and practice in their organization.
- *The chief architect.* The chief architect is either responsible for the overall corporate IT architecture strategy or is the member of the enterprise architecture team who has executive-level responsibility for the overall IT architecture and how it meets the needs of the business. Sometimes these individuals have both budget and authority, but unlike

the CIO, they may have the capability to become a full-time SOA champion. The chief architect is usually the CIO's chief advisor on architecture issues. As long as the CIO and chief architect see eye to eye, there's a good chance an SOA initiative will be successful.

■ *An LOB executive.* Having a business executive champion SOA is like a precious gem: rare and valuable. Few business executives have the combination of technical depth and architectural vision to champion SOA, but in organizations lucky enough to have such a person, he or she often can drive substantial business value out of the SOA initiative. As this person deals with business challenges on a daily basis, his or her word tends to carry a lot of weight with senior management. However, the greatest challenge business executives face when championing SOA is getting IT on their side. If the technology folks decide to resist rather than work together with the business folks, this champion faces an uphill climb. More frequently than not, the LOB executive's initiative will get pooh-poohed if only because IT believes that the exec simply doesn't have the technical chops to understand the nature of their problems.

■ *A senior architect.* Unlike the chief architect, senior architects generally lack the budget and authority to drive SOA adoption within their organization. Instead, these individuals must take the role of evangelists, communicating the value of SOA to every audience that will listen. They must be charismatic, thick-skinned, and determined. An additional challenge such champions face is the fact that they are always very busy, and thus they may not have enough time to champion SOA effectively.

■ *An IT manager.* IT managers without the scope of responsibility of the CIO often face the greatest challenges as an SOA champion. These managers tend to work within a particular department or IT silo, and can drive SOA initiatives from within their group. However, it can be very difficult for such an individual to build support for cross-departmental or enterprise SOA initiatives, because in many instances, senior management has become resistant to the constant wolf cries of the IT department, having tried to solve perennial problems with patchwork solutions in the past.

The lack of seniority of the SOA champion, in fact, often limits the scope of the SOA initiatives he or she can pursue in general. Departmental SOA initiatives are the most straightforward and least risky to implement, and many individuals within organizations can build support for such projects in their own departments. Cross-departmental initiatives are far more challenging, because of the political and organizational complexities involved in getting different departments to agree on the shared Services issues of control, funding, and governance, as well as the technical challenge of building truly reusable Services. Therefore, such champions must have some sort of political edge: the authority to drive cross-departmental change, a special advantage due to their communication capabilities, or another intangible asset they can bring to bear.

Finding an SOA Champion

Instead of asking how to find an SOA champion in the organization, it might be best to first figure out if *you* should be such a champion, because if you're asking the question in the first place, then you are a natural place to start the search. Whether you feel you are the right person or not, the key to identifying the SOA champion within your company is to find a person whose responsibilities put him or her at the crux of the business-IT relationship. In other words, look for a person who is responsible for solving key business issues and who has sufficient visibility into the IT resources within the organization to understand how the company might bring those resources to bear to solve business problems. For example, if your company is struggling with Sarbanes-Oxley compliance, a likely SOA champion will be an individual with some level of responsibility for the compliance initiative who also has standing within IT, either with direct responsibility (as with an architect) or indirect influence (as with a LOB executive with IT abilities).

If no individual or team is able or willing to intentionally take on the role as SOA champion within the organization, then the role by default falls to a business stakeholder. In other words, a LOB executive who has a budget and who is applying it to a particular IT project may be open to tackling that project in a Service-oriented way. Otherwise, it falls on the CIO to find a place for SOA in the midst of all his or her other important initiatives. However, if no executive clearly understands the benefits and costs of SOA, and no one else in IT is willing to step up and champion SOA, it is quite likely that an organization will implement poor SOA at best, if the architecture is Service oriented at all. Without a strong motivation to change, people naturally follow familiar, comfortable patterns, and such patterns today do not lead to SOA best practices. In other words, as long as SOA remains an emerging architectural approach, finding an SOA champion is a necessity for the success of any SOA initiative.

People fear change, after all, and our instinctive reaction to fear is fight or flight. Fleeing the danger is always the more comfortable option, and in large organizations, this flight appears as a dogged attachment to the status quo. In this way, resistance to change feeds on itself, immobilizing people just as the need for change is the greatest. The key to breaking this vicious cycle of inaction is *empowerment*. Give people the power to fight their fear, and they are more likely to push for change than to flee it.

Champions of change are those rare individuals who empower themselves to fight for the new approach they believe in. The secret to their success is their ability to empower their colleagues as well. Our advice, therefore, to the SOA champions out there: To bring about the necessary level of change that your organizations need to adopt SOA, you must empower your colleagues through knowledge and understanding. Champions above all else are teachers; instruct your colleagues on the practices, benefits, and costs of SOA, and they too will have the power to sell Service Orientation internally and bring about positive change in the organization.

CHAPTER 10

Tackling the Inertia in the Organization

In the 1600s, Sir Isaac Newton distilled the complexity of the laws of physics into three fundamental rules that guided the movement of objects in the world. The first of these laws was the principle of inertia: Any object in motion tends to stay in motion unless acted on by some external force. If Newton wasn't speaking about objects, we might think he was talking about organizations and people, because the same fundamental reality holds true: Every organization will keep doing what it was doing before unless some external force forces it to change. Although this sort of inertia is positive when the business implements optimized processes and good business practices, it can be a significant problem for the company where inefficiency, bad business practices, and political ugliness continue unabated. As we discussed in Chapter 1, it is this bad sort of inertia that has kept the ugly rats' nests of tightly coupled IT around. Using Service Orientation, we must tackle this inertia and shift the momentum of the organization toward good business behaviors and improved IT practices.

SELLING SERVICE ORIENTATION TO YOUR BOSS, TEAM, AND COMPANY

According to a well-known saying, the road to business success is littered with failed companies that had great technology. After all, a good technology or a good product alone is not sufficient to guarantee success in the marketplace. Successful firms also need effective sales and marketing to bring a well-understood product to the market. However, companies often forge ahead with their product development and implementation plans without answering the critical question: Who is paying for this solution, and what problem of theirs does this technology solve? Coming up with the answer often is surprisingly challenging for companies that are looking to implement SOA, because the broad, enterprise nature of SOA initiatives can make it quite unclear who the buyer is.

Service-Oriented Architecture: Everybody's Business

Because SOA is an architectural approach that abstracts broad, heterogeneous IT systems and applications, enterprise SOA initiatives touch many different individuals and groups within the organization. Furthermore, implementations of SOA require interaction with a wide range of technologies and capabilities including security, management, integration, business process, and development capabilities. Although not all SOA implementations require all of these items, most require two or three such capabilities. Such broad capabilities can be a mixed bag for companies looking to make use of SOA.

On one hand, the broad capabilities of SOA and the tools that support them offer significant business value over single-function technology solutions that address only one or two of the capabilities we listed, but on the other hand, it's less clear who in the organization is responsible for buying such solutions. In particular, SOA champions might call on application developers, enterprise architects, or network operations managers in the course of their efforts to sell Service Orientation internally. But which of these roles is truly responsible for paying for SOA implementations?

Application Developer Buyer

In many ways, application developers and their managers are responsible for a significant part of the implementation and maintenance of systems that participate in an SOA implementation. Application developers are first and foremost concerned with the effectiveness of the application they are developing and secondarily with higher-level issues such as reuse and business agility. Although it's true that most application developers take advantage of Service Orientation mostly as a way to simplify integration on a project-by-project basis, and many don't understand (or even care about) the fundamental nature of business agility, application developers hold the keys to many departmental SOA projects nevertheless. Despite their low-level, tactical use of SOA, application developers have some limited budget control, especially with regard to incremental projects at the departmental level.

SOA champions who are looking to gain support for larger SOA projects by first starting small should look to expose Services from individual systems, typically mainframe or other legacy systems. By so doing they will find significant traction with the application developer group. These projects will be mostly small, incremental ones that over time might contribute to an SOA in the long term, but most such projects use Services as a stopgap for their existing, tactical integration issues. As a result, over the long run, an SOA champion should look elsewhere in the organization to find the buyer for Service Orientation initiatives that consist of more than one project.

Enterprise Architect Buyer

Search a bit higher in the IT organization and you'll find the enterprise architect. Enterprise architects can be individuals with that title in their job description or can consist of a team of high-level developers and technical managers who have wide-ranging responsibilities in different parts of the organization. These users are not directly concerned with a particular tactical task, such as point-to-point use of Services for a legacy integration project, but rather concern themselves with trying to map the business needs to ongoing IT projects while maximizing agility and minimizing incremental IT cost.

Enterprise architects are the sweet spot in the organization for emerging SOA projects. These users might have control over departmental-level IT initiatives or may have cross-organization responsibilities for creating and recommending architectural approaches for all ongoing IT projects. As a result, these people care mostly about infrastructure and tools that help further their architectural goals. SOA champions can tap into these higher-level concerns by focusing on SOA run-time infrastructure as well as more critical aspects of building reusable, composable, and loosely coupled Services. These folks have money too—we've seen evidence that companies that have SOA purchasing authority centralized with the enterprise architect community start with small projects that rapidly blossom to become cross departmental or even enterprisewide in scale and cost.

However, the enterprise architect is not a well-defined role in many corporations today. In some cases, people who call themselves enterprise architects may actually simply be application developers or project managers; in other cases, they may be missing critical aspects of their role, such as network operations, security, and business process definition. SOA champions who hope to target the enterprise architect community either will have to wait until this role becomes more prevalent and well-defined or will have to continue targeting other buyers in the organization.

Network Operations Buyer

Companies today are dependent on their networks to enable their core applications and business processes, and any network disruption has a profound impact on the financial health of the organization. Yet despite the important role that networks serve, the application development and network operations worlds have traditionally been separate, disconnected domains. Developers usually build applications that run on servers, and network administrators maintain and configure the network that connects them, but rarely vice versa. As a result, these two sets of professionals rarely have the opportunity to work together directly.

One of the surprising side effects of the movement to SOA, however, is that this natural separation between application development and network operations is breaking down. Rather than simply maintaining the data center and being responsive to threats or performance issues as they crop up, the network administrator must now deal with application and Service management issues, including security and other policy considerations that apply to the Services and process they interact with. This new level of responsibility for such operations personnel also means that they will become a key part of the enterprise architecture team in the Service-oriented environment, because such network is seen as an extension of the application infrastructure.

In many ways, the network administrator is responsible for helping guide the development and implementation of SOA with the same goals as other members of the team: increasing business agility and asset reuse in the face of IT heterogeneity. The only difference between network administrators and software developers is that the former provide solutions in the form of hardware and networks, rather than software-based solutions alone.

Network operations personnel care most about the health and well-being of the network. They generally don't see Services as a part of a distributed, agile computing infrastructure, but rather as a foreign, alien body that they must deal with in a controlled manner. Instead of being proponents of SOA, network operations personnel are primarily disposed against these new technologies due to the threats they introduce to "their" networks. When network operations users do buy in to Service-oriented solutions or products, they do so out of *FUD*—fear, uncertainty, and doubt that those Services introduce—rather than the positive business changes that they represent.

As a result, many SOA champions will face a naturally skeptical and resistant audience when trying to sell SOA solutions to their network administration and management groups. Even when they do manage to convince those folks to part with their spare budget dollars, the implementations will tend to be tactically focused with little opportunity to provide additional value to higher levels of the organization. SOA champions shouldn't expect to find great supporters of agile SOA implementations within the network administration ranks.

Security, Governance, and/or Policy Buyer

In some companies, the role of security administration and policy definition is separate from network operations as well as from the application development and architecture. Security users are primarily concerned with defining and enforcing policies that meet with established corporate governance requirements and emerging IT policies and procedures. They apply these policies to all IT assets, whether software, hardware, neither, or both. As a result, their involvement with SOA stems from the emerging need to secure Services, just as they have secured the other assets under their control. A policy they define for portal access must apply as well to the Services that underlie the portal. Similarly, network access policies that they might have applied to the firewalls at the boundaries of the organization must now spread to all the systems that could potentially put the network at risk.

These security administration and policy management buyers thus care the most about Services security, contract, and policy definition tools. Although they care less about the aspects of business agility and reuse than the enterprise architects, their purchasing decisions do have an impact on the entire enterprise and can have significant relevance to the infrastructure of a company. Therefore, whoever is responsible for buying security and policy administration for the company has influence on the SOA purchasing decision for the organization as a whole.

Making the Case for SOA at the Highest Level: The CIO

Who, then, is truly responsible for buying SOA products within the organization? Until new purchasing patterns evolve, SOA champions will by necessity have to tailor their plans for the specific buying audiences they plan to target. This limitation is unfortunate, because the promise of Service Orientation is so broad within the organization. Indeed, every SOA project can influence the application developer, enterprise architecture team, network administration personnel, and security and policy managers. How can an SOA champion target just one buyer? Until a single audience within the enterprise emerges that can understand the broad message and has purchasing authority to implement SOA enterprise-wide, the answer lies in the ability of SOA champions to realize that Service Orientation is an approach that they can sell to specific audiences by touting different value propositions.

Enterprise architecture, and by extension SOA, is special in that requirements cross IT and business domains. While IT executives could delegate other IT projects, such as traditional integration, enterprise resource planning (ERP) implementations, and Web site projects to small, focused, and relatively isolated groups within the IT department, the same cannot be said for any SOA implementation that addresses a business need. Rather, SOA projects demand expertise from across the organization, including business users who can define needs and processes, application developers who interact with integration middleware and legacy systems, data center administrators, portal developers and administrators, folks who deal with security, and IT staff who manage and monitor back-office systems.

Indeed, pulling off a successful SOA implementation requires discipline and teamwork across the IT and business organization. The SOA champion eventually must convince the CIO of the merits of moving to a Service-oriented approach. Visionary CIOs will realize that cohesive enterprise architecture teams must operate as the backbone for realizing early SOA success. But in order to do so, they must stop implementing shortsighted solutions for short-term problems. Rather, CIOs must think more holistically of Service Orientation as a cross-organizational approach to solving a broad set of problems. Make no mistake, such changes are difficult, and require effective governance and tough discipline. Many CIOs will get it wrong. It takes the persistent, visionary, and effective SOA champion to turn mistakes into long-term successes.

QUANTIFYING THE COST AND THE RETURN ON THE SERVICE ORIENTATION INVESTMENT

In today's post–dot-com world of tight IT budgets, increased regulation, global competition, and accelerating change, companies (and governments) require quantifiable results from their investments in technology. No CIO will sign off on any investment in new technology without a solid expectation for how it will deliver value to the business. When people understand an established technology and how it will provide value over time, calculating the return on investment (ROI) for IT expenditures is often a straightforward process. However, calculating ROI on projects involving new technologies or emerging IT approaches like SOA is frequently more of an art than a science. (See Chapter 2 for an introduction to ROI.)

What makes calculating the ROI of SOA even more challenging is that architecture, by itself, doesn't offer specific features that companies can readily identify with some particular return. After all, architecture is an investment that companies must make in advance of any return and must continue to make over the lifetime of their SOA implementations. How, then, can managers calculate the ROI of their SOA initiatives before those projects take place? What are the tangible benefits of SOA that can result in a quantifiable ROI for the implementers? How should companies calculate the expected return that those tangible benefits will provide to the organization? Only by understanding the full range of SOA value propositions can companies begin to get a handle on calculating the ROI of SOA, and even then, it may be impossible to understand SOA's true ROI before some indeterminate completion date, because SOA addresses issues of fundamentally unpredictable business change.

Nevertheless, we'll do our best to give you the tools you need to evaluate the ROI of your SOA initiatives. This process starts with the fundamental business benefits of SOA. SOA provides benefits in four basic categories:

1. Reducing integration expense
2. Reducing development cost by increasing asset reuse
3. Increasing business agility
4. Reducing business risk through increase in visibility and control

These four core benefits actually offer return at many different levels and parts of the organization, depending on which set of business problems the company is applying SOA to. We explore each of these areas of ROI below and explain how to realize those benefits by applying Service-oriented approaches.

Reducing Integration Expense

Often the first projects that companies apply SOA to is for the reduction of the rats' nests of complexity that riddles their organizations and hobbles their ability to become agile and flexible. The only way to change the economics of integration is to move toward implementing loosely coupled integration approaches that reduce the complexity and hence the cost of integrating and managing distributed computing environments. The real win with SOA is in replacing or abstracting multiple tightly coupled and often proprietary systems Service-Oriented Processes composed of loosely coupled Services. The goal of any SOA project should be, first and foremost, to rid the organization of its rats' nests and thus provide the tactical, relatively short-term ROI of dramatically reducing the expense of integration.

Calculating the ROI for using SOA to reduce integration expense is fairly straightforward. Companies can compare their investment in standards-based SOA to an equivalent traditional integration middleware approach and then compare reductions in both the immediate licensing and configuration costs as well as the longer-term maintenance and change costs. In the short term, companies can realize significant and immediate ROI from simply moving from tightly coupled forms of integration to loosely coupled ones. Eventually companies can phase out their more expensive integration approaches altogether, without suffering from the traditional pain associated with ripping out the infrastructure.

However, there's no need to quit the Enterprise Application Integration (EAI) addiction cold turkey. Companies can realize ROI for SOA incrementally as well by implementing SOA side by side with their existing EAI projects, providing a modest and incremental but still significant cost reduction, with the goal of building ROI over the long term. Over time, this tactical ROI benefit of SOA will wane, however, as companies gradually replace their legacy middleware technologies with Service-oriented approaches.

Reducing Development Cost by Increasing Asset Reuse

Although reducing integration expense can often justify an initial SOA project, seeing SOA as nothing more than a way to reduce such expense is short-sighted. SOA may be viable even in an environment of homogeneity. In addition, an integration-centric mind-set doesn't provide a way to achieve ROI when companies require new uses for existing infrastructure—something we want to achieve since we value thrift. Instead, the reuse of existing Services provides an additional ROI for companies looking to implement SOA.

Companies spend very little of their time and budget building new applications that solve the evolving needs of the business. This lack of emphasis on new application development results from the fact that developers create each new application in isolation from the applications they built previously. As a result, each new application is a piece of the IT puzzle that they must integrate with other components, exacerbating the integration problem discussed in Chapter 2. Clearly, developers must build new applications in such a way that reduces not only the cost of development, but also maintenance over time.

One of the most important benefits of SOA is that users can create new business processes and composite applications from existing Services. In other words, Service reuse becomes the mantra, rather than application integration. As they create new Services that they can reuse for new composite applications, companies can realize significant return from their composite application development investment. As a result, the economics of composite application development that leverages SOA improves over time, as companies build and reuse an increasing number of Services.

It may even be possible to shift the 70% now spent on integration to new application development. The returns companies can realize in this asset reuse scenario for SOA are not simply the cost reduction of simplified integration, but also improved time to market, more responsive customer service, reduction in overall staffing, and a greater ability to outsource or offshore Service creation, implementation, and even composition. Any ROI calculation based on the asset reuse benefits of SOA must therefore take into account all of these parts of the SOA value proposition.

Increasing Business Agility

Although reducing costs and increasing reuse provide clear ROI for SOA, increasing business agility is the most promising benefit of SOA as well as the most difficult to quantify. Simplification of integration and improvement of reuse are technology-centric benefits; business users also demand greater flexibility from IT. Rather than simply creating requirements that they then toss over the IT development wall for months—long implementation cycles, business users want immediate control over their operations so that they can make rapid changes to their businesses as market forces change.

The ROI scenario required for calculating the value of this business agility benefit centers on the ability for business users to control business process definition and management directly. Through Service-Oriented Process, companies can delegate parts of their overall business process flows to different parts of the organization, each of which has direct and immediate control of the actual operation of the business. The resulting business returns from an SOA investment are dramatic improvements in business efficiency as well as the ability to embed a company's business processes inside the operations of suppliers or business partners.

Thus, the return here affects not just the bottom line of a company's operations, but also its top line. Increased business agility may result in the ability to capture revenue streams that the company previously considered to be inaccessible and affords companies ways to provide value to their suppliers and partners that can result in significant new business opportunities. By extending the reach of SOA to business users, the architecture can deliver ROI to the business as a whole, rather than simply the IT department.

Calculating the business agility ROI of SOA, however, can be extraordinarily difficult, because the new uses that businesspeople will apply their IT resources to are inherently unpredictable. After all, the whole point to agility is to be able to deal with unexpected change. Therefore, it often makes sense to restrict the business agility ROI calculation to a particular scope—for example, situations where product information or business processes regularly change in a predictable manner.

Reducing Business Risk Through Increase in Visibility and Control

Regulatory compliance is essentially a business agility issue, because such regulations are inherently arbitrary, and can change over time. Today, regulations such as Sarbanes-Oxley, the PATRIOT Act, and Basel II mandate changes within companies that drive IT implementations. The penalties of noncompliance can severely impact a company's financial position as well as the personal liberty of its executives. Many companies simply lack the visibility into their business operations that they need to make intelligent planning decisions and control their risk, let alone respond to the increased visibility that these regulations require.

Increased business visibility in the face of changing regulations is a concrete instance of the business agility benefit that SOA can provide. Specifically, SOA offers a risk-reduction capacity to companies looking for increased operations visibility. Governance, compliance, and general risk reduction have a quantifiable benefit distinct from increased business agility. Compliance and governance offer a reduction of liability; business agility offers an increase in business opportunity. All these benefits are important, but they speak to different parts of the corporate psyche.

Quantifying the reduction of risk in order to calculate the ROI of an SOA-based compliance project is also a tricky proposition. Just how much is compliance worth? The answer lies in how much noncompliance will cost a company. The ROI of risk reduction is much like the ROI of insurance or security: Its value derives from the prevention of an *unknown* expense.

Implementing SOA for the purpose of controlling business processes; establishing enterprise-wide security, privacy, and implementation policies; and providing auditable information trails are all examples of ways that SOA can reduce several of the risks facing companies today. In fact, the central technology offices of many large companies often find that the primary benefit of SOA is in regulatory compliance and the associated reduction in risk. Although the reduction in risk that SOA provides is tangible, it is difficult to quantify the true ROI of an SOA implementation where risk reduction is a primary benefit. At the end of the day, companies will find value in implementing SOA to reduce risk to some arbitrarily acceptable level and base the ROI of that implementation on the perceived avoidance of loss that the implementation addresses.

Composite and Iterative ROI for SOA

Because of the multifaceted nature of the SOA value proposition, ROI calculations for SOA projects can vary greatly from one project to another. Rather than seeking a single ROI goal for an SOA implementation, companies should take the same iterative, composite approach to ROI that they take for SOA implementation itself. For example, every time they define a new Service, they should also define a corresponding ROI objective for that Service. How much will they spend on this Service? What direct and indirect returns can they realize from this Service's implementation, in terms of reduced integration costs, improved asset reuse, or greater business agility? Furthermore, as the company reuses that Service, how will the composition of the Service with other Services into processes realize additional ROI for the business?

In many cases, SOA implementations can provide a clear, positive ROI from the first day a Service goes live. However, it is more likely that ROI expectations, like SOA implementations, should be iterative in nature, frequently assessed, and composite. In doing so, companies can both realize and quantify the return on investment of their SOA implementation.

MONEY, MONEY, MONEY: WHERE WILL IT COME FROM TO PAY FOR SOA?

Most entrepreneurs and salespeople know that in order to make a sale, a deal needs three key ingredients: need, urgency, and budget. It's hard to sell anything if the prospect doesn't have a need for it, and likewise it's hard to encourage a short-term purchase if there's little urgency to implement the solution today versus a few years from now. Most important, it's impossible to sell any sort of solution if there simply isn't any budget to make the purchase happen—even if the prospect needs the solution urgently. Given that we've spent much of this book discussing the need and urgency for implementing SOA projects, we'd be negligent if we didn't discuss the third key ingredient to making SOA happen: funding. Simply put, where is the money going to come from to pay for SOA?

Business executives generally seek specific capabilities, features, and functions from IT initiatives that address tactical business problems—but as we pointed out earlier, architectures don't have features. Executives typically require that the solutions they buy address immediate business imperatives, such as reducing expenditures, increasing sales opportunities, improving customer satisfaction, enabling new channels for interacting with customers or partners, or allowing their companies to gain greater insight or control over their daily operations.

Architecture initiatives, however, tend to be more strategic than tactical. Because architecture is essentially a discipline and set of approaches for designing complex systems, *by itself* it doesn't provide any of the *tactical* benefits that business executives typically budget for (although specific implementations of the architecture might in fact provide such tactical benefits). SOA initiatives are even less likely to provide specific tactical benefits than other architectural projects, because the core of an SOA project consists of building the Services abstraction layer, and abstraction layers themselves don't have features. As a result, one of the greatest challenges for those selling or seeking funding for SOA solutions is identifying a specific business imperative that depends on SOA, yet promises low cost and risk and also the greatest return. The challenge organizations face is in identifying the places in the organization where there is sufficient budget for SOA projects.

Funding Enterprisewide versus Departmental Projects

One of the universal rules of project funding is that it's always easier to fund a smaller, more tightly scoped project than a larger, broadly scoped one. Although there might be a handful of enterprisewide SOA initiatives of significant scope and size somewhere in the world today, these projects are a rarity, simply because of the amount of time, risk, and cost involved in implementing them. The larger the project, the more levels of management must participate, stretching out the sales cycle and raising the stakes for everyone involved. For enterprisewide SOA projects like those that corporate governance or regulatory compliance motivations drive, obtaining funding is a matter of getting buy-in at the very highest levels in the organization, often from the CIO or chief financial officer (CFO). Without their support, such projects rarely get off the ground.

It's no wonder, then, that most successful SOA projects to date are at the departmental or pilot level. Starting small not only gives a project a greater chance of success, but also enables incremental funding by midlevel managers who can use their discretionary budget to make things happen. Even though small projects won't have the strategic benefits of enterprisewide SOA initiatives, they often solve more tactical problems, such as the reduction of integration costs or enabling Service reuse for a particular, well-defined set of business Services. These projects typically have manageable budgets and can take a few months or less to implement. Furthermore, they can have an immediate ROI within a short time of their implementation.

However, selling SOA at the departmental level is not trivial. SOA champions should focus on short-term, tactical goals that solve immediate problems and enable the department to learn how to apply SOA for incremental returns. It's often best to concentrate on business goals for one to two quarters and then seek to implement SOA incrementally to meet longer-term goals while lowering cost and risk and providing greater agility. Simply put, departments require solutions that solve today's problems with today's budgets, but must also introduce an architecture that can solve tomorrow's problems as well without requiring much additional investment.

IT versus Line of Business versus Architecture Group Funding

Even at the departmental level, it is not entirely clear who should be paying for SOA. It's possible to argue that because SOA is primarily a concept that leverages IT to solve business problems, the IT department should fund as well as manage the solution. Today's IT budgets, however, face a daunting roadblock. Most IT departments find that the bulk of their budgetary dollar goes toward maintenance expenses, with only a small percentage left over to devote to strategic innovation. New SOA projects typically come from that innovation sliver of the budget, which puts IT executives in the difficult position of balancing their SOA projects with all their other strategic IT initiatives.

As a result, many companies are looking to fund SOA projects not from IT budget dollars, but rather from the line of business (LOB). Most coarse-grained Services should map directly to business imperatives, such as customer support, back-end operations, or reporting capabilities, after all. The sales, marketing, customer support, or operations groups should directly contribute their dollars to make those Services happen. In many ways, the LOB should consider the IT department to be a third-party service provider to the organization, supplying the infrastructure and know how to build the Services, but funded from the LOB. In fact, by applying this logic, companies can easily build an abstracted Service model that represents the business needs for Services independent of the IT department's tactical needs. The IT department can then recoup any of its costs using chargebacks or other means for charging the LOB for the use of its resources.

A third, more innovative answer to the SOA project funding conundrum is for enterprise architecture to be neither the responsibility of the IT department nor the LOB, but rather funded as a strategic department itself as part of the office of the CFO or CIO. Forward-looking companies are coming to realize that enterprise architecture is a strategically important capability that requires its own funding, line of control, and business metrics—in other words, enterprise architecture can be a separate LOB in its own right. As such, it makes no sense to separate this capability organizationally without giving the architecture group its own budget. Enterprise architecture as a separate LOB is a new and potentially risky concept, yet some companies have already taken the bold step of creating such a separately funded architecture group that has control over SOA projects across the enterprise.

Robbing Peter to Pay Paul

What happens when there is no separately funded architecture group, and neither IT nor the LOBs have any budget to fund SOA projects, in spite of any need and urgency? In that case, companies should be looking to recover costs from existing IT projects to fund incremental SOA projects. In other words, IT executives should fund SOA initiatives out of the maintenance portion of their budget, rather than the innovation portion.

In particular, companies should look to recover the wasteful expenditure on tightly coupled integration projects, which should go by the wayside in any case in order to implement Service-oriented initiatives. It simply doesn't make sense for companies to complain of a lack of money for relatively small SOA projects while they spend millions on maintaining brittle, tightly coupled integration projects that do nothing to advance their architectural goals. After all, the best way to get out of a hole is to stop digging.

The best way to both advance SOA initiatives and obtain budget for them is to reduce the expenditure on EAI maintenance. Companies can stop throwing money into the bottomless pit of IT spending by taking the first step on the path away from tightly coupled integration to the benefits of agility, Service reuse, composition, and less expensive integration overall.

No executives will fund an SOA initiative by reducing EAI maintenance costs unless they have a clear picture of the ROI they can achieve by making such a choice. We provided an idea of the sorts of return that SOA can provide the organization in Chapter 8. It's important to keep in mind, however, that every emerging technology approach faces the challenge of entering a marketplace where companies have no established line item in their budgets for the innovation in question. Many technologies fail because they simply do not provide sufficient business justification for creative funding approaches. To avoid this trap with SOA, companies must focus on the here-and-now of business issues, applying Service-oriented techniques to derive ongoing business value, and leverage incremental success to ensure continued funding for greater reward down the road.

REACHING THE SOA TIPPING POINT

Most technologies that become indispensable down the road first go through a phase in which relatively few people make use of the technology—and then they suddenly become widespread and ubiquitous. The term *tipping point* refers to this dramatic moment when something obscure suddenly becomes commonplace. A closely related idea to the tipping point is the notion of the *network effect,* first coined by Ethernet inventor Bob Metcalfe, which states that the usefulness of some network of things increases in direct proportion to the number of things connected to that network. In other words, as you connect more resources to the network, the desire to connect additional systems to consume those resources grows, in turn providing an increased motivation to add additional resources to the network. As applied to Service Orientation, these ideas really say the same thing: At first, only a few people will make use of the Services available on the network, but at some unknown future tipping point, those Services will go from obscurity to ubiquity.

When does this tipping point happen? In order for a company to experience rapid adoption and growth of the Services in the network, there must be enough of the right Services on the network in the first place. An organization is better able to achieve the business goals of greater business agility, increased IT asset reuse, and the reduction of complexity through the abstraction of heterogeneity, the more critical, business-focused Services are available on the network. Once a few important Services are available on the corporate network, then various people will see reasons to utilize those Services and perhaps expose Services of their own, perpetuating the chain reaction of growth, leading to a critical mass of available Services. Indeed, eventually most individuals will participate in creating or consuming Services in one way or another as the use of Services spreads on the network.

In fact, it is possible for companies to have hundreds of Services available, even though they have developed only a small fraction of that number internally. The ease of new Service creation and the fact that newly purchased software will increasingly expose Service interfaces as their primary means of interaction will result in hundreds or thousands of Services on the network. Users don't care whether their own IT departments developed a Service—they just want useful Services that meet their requirements. Therefore, a key indication that a company has passed the SOA tipping point is that the demand for and the supply of Services explode.

Such an explosion in demand is a familiar occurrence. For example, the rapid spread of wireless networking forced companies into the same sort of technology adoption mode. In the beginning, only a few thought-leading individuals in the organization took it on themselves to introduce wireless access points on their network, because they found value in the technology for themselves but didn't have enough buy-in across the organization to mandate wireless networking for the whole organization. The first wireless networks consisted of a few installations among small groups, usually a result of somebody putting a small wireless access point in a cubicle, attached to the internal network.

Soon the number of wireless consumers began to grow as others discovered these renegade access points and found them useful, which in turn led to an increased demand for new wireless access points. At some point, the growth of wireless networking was unstoppable. Some companies planned for this growth of wireless, but many were caught unprepared for the network management and security headaches that resulted. If a technology be useful and exhibits a network effect, then it will spread regardless of the foreplanning of the folks in central IT. Don't let the widespread adoption of Services catch you equally unprepared.

The fact that an increased supply of Services leads to an increased demand that perpetuates the network effect will be the essential indicator that we've passed the tipping point for SOA. At that point, the focus of attention will shift from producing new Services to consuming and composing existing ones. The result will be an entirely new set of opportunities for those looking to implement SOA in their organization. These new opportunities include:

- *Competition among Services.* Users will require a choice among Services to consume. More than one Service will provide essentially the

same functionality, so Service providers will have to compete on capabilities, reliability, and value.

- *New models for consuming Services.* Paying to use Services will
  become a commonplace reality. Business-to-business marketplaces for
  Services will rise, and within organizations, enterprises can establish
  chargeback infrastructures to distribute the cost of providing Services
  across the organization.

- *Applications you buy won't come with user interfaces anymore.* Business application vendors will be able to assume that users have adequate consumer applications and, therefore, those business applications
  need not come with their own interfaces. Once Service consumption is
  a foregone conclusion, the software that companies buy will simply add
  to the collection of Services a company uses.

None of these eventualities can take place unless Service consumption
has already reached a tipping point within the organization. The business
and technical benefits that SOA offers companies are significant, and the
technological barriers to adoption are low. Consequently, Services built the
right way will expand beyond the purview of the people who built them.
Through the power of the tipping point, therefore, companies will overcome
the inertia of Service adoption. It is better, then, to plan for this change than
to be caught off guard.

RETURN OF THE LUDDITES

At some point before it gets to the Services tipping point, a business has to
shift its mind-set from existing siloed IT organizations focused on separate
solutions for different IT problems to a cohesive architectural view of IT as
a collection of Services responding to ongoing, changing business requirements. From a technical perspective, Service adoption might reach a tipping
point, but from an organizational perspective, change might be much slower
in coming. What happens when Service use outpaces the organization that
must use, manage, and control those Services? The answer is friction, chaos,
and revolt.

Unfortunately, this sort of revolt against new technologies is not a new
thing. Take, for example, the major upheaval of society that happened as a
result of the Industrial Revolution. For those people who were in the manufacturing, agriculture, and commerce industries, the adoption of new
technology that did the work of skilled craftsmen was certainly a revolution—one that a few extremists sought to reverse. For hundreds of years,
craftsmen in England had manually produced high-quality textile goods
that dominated world markets and export trade. Using methods passed

down through the generations, artisans created these goods by hand, usually in their own homes. In the early nineteenth century, the availability of cotton and the growth of worldwide trade spurred increased demand for woven textiles. With the advent of steam- and water-powered machinery, the emergence of textile manufacturing as an industry along with inventions that enabled rapid production of textiles threatened the long-standing way of life for these textile artisans.

They found that power looms were quickly making them obsolete by shifting the balance of power away from individual artisans to factory owners who could afford to invest money in expensive machines. The weavers complained that the mass production of textiles resulted in poor quality, allowed factory workers to employ less-skilled laborers, and was contributing to a worldwide glut of cotton products, but that couldn't stop the tide of industry. Indeed, many weavers quickly found themselves not only without a job, but without any marketable skills at all.

To the rescue of these poor lost souls arose the now-legendary Ned Ludd, who led a group of rebels who sought to destroy these looms so as to guarantee the weavers' future livelihoods. Throughout the English countryside, workers began to rebel against factory owners, breaking into their facilities at night and smashing their automated looms. It took the full force of the English army to put down this revolt. As a result of this insurrection against the unstoppable tide of progress, the term *Luddite* has come to mean anyone who opposes the advance of technology due to the cultural changes that are associated with it.

IT's New Luddites

For virtually every SOA project, organizational, human issues are far more difficult to resolve than technical ones. People are only just so flexible, after all, and groups of people tend to be less flexible than many of the individuals within the group. There are many reasons for this human inflexibility— fear of the unknown, resistance to change, limited attention spans, and our core personal motivations to follow enlightened self-interest and avoid discomfort and risk.

Any significant technology change also has a corresponding cultural and organizational change that goes with it, and the move to Service Orientation is no exception. Indeed, many people stand to lose their current positions as companies seek to reduce their dependence on tightly coupled integration middleware and large, brittle IT projects. Although the days of smashing machinery as a protest against social change have gone (let's hope), there is reason to believe that some technologists will take up a more passive form of resistance, because they feel that the move to Service Orientation threatens their very livelihoods. One particular group, as discussed in Chapter 7, consists of managers in charge of IT silos. Clearly, as we move to concepts of shared, composable Services that are available to the organization as a whole, those layers of middle management will simply disappear.

However, SOA won't impact just middle management, it will also impact IT specialists. *IT specialists* are technologists who are experts at their particular field. These folks know all the ins and outs of complex, often aging systems such as mainframes, network devices, databases, customer relationship management (CRM) systems, complex enterprise applications, and the minutiae of coding in the most esoteric of languages. IT specialists are generally seasoned, senior individuals, with 20 or more years of experience in their particular field, and they act as a subject-matter resource for others within the organization. They fill the important and necessary role of making sure that the complex interconnection of disparate systems all functions in a way that works for the organization. However, it is precisely all that complexity and brittle interconnectivity that makes companies so resistant to change in the first place. If those complex, brittle, and inefficient systems have to go, so too do the specialists who are needed to keep them working.

Thus, these IT specialists are often resistant to supporting the move to SOA. Clearly, these individuals have built their careers by focusing on a particular technology; new approaches or technologies can be threatening to them. The problem is that many of these specialists think that they could do the very same things in a more efficient way utilizing the tools and technologies specific to the infrastructure they are most familiar with. As a result, they often refuse to listen to the architects or cooperate in overall SOA projects.

But it's not just the techies who have cause to revolt. Many line-of-business users and controllers of various business processes will feel that Service Orientation puts too much control into the hands of people who know too little about how the organization "truly works." Those folks who have spent their lives doing a particular task do indeed know that task well, but they often forget the context of that task among all the activities that contribute to how the business works. An organization might find that after adopting a Service-Oriented Process, it can eliminate many redundancies or inefficiencies, thus eliminating some jobs and support roles that specifically dealt with the older, inefficient processes.

Controlling the Revolt Through Deliberate Education

In fact, one of the greatest challenges that SOA champions face is in promoting acceptance of the new architectural approach, both within lines of business and among IT personnel. One technique for organizing architecture efforts within the enterprise is to form enterprise architecture (EA) teams or councils, with a mandate to provide architectural leadership across the organization. These teams are often the driving force behind SOA in their organizations, yet executive management frequently doesn't give them adequate authority to dictate any architectural practices to IT. We call this situation the ivory tower problem, because these EA teams find themselves making architectural recommendations without any way of enforcing their recommendations.

One approach to addressing the ivory tower problem is to give sufficient power and enforcement to the EA team by strengthening the mandate they receive from executive management. If the CIO or another executive is an effective champion of SOA within the organization, then frequently that person can drive change down into IT. However, many companies don't have an executive champion with a clear mandate for SOA, and even in those organizations that do, many times the EA team will find that certain members of the IT department are resistant to the changes that SOA represents to their day-to-day responsibilities.

One approach to addressing this challenge is to build acceptance for SOA within the broader business and IT communities by involving them early on in an education process around SOA. This approach brings individuals from various groups together to go through an ongoing education process, essentially going over the benefits and implications of SOA on a frequent enough basis that they come to understand and support the changes that SOA requires. This education-centric approach to winning over those people who are most resistant to SOA is especially helpful, because it helps promote the idea of SOA across the lines of business as well as IT.

Developers, however, present a dual challenge: They require the low-level technical details of how SOA differs from what they are doing today, and it can be difficult to speak with them without first speaking with the relevant technical specialists, who are generally resistant to change and new ideas. To work around the specialists' intransigence, focus on educating the developers. Over time, the specialists should gradually come around to the Service-oriented way of thinking, as many of the developers they work with on a daily basis become accustomed to the new approaches, and the specialists come to realize that SOA is a foregone conclusion for the organization.

SOA represents a doubly threatening source of change for technical people, because it represents changing technological approaches as well as broader organizational changes as companies implement shared Services and composable processes. SOA champions, therefore, must also take on the role of change agents, working with people on an individual basis to address the issues that make them reluctant to change. An organization that plans to fully embrace Service Orientation will have to fully embrace the organizational and cultural changes that the new approach requires. In order to make those changes, we need first to understand what the new IT organization will look like once a company moves to Service Orientation.

NEW SERVICE-ORIENTED ORGANIZATION

Although it is certainly possible for SOA champions to bring IT specialists around to the Service-oriented way of thinking through ongoing, repetitive, and methodical education, middle managers who had heretofore managed various IT silos are still left out in the cold. At the very least, SOA will require significant changes in the way companies organize IT. Whereas before, different organizations managed the portal team, or the ERP application, or some other IT-centric division, Service Orientation mandates the use of shared Services that touch on multiple different technologies, systems, and organizational units. As a result, the siloed management of IT breaks down, as users from across the organization and beyond can now consume those Services and compose them into processes. The sand is shifting under the feet of such managers, and some will find their job responsibilities going away—but there is hope for many of them.

Managers who clearly understand that their role is to make their company successful in achieving its business goals, rather than simply focusing on the operations of their own bailiwick, are the people most likely to be able to weather the shift to Service Orientation. After all, their skills will still be in demand—it's just that what they'll be managing will be different. Instead of the old IT silos, companies will need people to manage the Service domains (which we defined and discussed in Chapter 8) that will be central to how a company deals with ongoing change in a Service-oriented manner. Because Service domains are business-focused collections of Services, they differ fundamentally from the IT-centric silos that Service Orientation seeks to break down. So, rather than having a portal manager, we will have managers of Customer Services, Finance Services, and Supplier Services, for example. As companies shift to SOA, organizations with a hierarchical culture will find that their middle managers can still find themselves gainfully employed by managing Service domains.

Of course, Service Orientation enables companies to move away from rigid hierarchies to more flexible, flatter organizations. Here's where the business context of loose coupling kicks in. Service domains as *business* entities should be loosely coupled from other such domains, as well as from the consumers of the Services in the domain. For example, one Service domain might be the external, customer domain; another might be the internal accounting domain. Each domain should have a contractual relationship with the others, so that all domain managers can make changes to the inner operations of their domains without impacting the other domains. In such a loosely coupled environment, then, we augment hierarchical management with cooperation in a flattened organizational layer.

SOA Governance and the New IT Power Structure

We're not saying, of course, that Service Orientation will lead to the end of hierarchical corporations. We will go so far as to say, however, that Service Orientation can transform how those hierarchies operate. Recall our discussion of SOA governance from Chapter 8. Governance is essentially the way for senior management to establish and communicate the policies of the corporation, give the rank and file the tools to follow those policies, provide management with the visibility necessary to confirm that people are following the policies, and mitigate any problems they might find as a result. SOA governance, in particular, is governance in the context of SOA, where we are now able to distill those corporate policies into metadata that the Services can understand and act on automatically and to use Services as a way to enforce governance throughout the organization.

When we discussed the automation paradox in Chapter 4, we talked about processes that were difficult to automate through ordinary mechanisms, but those on which Service Orientation can make a significant impact. Human management processes are perfect examples of difficult-to-automate processes that Service Orientation can wrest from manual control Now, we're not saying that human managers won't be necessary because some computer will be doing their jobs—that's the *Modern Times* big-gear view of automation. Rather, Service Orientation provides a way to enable line-of-business managers to have greater control of their day-to-day work to work with Service-Oriented Processes that are a mix of automated and manual activities.

The role of top-level executives in the Service-oriented organization therefore consists of creating overarching business strategies that translate into corporate policies that companies can implement in a loosely coupled, Service-oriented way and of establishing corporate governance that dictates how Services and tools that power those Services represent, enforce, and communicate those policies. Then managers must work within that governance framework to deal with issues as they arise.

Building Cross-Functional Teams

As we discussed in Chapter 9, in order to implement SOA, companies must pull together diverse teams of people who may not have worked jointly before. Architects, developers, security experts, business analysts, business process experts, network administrators, and more—all serve an important role in an SOA implementation project. Once a company has SOA up and running, however, cross-functional teams are every bit as important as they were during the SOA rollout. We now have three different lines of control: senior line-of-business management communicating policies through SOA governance tools, managers of Service domains coordinating the business use of Services, and Service-oriented architects providing oversight of the architectural implementation in operation. Each type of manager may call meetings for different purposes.

The line-of-business executive might call a meeting with business and IT representatives who work directly with that manager's department, including business process specialists and possibly some Service domain managers, but rarely with any architects. The Service-oriented architect, however, must meet with technical architects and business process architects, as well as with infrastructure personnel such as developers, network managers, and security specialists. They will also be working closely with the Service domains. Finally, Service domain managers will be most interested in meeting with the technical staff responsible for the Services in their domain, including technical project managers, developers, and technical architects.

The Service-oriented architect's role is different from today's typical enterprise architect as well. Today, people generally consider architecture to be a *design time* activity, in that architects do their work designing a system before that system goes into operation. With that perception, the belief might be that once the system is up and running, it's time for the architect to move on to something new.

In the Service-oriented organization, however, the work of the architect is never done. As we discuss more fully in Chapter 11, the design and the operation tasks in a working SOA implementation are all ongoing, intertwined activities, as various IT groups create and modify Services and various lines of business create and modify processes with those Services. Just as with the great classical music composers, who both composed the music and conducted the orchestra, the Service-oriented architect must play both a design role for the architecture as well as be the "conductor" or overseer of the architectural implementation in operation.

IT departments must make a few additional organizational changes to ensure that the new cross-functional teams are effective:

■ *Employ an IT-dedicated financial officer.* It is probably fair to say that most folks in IT don't have an adequate understanding of finance and business economics in the first place to understand how their department will positively impact the business. A Service-oriented organization will have to broaden the financial knowledge of the people responsible for defining and measuring Services to include financially savvy individuals who can make say whether a Service is really contributing value to the company.

- *Give architects dotted-line responsibility to the CIO.* Architecture is the one activity within IT that is not focused on the tactical issues of implementing technology or meeting short-term business requirements. Rather, architecture is the practice of dealing with ongoing and unpredictable business change. Companies should give the architecture team the highest possible visibility to the executive in charge of the IT organization, usually the CIO.

- *Implement metrics for each Service* Services represent current and future business requirements. Therefore, companies should measure the effectiveness of a Service by how well it meets the business requirements, instead of evaluating the underlying IT systems that implement that Service. Far too many techies in executive management simply apply performance metrics, such as uptime and availability, to Services as a way of measuring their value. However, these metrics are not directly relevant to the business. More important is whether the Service is returning actual business value and ROI.

- *Compensate IT right.* It's important to compensate IT employees on key business metrics, such as financial performance, customer satisfaction, the ability to meet deadlines, the reduction of overall business spending, and quality metrics. Once executives tie compensation to these goals, it's amazing how quickly behavior changes. Service-Oriented Enterprises should organize IT people around Service domains—particular sets of Services that fulfill different business needs. Once the Service domains have business metrics applied to them, those metrics can also apply to the individuals who are in charge of them.

- *Aim for transparency.* One of the side effects of Service Orientation is transparency, which means that IT capabilities as well as IT deficiencies are visible for all to see. IT failures become more apparent, as do inadequacies and missed opportunities. Service Orientation is a knife that cuts both ways: In order for IT to enable businesses to respond in an agile, flexible fashion, IT must be sufficiently transparent to the business so that it can see where the bottlenecks are.

Who Is the Master of the Requirement?

A properly operating Service-oriented organization, therefore, is a fluid affair, with ongoing change a way of life, not an unwelcome, occasional guest. In spite of this fluidity, however, Service Orientation helps companies focus on competitiveness, by providing the agility to run circles around the competition. The challenge a company faces, then, is how to leverage the agility benefit of Service Orientation without letting the company go off into the weeds.

The answer is right under your nose. How do today's large enterprises handle the same challenge, given that they have perhaps tens of thousands of people, yet must steer their ship in a single direction? The answer lies in the nature of human management. Executives, after all, cannot be effective if they micromanage—that is, if they expect the people to report to them to do just what they tell their reports to do. Instead, effective managers communicate policies and instructions on a broad level, and let the people who work for them use their own innate skills to take those instructions and fill in the missing details. In large organizations with many levels, instructions from on high receive increasing levels of detail as they work their way down. The best companies, then, are able to incorporate the strengths of their people at each level to actualize the intentions of senior management in effective ways.

Service Orientation doesn't seek to change this fundamentally human approach to running large organizations—instead, it seeks to *improve* it. The CEO still leads the executive team in setting corporate policy and steering the company as a whole. The hierarchical organization still disseminates that policy and allows the strengths of each individual to build value for the organization and its customers. What Service Orientation brings to the table is greater agility at every step of the process. Service Orientation adds lubrication to the tight linkages of the corporate hierarchy, allowing flexibility without jeopardizing control. Companies have always had to change, but now change becomes an expected part of the day-to-day operation of the organization. And IT, instead of being an expensive drag on the flexibility of a company to respond to market forces, now becomes a valuable source of flexible tools that all parts of the organization can use to meet the requirements of the business.

CHAPTER 11

Build Agility with Agility

We promised at the outset that this book would be a business book, not a technology book, but we didn't mean that we would ignore technology altogether. We have doled out measured portions of technology, because, after all, we really mean this book to marry the concepts of IT and business. However, we couldn't call this an eBusiness book because of the dot-com stigma still associated with the term. Besides, eBusiness hasn't yet resolved the long-lived problems of inflexibility that Service Orientation is more specifically focused on. Nevertheless, by considering IT capabilities to be business resources, we both bring new life to the tired eBusiness term by providing a thorough grounding in Service Orientation as the raison d'être for eBusiness.

As a recap, we've thoroughly covered what's wrong with IT and how business uses IT today, as well as what Service Orientation is, why you would want it, what steps you should take to implement it, and how your business can succeed with it. In this chapter, we return to the IT department—not with technical minutiae by any means, but rather with how the department must change the way it builds, manages, and evolves the technology that underlies your company's Services.

DEATH TO THE SOFTWARE DEVELOPMENT LIFECYCLE!

Bringing Service Orientation to the IT department sacrifices a number of sacred cows, not the least of which is the *Software Development Lifecycle* (SDLC). The SDLC is a concept that details the various stages of the life of software systems (which include hardware, although we'll talk about the SDLC as if software were all that mattered). The concept of *life* here embodies the same things that we associate with the life of a human, such as conception, birth, childhood, adolescence, going out into the world, maturing, getting old, and finally dying. Just as all living things go through such a lifecycle, the theory behind the concept of the SDLC is that software in the enterprise does too. Here, then, are the important phases in the lifecycle of a piece of software, according to the SDLC theory:

- *Business requirements gathering* (i.e., **being conceived**). Traditionally, business analysts on the requirements-gathering team sit down with line-of-business representatives and distill all of the use cases necessary to describe precisely what the business requires of some new piece of software. The result is a set of documents that outline the concept at hand and what functionality IT needs to fulfill the business requirements.

- *Design* (i.e., **being born**). Architects take the requirements documentation and create a complete, detailed description of what the developers are supposed to build. In this phase, IT projects go from concept to plan.

- *Implementation* (i.e., **childhood**). The developers build the system according to the architects' design.

- *Testing* (i.e., **adolescence**). The quality assurance (QA) team takes the requirements documents and ensures that the developers built a final project that meets those requirements. If they find any problems, either with the way the system works or a deficiency in the way that the system met the requirements, the developers fix them, until the working system passes all the tests.

- *Deployment* (i.e., **going out into the world**). The developers and operations personnel put the working system into production—in other words, move it to the live environment so the company can actually use it.

- *Operations* (i.e., **maturing**). Once the system is up and running, it is now considered mission critical and under the management of the operations staff. The working system must meet its ongoing business needs, with occasional maintenance and fine-tuning to improve the efficiency of the system.

- *Sunset* or *legacy* (i.e., **getting old**). New technologies appear that make the working system seem obsolete or, at the least, no longer cost-effective. The company comes up with a plan to retire it and begins to phase out its use.

- *Retirement* (i.e., **death**). Finally, the system is taken out of production and all costs are reduced to zero.

The SDLC makes so much sense and is so intuitive that IT departments have been following its steps since the dawn of business computing. In fact, over time, various experts have fleshed out the broad precepts of the SDLC into a specific methodology that they call the *waterfall methodology*. The idea behind the waterfall methodology is that it's important to finish each step in the lifecycle before starting the next one, and furthermore, there should be a specific checklist of tasks the team must complete to finish each step before they move onto the next. Just as a waterfall follows the path of least resistance from higher levels to lower ones, the waterfall methodology specifies a step-by-step road map for following the SDLC.

In spite of its intuitive nature, however, the sad fact is that *the vast majority of all software projects that follow the waterfall methodology fail.* In fact, at least 85% of such projects fail in one way or another, either by going over budget, taking too long, failing to deliver the required functionality, or in extreme cases, never even reach deployment. A few of the numerous reasons why the waterfall approach doesn't work are:

- *The technical team understands the requirements poorly.* The business folks speak in terms of the business, but the techies speak in technical terms. Sometimes they simply don't see eye to eye on what certain concepts mean. Simply put, business and IT speak different languages.
- *People communicate poorly with each other.* This pitfall is the principle of the game of telephone we all played as children. Remember sitting in a circle, where one person whispers a phrase to the next, and when the phrase comes full circle, it's entirely different from the original phrase? Well, human communication is essentially imperfect, so when the business users talk to the analysts, and the analysts talk to the architects, and the architects talk to the developers, you're bound to have problems. Furthermore, many times the business users poorly articulate their needs, and in turn, analysts poorly describe those needs.
- *Problems crop up later rather than earlier.* Testing naturally comes after development in the SDLC, right? Well, if there's a problem, it's far more time consuming and expensive to fix it after development than before it. The earlier you can catch a problem, the better—after all, it is much easier to fix a problem with the design than with a poorly working implementation. Unfortunately, the way most businesses run their SDLC, testing comes so late in the project that there is no incentive to do anything about serious and significant problems.
- *It's hard to make adjustments along the way.* According to the SDLC, once the design phase is done, it's done. Similarly, once the implementation is done, it's done—there's no turning back. The waterfall methodology is like driving a car on autopilot, where you point the car in one direction and then leave the steering wheel alone. What's the chance you'll keep going in the right direction for long?
- *Business requirements change.* Even if the developers are able to deliver exactly what the business folks wanted, their requirements simply may have changed in the meantime. The SDLC doesn't even come close to factoring in the possibility that somewhere in the middle of the process something will change.

Iterative Methodologies to the Rescue

You'd think that the industry experts who hammer out recommended best practices would have realized that the waterfall methodology didn't work, and in fact, most of them have. As it happens, the 1990s saw the rise of several new, *iterative* methodologies, like the Spiral Methodology and the Rational Unified Process, as IT spending and project development skyrocketed. These methodologies improved on the waterfall SDLC by propounding a phased lifecycle approach, where various steps overlapped with one another. Each IT project then goes through several iterations, where each iteration breaks some new ground and wraps up some part of the project, all the while allowing the team to rework and improve what they've come up with.

In an iterative approach, for example, the requirements may not be entirely complete when the design begins. Instead, the architects visit with the users and the analysts during the design process to ensure they're on track, giving the analysts time to improve the requirements documentation. Likewise, once the developers start building out the design, they confer with the business users and the architects to keep themselves on track. The requirements documents and the design might improve a few times as the project progresses. The iterations then continue along these lines until the system is fully operational.

Iterative methodologies clearly address the first four problems with the waterfall approach we listed. Iterative approaches are more collaborative, improving communication and providing for a way to resolve misunderstandings. Problems are also more likely to crop up earlier in a project, when it's easier to fix them. Iterative methodologies, however, don't address the final issue—continuously changing business requirements—very well at all. If requirements change is limited and occurs relatively early in a project, then yes, an iterative methodology can adjust the course of a project to the new requirements reasonably well. But what happens when requirements change is ongoing, even after deployment? Remember, iterative approaches still follow the general flow of the SDLC, so projects must always reach a completed state. If a project team is building software in an inherently inflexible way that assumes a final state, then it doesn't matter how iterative the methodology that the team follows happens to be; that software will still be inflexible once it's in production.

Traditional iterative methodologies, therefore, aren't up to the task of building SOA deployments, because the goal of such deployments is to build IT systems that deal well with ongoing change. What we need is a more agile approach to building software that inherently allows for such change. Furthermore, Service Orientation actually requires a rethink of the SDLC itself, because Service-oriented projects are never actually *complete*. It's important to deploy SOA projects in a tentative state, with the explicit acknowledgment that any deployment can change at any time. And if there's no deployment step per se, then requirements gathering, design, development, and testing continue indefinitely, and operations, sunset, and retirement might also take place at any time. The whole SDLC arch of beginning, middle, and end really doesn't apply to the flexible, ever-changing vision of Service Orientation.

LEGO BLOCK MODEL OF SERVICE ORIENTATION

Service Orientation requires a new way of thinking about the SDLC, but we wouldn't go so far as to say that we have to throw out all the ideas from the SDLC. After all, even in a Service-oriented IT shop, we still have to think about how to develop, test, deploy, and retire systems and software. The fundamental change that Service Orientation introduces is that the lifecycle is at a much smaller scale and a lot more iterative than what most firms are used to. In traditional enterprise IT, projects tend to be large, expensive, and time consuming; in Service Orientation, you can consider creating or modifying each individual Service and its underlying software as a separate project. In essence, we move from large IT projects to "microprojects," each with a discrete lifecycle of its own, but part of a continually evolving whole.

Think of how your body works: You have hundreds of thousands of cells in your body, each with a discrete lifecycle of its own and constantly being created, living, and then dying, but your body seems to operate without any interruption. That's because the human body as a whole is changing all the time, but not in a single set of steps. Rather, the body is changing hundreds of thousands of times a day in such a way that each lifecycle contributes to the overall, changing requirements of the body on a daily basis.

Recall that an atomic Service exposes specific technical functionality—typically, a basic operation on a particular business application. Composed Services offer broader, business-centric value, and typically make up several atomic Services. The distinction between atomic and composed Services is a philosophical one—after all, in a loosely coupled environment, Service consumers don't know if the Service they are consuming is atomic or composite. However, the developer of Services needs to be aware of the difference because atomic Services should have their own mini-SDLCs. Developers build atomic Services by writing software, so they should follow an appropriate software methodology. Business users create and evolve composed Services without having to write any new software, because they have the luxury of simply composing together existing Services. So, while you can treat each atomic Service as if it were a piece of software, you can't think of any significant Service Orientation project which uses Service-Oriented Processes as a traditional software project that follows an SDLC.

Indeed, with the exception of creating atomic Services, SOA projects look very little like traditional software projects. Instead, large Service Orientation projects involve many Services that are expected to change frequently—either atomic Services that developers must create or modify on an ongoing basis, or composed Services that the business might rework on a moment's notice.

You can think of a Service Orientation project as building something out of Legos, where each atomic Service is a different Lego block. Before we have any blocks to assemble, we must first build the block itself. Creating each Lego block means molding the plastic—a very technical process. However, once we have enough blocks in our collection, we never have to think about molding plastic ever again. Building something out of Legos, once we have them, doesn't involve anything nearly so technical; simply plug the blocks into each other, and if you don't like what you make, then take the blocks apart and build something else. If we find that we are missing a Lego piece that we need, such as a wheel, we go out and purchase it, or if we have the technical skills, we can mold it ourselves.

However, the traditional SDLC looks nothing like the Lego block approach. Instead of easily interchangeable parts, traditional enterprise software projects require companies to build large, custom-molded individual blocks that had the desired shape right out of the mold. Nothing to assemble later, but if requirements change, you're out of luck.

Have Bumps, Will Build:
The Agile Methodology Movement

Any kid knows that the secret to Legos are the bumps. Every Lego, regardless of its shape or purpose, has the same shape bumps on the top and dents in the bottom so that they fit together every time. With Services, the bumps represent the *contract*. When the development team members need to build an atomic Service, they must look to the contract to know what to build. As long as they follow the contract, they can be sure their bumps fit into all the dents out there, even if they know nothing about the Service consumers except what the contract tells them.

Given that building atomic Services is an ongoing, ever-changing task, and Service-building teams get their marching orders from the Service contracts, what is an appropriate methodology for creating such Services from scratch when they don't already exist? Clearly, an iterative approach makes sense, because of the fluid nature of such projects—but a traditional SDLC-based iterative methodology just won't do. We need a much more agile methodology. Lo and behold, there's just such a thing—and it's called *Agile Methodology*. In fact, there's a whole Agile Methodology *movement*, with a variety of individual methodologies that people consider to be Agile, such as Extreme Programming (XP). We'll consider Agile Methodologies as a group and identify particular techniques that make sense for Service Orientation.

The goal of Agile Methodologies is to build just what the user wants, avoiding extraneous work on documentation and other things that aren't software. The focus of Agile Methodologies is on people and working programming code, not on process or documentation. The core strength of Agile Methodologies lies in their agility—the ability to deal with changing requirements. One of the most important Agile Methodology techniques is how the approach recommends adoption of the methodology itself. You're not supposed to adopt Agile Methodologies in an all-or-nothing manner; the agile approach to adopting an Agile Methodology is to adopt only those aspects of the methodology that solve the pressing problems in the existing development process. Therefore, even though there are ideal descriptions of Agile Methodologies, in reality, teams that implement some form of an Agile Methodology typically pick and choose those aspects that are appropriate for their needs. In fact, that's just what we're going to do in this chapter.

The core tenets of Agile Methodology that enterprises moving to Service Orientation should pay particular attention to include:

- *Maintain a focus on simplicity.* Services should be as simple as possible, but no simpler. If something adds needless complexity, remove it. If there are two ways of solving a problem, choose the simplest.

Jargon Watch: Extreme Programming

One of the most popular agile methodologies is *Extreme Programming* (XP). XP provides a flexible process for building software systems in environments where requirements are unknown or in flux. XP requires that a user representative work closely with the development team, helping to write tests that guide the daily work of the developers. All members of the team pitch in on the design, which is kept as minimal and informal as possible. All team members are responsible for all of the code, and anyone can rework any part of the project. Developers tackle XP projects iteratively, first writing a test, then implementing just the code necessary to pass all the tests.

- *Operate with small teams focused on speed and efficiency.* Teams working on Service Orientation projects often have a wide mix of members (e.g., architects working with developers, or business analysts working with line of business personnel). Each of these teams should be small enough to work well together, so that each member can understand all the issues facing the team. Avoid unnecessary distractions so the teams can focus on working efficiently.

- *Write tests first and work until all tests pass.* Writing down a test forces team members to think about what their task at hand is actually supposed to do. Similarly, if their current task passes the tests, then they know they are done with the task. In the Service-oriented construct, this means that teams should build the contracts first and then the tests necessary to prove that a contract works *before* writing any code. If a contract can be tested without even writing code, all the better.

- *Refactor when necessary.* *Refactoring* means reworking existing code to make it more efficient without changing its functionality. Typically, a team should refactor when there is code in two places that does the same thing. Taking a Service-Oriented perspective on refactoring means reworking Services so that they are more efficient. For example, if two Services have overlapping functionality, it makes sense either to combine them or to create a third Service that contains the common functionality. Refactoring can also lead to performance and security improvements, and can streamline the business processes that rely on the Services.

- *Maintain a focus on the users and their requirements.* One of the core concepts in XP is the idea that a user representative is a core part of the development team and helps to write functional tests to ensure the team doesn't build something the user doesn't want. With SOA, the contract stands in for the user among the technical teams. Remember, the Services form a layer of abstraction between the technology and the business users, and thus the users and the techies do not need to work together directly as long as the contracts are complete, accurate, and up-to-date. In SOA, the mandate is to maintain a focus on the contract.

As companies move to adopt Service Orientation, their application development processes will change. In fact, Service Orientation promises to transform the basic definitions of *application* and *development* themselves as a result of the shift of responsibility for application development into the hands of business users as they compose Service-Oriented Processes. After all, in the Service-oriented context, an application is a set of Services and processes. It's crucial, therefore, for developers as well as business users to understand the changing nature of applications and the techniques for creating and managing them within the context of Service Orientation.

FOUR PILLARS OF SERVICE-ORIENTED DEVELOPMENT

We can call the new type of application that Service Orientation mandates a *Service-Oriented Business Application* or a *Composite Application*. Such composite applications consist of Service-Oriented Processes that compose Services and other processes to provide flexible functionality to the business. Because Service-Oriented Processes are continuously changing, so are composite applications. Therefore, the development of such applications is centered on the configuring of processes, policies, and contracts rather than the development of code to build new Services.

Just as playing with Legos is more about putting the blocks together than molding new parts, so too is the Service-Oriented Business Application. The application developer's role will change as well. Most composite application developers are business analysts who work with tools that enable the configuration of metadata, thus enabling them to create and manage business logic without having to do any programming.

Although moving business logic to the composite application level is a noble goal to be sure, there's no question that a large portion of the business logic in today's organizations will remain locked away in existing business applications. It's important to keep in mind, therefore, that two basically different kinds of applications will continue to exist simultaneously in the Service-oriented organization: composite applications that business analysts create and manage, and the existing legacy business applications that will continue to exist below the Services layer of abstraction.

Clearly, the Services layer of abstraction plays a pivotal role in SOA. This abstraction derives from the contracted nature of Services. As long as each Service meets its contract, business analysts need work only with the metadata contained in such contracts, without needing to know the implementation details of the Service. Likewise, developers must build only components with Service interfaces that meet those contracts. They need have no knowledge of the consuming applications beyond the metadata in the contract.

Service-oriented architects, however, must have the big picture of the SOA implementation that crosses the Services layer of abstraction. They must create and manage models of the business requirements, Services, and the underlying implementation, as well as a model of the Services themselves, which we call the *Service model*. As a result, there are two spheres of Service-oriented development: the sphere of business activity above the Service model and the sphere of technical activity below it.

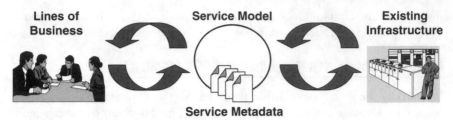

EXHIBIT 11.1   Two Spheres of Service-Oriented Development

Two Spheres of Service-Oriented Development

To illustrate this concept, Exhibit 11.1 shows at a high level how building and managing an SOA implementation involves working in these two spheres. It also shows a clear methodology for translating requirements across the Service model when appropriate.

One of the challenges of Service-oriented development is in following an approach that maintains the business agility benefit, which, after all, is one of the main value propositions of SOA. The secret to building for agility is to remember that composite applications have the meta-requirement of responding flexibly to changes in the business environment. The traditional gather requirements/design/build/test/deploy waterfall methodology for software development fails to address this meta-requirement of agility. Service-oriented development, therefore, requires a different approach to represent the business requirements to IT and to represent IT capabilities to the business. As a result, Service-oriented development follows one of three basic scenarios.

In the first scenario, shown in Exhibit 11.2, business analysts work with business users to understand and gather current business requirements. These analysts then work with composite application tools to configure and compose Services and processes to meet those requirements. In this scenario, the available Services are sufficient to meet the needs of the business—no

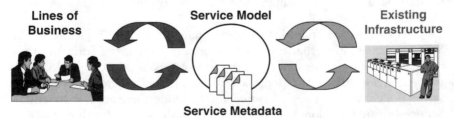

EXHIBIT 11.2   Composite Application Development

new plastic needs to be molded. The analysts work in an iterative fashion with users, adjusting the processes as needed to fine-tune their functionality. Business analysts work to satisfy specific business requirements, without the need to involve IT because they are simply recombining the existing Services to meet new needs—working with the Lego blocks they have, as it were. They are thus able to respond quickly to changing business requirements on an ongoing basis as long as they have all the blocks they need.

However, what happens if the line of business requires functionality that current Services are unable to provide? In this second scenario, shown in Exhibit 11.3, business analysts find that the existing Services in production are insufficient to meet the needs of the current set of business requirements. As a result, they describe the newly required functionality by creating or modifying Service contract metadata in the Service model. Basically, they provide instructions to the programming staff by establishing requirements within proposed Service contracts.

The developers then code to the contract by developing Services that meet these new contract requirements, without having to know the specific usage scenarios for those Services beyond the information contained in the contract. Service contract metadata therefore form the requirements documentation necessary to create or modify existing components in order to expose Service interfaces that satisfy those contracts. The contract becomes the embodiment of the Service as it is currently operating, as well as documentation that describes how to consume that Service. At that point, business analysts can incorporate the required working Services into their processes.

The third scenario involves changing only a Service to operate better. In this scenario, there is some technical reason for changing the programming of a Service without changing that Service's contract—in other words, refactoring it. For example, refactoring might be called for if the IT staff members determine that they must make changes to satisfy some Service-level requirement, say to maintain the scalability of the underlying components. Another example would be when IT decides to replace a legacy application

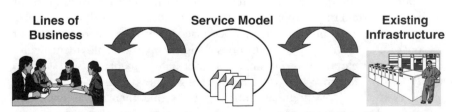

Lines of Business   **Service Model**   **Existing Infrastructure**

EXHIBIT 11.3   Service Creation or Modification

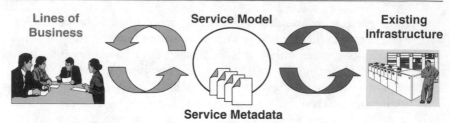

EXHIBIT 11.4   Service Refactoring

or other part of the existing infrastructure. Refactoring may also take place to streamline components by removing redundant parts of the code, as we show in Exhibit 11.4. The critical point to this third scenario is that the business users are none the wiser about any changes, because the contracts remain the same, and ideally, IT addresses any potential performance issues before they affect the business.

Four Pillars of Service-Oriented Development

All of the preceding scenarios share some common elements that distinguish Service-oriented development from other forms of development that typically rely on the waterfall methodology or other traditional application development approaches. Specifically, companies must understand four pillars of Service-oriented development:

- *Pillar 1: Iterative development.*   We're representing each sphere of development with a pair of arrows to indicate the fundamentally iterative nature of Service-oriented development. Business analysts must work iteratively with business users, both to satisfy the original requirements and to maintain agility as those requirements change. Likewise, developers must continually iterate their code to satisfy ongoing changes to the Service contracts.
- *Pillar 2: User involvement.*   Unlike the waterfall approach, where users specify requirements at the beginning of a project only, business users continually drive Service-oriented development. The meta-requirement is for a system that responds well to change, and as a result, the requirements definition phase of any Service-oriented project is actually a set of ongoing activities. At no point does design stop and deployment begin. Rather, development is ongoing, as is user involvement.
- *Pillar 3: Contract-first development.*   Business analysts work with users to distill requirements into contracts that then act as marching orders for the developers. Such metadata represent both the requirements and the test plans that analysts can execute to guarantee that

Services meet their requirements. In other words, contract-first development is an example of test-first development, and both approaches are examples of metadata-driven application development.

- *Pillar 4: Refactoring.* The Services layer of abstraction affords IT the luxury of a curtain that hides the inner workings of the technology from the business. Rather than an excuse to maintain a poor infrastructure, this abstraction layer actually gives IT more leeway to make continual improvements to the technology. Refactoring is thus the underpinning of reuse, as IT may now work to streamline technology across platforms to meet the needs of the business. As a result, a Service-oriented company should become more efficient, flexible, and agile over time as they squeeze out unnecessary complexity, redundancy, and costs iteratively over time.

In none of these scenarios does the IT department determine which Services to build. IT must build only Services that meet the requirements that the contracts specify or refactor Services to provide better business return to the organization. Rather than IT dictating the terms for building application functionality, it is the business side of the organization that determines how to build and consume Services. By following these Agile Methodology techniques, companies can be well prepared for building, managing, and evolving IT that leverages ongoing change.

Remember that Agile Methodologies value individuals and interactions over development processes and tools, working software over comprehensive documentation, customer collaboration over negotiation, and responding to change over following a plan. To be successful, Service-oriented development must follow these principles as well. Service-oriented development borrows from and extends the concepts of XP and other Agile Methodology approaches. Nevertheless, companies that wish to become Service-oriented must follow the four pillars of Service-oriented development.

NOT YOUR PARENTS' REQUIREMENTS GATHERING

When we talked about SOA pilot projects in Chapter 9, we discussed the usefulness of having SOA as the ulterior motive for the project. The explicit motivation, however, was to address some particular set of business requirements. This approach makes sense within the context of a pilot project, because it aligns with the goals of tackling a pilot in the first place—building acceptance, lowering risk, and getting the hang of the new, Service-oriented approach. However, as companies roll out broader SOA implementations, from cross-departmental to enterprise initiatives, the technique companies should take to gather and implement business requirements should be entirely different.

In fact, the Service-oriented architect must keep in mind two different types of business requirement: short-term tactical requirements and the strategic meta-requirement of agility. From the architect's perspective, the meta-requirement is far more interesting and important, because it promulgates SOA as rats' nest untangler. As you may recall, rats' nests came to be in the first place because, over time, IT makes the most expedient choice over the more strategic one, adding new layers of complexity and leading to an increasingly brittle mess. By focusing on the meta-requirement of agility, we can break this cycle of increasing inflexibility by giving the architect a way to keep the SOA initiative on track, not only untangling the current rats' nest, but avoiding the creation of a new one as well.

Fleshing Out the Meta-Requirement of Agility

In the ideal world, the architect would be able to design a system that was infinitely agile: It would be able to respond to any unpredictable, farfetched eventuality that happenstance could throw at it, from natural disasters to political coups or even aliens landing, for that matter. Sure, maybe we can design SOA to be up to the task of such agility, but at what cost? In the real world, there's always give-and-take between the level of agility a company truly requires and the amount of money it wishes to spend to achieve it.

The fundamental goal of loose coupling requires that when you build a Service, you shouldn't have any information about the consumers of that Service beyond the information in the Service contract. In reality, however, what we mean is that you don't need to have any information within a specific *context,* and that context sets the constraints for the meta-requirement for agility. For example, if you know that only consumers internal to your organization will ever be allowed to access a particular Service, and that there will never be more than 1,000 such consumers, then that 1,000-consumer limit places a constraint on the meta-requirement. If you plan to expose your Service to all of your million customers, then you have a different constraint. The scope of the Service can thus be defined in such a way that agility is maximized within bounds.

Many such constraints address the nonfunctional aspect of the meta-requirement. Understanding the maximum number of consumers a Service might have indicates how scalable the Service must be. Likewise, providing constraints in the contract that determine how much downtime the business will allow for a particular Service will tell the architect how fault-tolerant it should be. Building scalability and fault tolerance into the Service infrastructure comes with significant cost, so it definitely makes sense to deal with such nonfunctional requirements as part of the architectural plan. It is important to note that a contract can specify any terms that the consumer

Jargon Watch: Functional versus Nonfunctional Requirements

When business users describe their requirements for a particular application, some of the things they list are *functions* of that application—in other words, what the application is supposed to *do*. These requirements are predictably called *functional requirements* because they detail what a Service does. However, there's a whole class of requirements that are *nonfunctional*, in that they describe properties of the application that aren't its functions. Typical examples of nonfunctional requirements include how many users might be able to access the application at the same time (scalability), how important it is for the application to be working all the time (fault tolerance), and how secure the application is. Sometimes we call these nonfunctional requirements *policies* that govern how a Service works. Policies and contracts together form the core of the functional and nonfunctional requirements for a Service.

In the context of SOA, the implementation should be able to address new or changing functional requirements with little or no additional programming—essential to providing the agility benefit of the architecture. Architects handle the nonfunctional requirements of SOA, however, in a more traditional fashion: Basically, plan for the worst, within reason, and go from there.

and provider agree to, but that doesn't mean that we should allow any arbitrary terms to make their way into the contract. Rather, it's important to limit the types of terms a contract might have in order to limit the cost and complexity of building the Services.

Planning for Change

Even after the architects have fleshed out all of the nonfunctional constraints on the architecture, it's still important to build a certain amount of flexibility into those constraints. After all, you may have underestimated the maximum number of consumers or the business's requirements for fault tolerance or security at some point in the future. You clearly can't afford to support such capabilities out of the gate, but it does make sense to have a plan for addressing such changes as well as a mechanism for giving you an early warning that you'll need to make the changes before something breaks. In essence, we need an iterative and agile approach for dealing with contract and constraint changes in addition to changes to the Service itself.

Fortunately, we have a bit of knowledge about how to deal with changes in constraints and assumptions of how Services should behave. We can combine aspects of our Service-oriented development approach with the way that we handle scalability and change issues for today's large Web sites. For example, an unexpected increase in traffic might cause a data center to bring more servers online or maybe to outsource peak capacity needs to a service provider. We're not reinventing the wheel with SOA, after all—we're simply building this level of flexibility into the Service interface.

In fact, planning for change is important to addressing functional requirements as well. From the architect's perspective, in fact, architecting to meet functional requirements is *entirely* about planning for change. The specifics of the functionality the business requires on a daily basis are in the realm of the business analyst and business process architect, and affect IT only when the available Services aren't able to meet the requirement. In a properly designed SOA, therefore, architects need not concern themselves with the daily ebb and flow of new functional requirements, as there is already a methodology in place by which those changes are factored into account. Architects, however, should think in terms of the lifecycles of the Services that must meet those requirements.

As we explained at the beginning of this chapter, SOA projects don't have traditional lifecycles. Individual Services, however, do go through their own lifecycles as shifting functional requirements dictate. In fact, to meet different constraints, a Service can have multiple contracts for different consumers at the same time. Conversely, a single contract can map to a range of Services, providing them with a single set of constraints and shielding the Service consumer from having to know which Services are satisfying the contract. This "many-to-many" aspect of Services makes it possible to handle ongoing changes to contracts and constraints without having to think about redeveloping the underlying Service.

The lifecycle of a Service reflects its inherently dynamic nature, because each Service may have several different contracts that represent different capabilities to different consumers. The Service itself must be able to meet each contract, even as the set of contracts changes. Keep in mind that we iteratively design a contract; thus, it might be in different states of completion at different times, including in development, ready to be implemented, in production, and deprecated (obsolete, but kept around in case a consumer requires it). The contracts as well as the information about their current states are all metadata, and the Service infrastructure should be able to support changing contract states with no additional programming. It is up to the architect, however, to design the Service infrastructure to support this essential capability.

Unfortunately, reality places some limitations on how well the SOA implementation can respond to changing functional requirements. These limitations typically derive from the existing technology. After all, under the Services abstraction layer you still have databases, legacy applications, and the like. It's critical for the Service-oriented architect to be able to understand the real-world limitations of the existing technology, in order to provide a realistic design for the architecture. After all, as we explained earlier, loose coupling is actually a relative term. There still is some measure of coupling here, and it's that level of coupling that always keeps us grounded in reality.

Work in Progress

In some parts of Greece, property taxes kick in only when the owner completes construction on a building. The result is that people always leave some small part of the building incomplete. You'll see a bit of rebar here, or some unfinished lumber there, often for years, and nobody seems to mind. Well, SOA is like that too. There's no requirement that you actually *finish* your SOA rollout. Some parts of your IT infrastructure may be working just fine, thank you very much, so there's no pressing reason to rearchitect them. That doesn't mean that there's anything wrong with that part of your IT that is Service-oriented. Just like the Greek buildings, SOA can be a work in progress indefinitely. As long as the business is realizing benefit and return on investment (ROI) from SOA projects, it is perfectly fine, if not preferable, for SOA initiatives to be works in progress.

As an enterprise architect, the Service-oriented architect must keep this principle in mind. After all, SOA is the *means,* not the end. The goal is not to implement SOA, but to solve a business problem. It's better to have an architecture that is constantly changing than a business whose needs are never met. There will always be costs associated with IT change, and the architect must always weigh the benefits to moving to SOA with the costs—not just on an enterprisewide basis, but often on a piece-by-piece basis as well. Because SOA has overhead and additional complexity associated with it, when the business tosses the architect some new requirements, he or she must always make the call as to whether a Service-oriented approach or a more traditional approach makes the most sense for addressing those requirements.

Unfortunately, there are no hard-and-fast rules that can guide this decision, because it's utterly dependent on the company's specific situation—

both its existing IT infrastructure and its corporate culture and other organizational limitations. For this reason, architecture will always remain
partly art and partly science.

BUILD, BUY, OR REPURPOSE?

Because Service-oriented architects live in the real world of tight budgets
and existing assets, they should approach all IT investment decisions with a
three-part question: Should they buy, build, or repurpose their IT resources
to meet their emerging business needs? Such fundamental investment questions apply to all aspects of IT, ranging from network devices to application
software to professional services needs, as well as SOA implementations.

However, one of the significant shifts in thinking that Service Orientation
introduces is the notion that business logic is not engrained in programming
code, but rather in the declarative metadata that describes a Service and how
it interacts with other Services. In essence, Service Orientation advocates a
movement away from code-centric development to configuration-centric
composition. This shift to metadata-driven development introduces new challenges to how organizations purchase, repurpose, or develop Services.

Rather than dealing with traditional development lifecycles, companies
must now understand how to continually iterate the development of their
Services, and therefore the metadata that surround their Services as well.
Just as companies have the choice of developing applications in-house or
purchasing their IT assets from third parties, so too must they resolve the
issue of whether to create and maintain their Services and associated metadata themselves, repurpose them from existing assets, or purchase them
from third-party suppliers.

Building Services from Scratch

When faced with a mandate to implement an SOA, the first thing that most
IT managers feel compelled to do is to start developing Service interfaces for
their existing legacy systems. But what does it mean to "develop a Service"?
Developers must deal with two different sorts of assets when building Services in an SOA: the application logic that underlies a Service interface and
the Service metadata themselves.

Application logic development that underlies a Service is much the same
as it has always been, with one key difference: Developers should not hard-
code business processes or any other business logic into the application, but
rather leave them for the metadata to handle. In a Service-oriented implementation, security and reliability considerations likewise should be relegated to the Service interface and policy contracts that surround a Service,

rather than to its underlying code. The real kernel of functionality that remains abstracted beneath the Service interface simply provides the implementation that guarantees the service level agreed to in the Service contract.

Most important, companies should realize that putting Service interfaces in front of existing application logic is not all that challenging. Because adding Service interfaces to legacy systems is straightforward, the real development work comes from defining Service contracts and creating the process, security, management, and other metadata that sit on top of the Services themselves. Simply wrapping legacy systems with Service interfaces is not sufficient.

Building business Services "from scratch" really means coming up with the policies and other metadata that govern how the Services work. In this context, it makes more sense to build such Services in-house than to source them from third parties. Although it's possible to purchase the underlying code that makes the Service work, it's hard to make the same case for Service metadata. Therefore, companies should look to build their own Service metadata and composite business Services.

Repurposing Services

One of the major tenets of Service Orientation is that companies should reuse Services as broadly as possible to support changing business requirements. Companies should expect their investment in Services to shift gradually over time from Service development and exposure to composition focused on Service reuse. Rather than spending time and money trying to figure out which new Services to build, companies should focus their efforts and resources on identifying existing Services in the enterprise, composing them into new processes, and refactoring them as necessary to support new capabilities.

Thus, the significant question that architects must grapple with is which Services to build from scratch and which to repurpose to meet changing needs. The answer to this question depends on the particular circumstances of the business and the scope of its existing Services. Furthermore, many of the Services that companies might have in the early days of their SOA projects will not be amenable to much refactoring, because they might come from prepackaged enterprise application suites or simple extensions of legacy application programming interfaces (APIs).

That said, companies that have properly defined their Services in a top-down fashion by starting with an overall architectural plan, rather than building their SOA from the bottom up by building Services as legacy wrappers, will be better able to repurpose and refactor their Services. Therefore, companies that develop composite Services will be able to extract continuing value from their Service investments. On the flip side, companies that only focus on Service development and not composition or reuse will hardly get the chance to benefit from the agility that SOA promises.

Of course, Service metadata that define security, policy, reliability, and business logic for interacting with Services should be amenable to repurposing. Companies should try their hardest to create Service metadata once and repurpose them as many times as possible to meet ever-changing business requirements. The real development effort here is not one of creating Services from scratch, but rather developing from the start the most agile, flexible Services that the company can later repurpose to meet new needs.

Buying Services

If companies can repurpose Services, then they can also purchase them from third parties, as a logical extension of the basic ability to reuse Services. In many cases, companies may find that the Services they are using the most do indeed come from external suppliers, rather than their own development shops. For example, enterprise application vendors are increasingly providing Services for consumption in corporate SOA implementations. However, a business-centric, process-driven SOA is likely to compose these Services with other Services that may or may not come from that technology supplier. Even in situations where the bulk of the Services might come from a third-party vendor, the business logic itself should be in the composite metadata, which the company most likely develops from scratch in-house.

The forward-looking question is whether companies will purchase *composite* Services from third-party vendors. This question actually doesn't have anything to do with technology, but rather is one of business process outsourcing. Buying a business-focused Service from a third-party vendor should be the same thing as outsourcing an entire business process to that vendor. The Service would appear to be a process the company outsources in its entirety. As a result, companies looking at purchasing such Services must think first about whether they want to outsource that process in the first place.

Although a third party can readily supply the underlying implementation of a Service, it's not clear what sort of metadata a company will realistically be able to purchase from a third-party supplier. Every company's security, reliability, process, and management criteria differs significantly. The most that a company can expect from a vendor are technologies for managing metadata or tools to simplify their creation.

Maintaining a Corporate Memory

In reality, most companies will find that they have to adopt a hybrid of all of the preceding approaches for their Service development and maintenance.

Existing technology vendors will prepackage a wide variety of Services that a company will use; other Services will emerge when companies extend their legacy systems using in-house resources. As companies devote more effort to developing Services, it's clear that the one thing they will need most of all is a corporate memory for how they create and evolve their Services over time.

A corporate memory is simply the ability for an organization to retain knowledge and experience that will help it as new situations emerge. Many companies tend to embed their corporate memory in the form of inflexible processes that tend to bog down their ability to respond to ongoing change—not the kind of corporate memory you wish to have. Rather, the kinds of memory we are talking about here are experiences and methodologies that a company can call on when appropriate to meet new needs.

Specifically, companies should maintain a memory for how they develop agile applications out of loosely coupled Services. If one division of the organization decides to build a Service to meet some specific needs, the company should make sure to communicate and save the reason that it built the Service so that in the future, different parts of the organization can either leverage the existing Service for reuse or decide to build a new Service if the assumptions that governed the decision to build versus reuse are no longer valid. Similarly, companies should not purchase the same Service twice if there's no reason to do so. Obviously, companies need a memory for why they made certain decisions as well as the assumptions underlying the decisions to build, buy, or repurpose existing Services.

REUSE: THE HOLY GRAIL OF IT

Environmentally aware consumers know that in order to produce less waste and increase their earth-friendliness, they need to practice the "3 Rs:" Reduce, Reuse, and Recycle. Just so with IT. In this case, we've talked about reducing the costs associated with IT, and we've talked about recycling existing legacy assets and Services into new Services as part of our exposing and refactoring efforts. However, we haven't spent enough time talking about how reuse works to enable agile, flexible IT.

Reuse seems to come up as a constant theme in each new, successful IT movement. The object-oriented movement of the late 1980s and early 1990s pushed the reusability of object assets as a primary reason to move to that new technology. The client/server movement that preceded it expounded on the values of sharing server assets to increase business logic reuse. Even the development of COBOL in the mainframe days had reuse as a core benefit. Nevertheless, reusing software assets has been extraordinarily difficult to achieve in practice, and the benefits of reuse have always been just out of reach. So, why do we care so much about reuse, and why have we still not been able to achieve it in practice?

In many ways, reuse seems to be the holy grail of IT. Business is constantly complaining about the high costs and inefficiency of IT. "If only IT could be reusable, like the office chairs we buy," bemoan those in business management. Business users are continually perplexed why IT seems to implement the same functionality over and over again, seemingly changing only the technologies and terminology. How many times can a business implement a customer database or an ordering system? It seems to the business that either IT doesn't understand what the business wants the first time, or maybe it's incredibly incompetent at meeting their needs, or both. Reuse seems to be that unattainable goal that business strives for in their relationship with IT.

Undeniably, reuse has the potential of significant benefit to the business. Not only does the possibility of reusing IT assets reduce the cost of long-term development, but it also allows the business to replace systems more effectively when they are no longer productive, increase the efficiency of the business as a whole, and enable synergies between different business units where none had existed before. In many ways, reuse seems to be a different way of saying business agility. In fact, business agility requires reusability.

Reuse the Old Way

The truth of the matter is that reuse happens all the time. The problem is that it's not happening in an agile and sustainable way. When faced with the need to reuse some bit of software, most developers turn to the tried-and-true method of simply copying and pasting bits of code from one system to another, with a few tweaks and changes along the way. This type of reuse is a way to shorten some development time and allow a developer to make use of the work that someone else has done.

However, these copy-and-paste methods of reuse are brittle and inefficient, and introduce a number of major problems. This approach works only as long as the developer doesn't make any modifications at all to the underlying code. Once any sort of change creeps in, we now have to deal with multiple versions of the same piece of code. Each version of the asset is now a *branch* of the original source code. Instead of having one asset to manage, we have two, instantly multiplying our problems and costs. Also, this method of reuse is error-prone and labor-intensive. A copy must be an exact duplicate, which is rarely the case, because there's always something to tweak or improve—introducing the possibility of errors and bugs along the way.

Finally, cutting and pasting loses the context of the original asset. Any links and sources that reference the content might also have to change. The person who originally created the asset might have had one thing in mind when he or she built that particular bit of functionality, and the way that another person is using it might be completely different, altering the way that it works and possibly making it fail in new and unpredictable ways.

Object-oriented coders sought to alter this cut-and-paste method of reuse by introducing the concept of code libraries. Developers either loaded a particular library when they built a new system or when they deployed the system to their customers. Code libraries clearly reduced the need for developers to write or copy code as much as they used to, but they introduced a whole new set of problems that pushed reuse that much farther out of reach.

The first problem is that even though code libraries centralized the code, that code remained fundamentally tightly coupled and brittle. Any change to a shared library instantly causes problems for every application that relies on that library. Instead of having multiple independent systems, we now have a single point of failure that can take down several applications at once. Another problem is that libraries are tightly coupled to their specific platform. If an organization wants to change its platform, all of those libraries instantly become useless. Such reuse is clearly not agile. We need reuse that can change as frequently as business requirements change, even when the organization wants to make a change to its underlying technologies.

Reuse the New Way

Perhaps the real problem of reuse is that building for reuse means building an asset that is by definition beyond its immediate and specific business requirements. How can a developer ever hope to build a reusable asset if the specifications for reuse are by definition unclear, imprecise, and apt to change frequently? Is reuse even possible if it's impossible to define the specific functionality for a reusable asset? And if a developer must create some reusable code, how will he or she know when it is done?

In many ways, reuse is not in the eye of the person building the asset, but rather in the eye of the people who use it. A developer can code thousands of versions of an asset for every possible scenario and foreseen consequence, but find that people use only a few of them. On the flip side, the developer might find that no one is using those assets at all because, despite all the different variations, they still don't meet a particular and specific need. So, the real challenge is to make reuse a reality in the eye of the user rather than in that of the developer.

The new mantra for reuse in the Service-oriented context is the notion of *broad applicability*. Instead of sharing code, Service consumers share Services when they're up and running. Clearly, we aren't multiplying a Service for different purposes by copying and pasting it multiple times, and neither are we using a Service in the same way as code or linked libraries. Mainframe systems, application servers, or data sources might provide Services for that matter, and there's no dependence on the particular choice of underlying infrastructure, which removes one of the problems that libraries faced. Instead, by putting the variable aspects of a Service in the Service contract, rather than in the underlying code, we can build a shared Service that is broadly applicable to many different processes and consumers.

If a Service is responsible for providing customer data, for example, but a dozen different consumers want the Service to present those data in different ways, we're presented instantly with a reuse conundrum: Should we make a dozen different Services, a dozen Service contracts, or a single contract with enough variability to handle the disparate needs? In the first case, we wouldn't want to create a dozen different Services, because that would defeat the goal of reuse. A single, overly complex contract would not be agile. A dozen different contracts for a single Service is a lot more manageable, and agile as well. Instead of managing a dozen Services, we now have to manage a dozen contracts, but that is a significantly easier task. We don't have to mold a bunch of new Lego parts, but we do have to make sure that the pieces do connect together well and fit the business need. Broad applicability, therefore, depends on the management of Service contracts.

Building broadly applicable Services, however, still doesn't guarantee reuse if people can't find those Services or understand how to use them. In addition to being broadly applicable, therefore, Services must also be consumable. *Consumability* means that people actually are able to reuse the Services. There must be a registry or repository that serves as a clearinghouse for available Services. Users must know how to use that clearinghouse to find the Services they need. Consumability also requires that there be sufficient information about the Services so that people know which Services are the right ones, and how to actually use them—and yes, this additional information is more Service metadata that the company must manage.

The Holy Grail of reuse is therefore finally within reach, because Service Orientation takes a practical approach to reuse. It's human nature to reuse something only when it's flexible and easy to find and use. By building Services to be broadly applicable and consumable, we're making it easy for people to reuse them. It's that ease of reuse that was always missing before—but now, through the power of Service Orientation, reuse is easy.

CHAPTER 12

Becoming a Service-Oriented Enterprise

One of the great things about writing a book as forward-looking and far-reaching as this one is that by the time we get to the final chapter, we get to throw off the shackles of explaining basic concepts and illustrating short-term practicality and wax futuristic on the long-term potential of Service Orientation. As any futurist is wont to do, we'll consider a scenario for the future—the scenario of the Service-Oriented Enterprise. Assuming companies around the world take all the advice in this book, and successfully navigate the pitfalls of implementing enterprise SOA and leveraging the power of Service Orientation across their businesses, then what will their companies—and the world at large—be like?

MAKING IT MATTER

We'll begin our trek through the future of Service Orientation with a look at the changing role of IT within the organization. Today IT serves a *tactical* role within most companies. In many organizations, IT has traditionally been a cost center. In the early years of computing, people saw IT solely as a means to automate existing business functions in the enterprise. When companies used hulking mainframes to store transaction or customer data, for example, there was no reason to expect that the IT department supporting that mainframe would somehow figure out how to turn the IT system into some kind of money generator for the organization.

As the early days of IT (affectionately known as *data processing*, or DP) gave way to a more business-centric perspective (then known as *management of information systems*, or MIS), companies hired chief information officers (CIOs) to run their IT organizations and gave them profit and loss responsibilities. CIOs ran IT as a business, offering services to other departments within the organization in return for some form of internal compensation.

Over time, technology reached a point where IT was not simply automating existing business functions and offering various services to other parts of the organization, but introducing new business capabilities, especially as companies entered the eBusiness era. Whereas before IT simply made existing business models work more effectively, IT now enabled entirely new business models. Nevertheless, it soon became clear that such profit-making initiatives were also entirely tactical in nature, because having a Web site or an eCommerce capability did not provide any differentiation in the marketplace, since soon every company was able to build such capabilities itself.

As Nicholas Carr pointed out in his seminal *Harvard Business Review* article, "IT Doesn't Matter," although IT remains essential to the competitiveness of companies, it doesn't provide any *strategic* differentiation that distinguishes one company from another.[1] Even when IT acts as a profit center for an organization, there is nothing about the way that IT enables such profit-making capability that other companies can't quickly duplicate. But far worse than simply failing to provide any strategic benefit, the IT department in most companies has slipped into a mode where it is seen neither as a contributor to the top line nor as a reducer of overall corporate expense. Rather, IT has garnered the reputation that it is little more than overhead—just a cost center for the organization.

Carr's detractors were quick to point out that running IT as a business

Jargon Watch: Strategy

In his seminal work *Competitive Strategy: Techniques for Analyzing Industries and Competitors*, Michael Porter defines two basic types of corporate strategy: *cost leadership* and *differentiation*.[2] Cost leadership strategies are the Wal-Mart style compete-on-price approaches. However, it's the differentiation strategy we're talking about in this book, which Porter defines as such: "A differentiation strategy calls for the development of a product or service that offers unique attributes that are valued by customers and that customers perceive to be better than or different from the products of the competition." The key, therefore, to the way we're using the word *strategy* is in the differentiation from one company to another. Essentially, your company's strategy should be how you can do something different from your competitors in a way that they will find difficult to copy.

[1] Nicholas Carr, "Why IT Doesn't Matter," *Harvard Business Review*, May 2003.
[2] Michael E. Porter, *Competitive Strategy: Techniques for Analyzing Industries and Competitors* (New York: Free Press, 1998).

doesn't just mean managing to the bottom line or simply wanting to reduce all spending and minimize investment on new technologies. Companies must think about how their investments will return incrementally *more* to the business over time, after all. Simply improving business processes and methodologies is not enough. These detractors, however, largely miss Carr's point. Countless business improvement experts expound on the idea that improving anything in business is simply about implementing some new process or other. Although certainly initiatives such as Six Sigma have helped companies get a grasp on how they go about delivering IT functionality, none of these initiatives provides for *strategic* differentiation.

Service Orientation: Providing Strategic Differentiation to Companies

We'll explain how SOA can offer strategic differentiation, but it's important to point out that SOA doesn't necessarily offer such differentiation to the organizations that implement it. It is all too easy for SOA to fall into the trap of simply being another approach that IT uses to meet tactical business needs. Many of the benefits of SOA we discussed in Chapter 8 fall into this category of tactical improvements: reducing the cost of integration, sharing Services, smoothing mergers and acquisitions, and enabling regulatory compliance, for example. Even leveraging SOA to shift the cost of IT from in-house to an outsourced organization is an inherently tactical maneuver. SOA doesn't become a strategic differentiator simply by playing a shell game with who is supplying IT functionality. Moving or relocating the IT department, or even incorporating the IT department as a subsidiary, doesn't fundamentally change how an organization leverages IT.

There is one benefit to SOA, however, that offers hope—the business agility benefit. After all, SOA is more than simply applying a new methodology to the same old IT practices. Businesses need to think about what Services are doing, who is defining them, and what specific and positive return they generate for the company. Then they must leverage SOA to enable businesses to get incrementally greater returns from IT as they use existing Services in *new* ways to take advantage of unpredictable business change.

Recall that our definition of *business agility* had two parts: Respond quickly and efficiently to business change, *and leverage that change for competitive advantage.* It is the second part of the agility benefit that offers hope to companies looking to escape Carr's conundrum. Such a benefit, however, does not automatically provide a strategic differentiator. We definitely recommend that companies use Service Orientation to leverage changes in the business environment for tactical competitive advantages, such as bringing a product to market more quickly or simply bringing a better product to market. Service Orientation, after all, cannot give a company a strategy. A Service-Oriented Enterprise, however, will have strategy that it is *uniquely* able to implement solely because of its adoption of Service Orientation.

Examples of such differentiators are necessarily futuristic, but let's put on our future-vision goggles and have a go. Let's say that sometime in the future a telecommunications company's strategy includes developing a create-your-own-service product offering for their customers. Through the power of Service Orientation, it enables its customers to pick and choose from a range of sophisticated telecom capabilities and assemble them into a new service unique to each customer. Furthermore, customers are able to rework this service any time they like. So, if a customer thinks it would be a good idea that whenever a particular show came onto the telecom-provided digital television service, the TV launched a multimedia conference call that brought together a group of the customer's friends into an online, interactive viewing experience via their mobile phone/personal digital assistants (PDAs), then the customer can simply go to the telecom company's Web site and set such a service up.

Such an offering would be strategic if it uniquely differentiated the company from its competitors (that's the definition of *strategic*, after all). And there's no way a company could offer such a dynamic, continually changing service if it wasn't Service oriented. Furthermore, the power of this service is that customers can take it wherever they want to go—essentially, the marketplace itself determines the nature of the product on a day-to-day basis. The whims of the marketplace, after all, are among the most fundamental sources of unpredictable business change. This telecom, therefore, is using the power of Service Orientation to leverage such change for competitive, strategic advantage.

When Carr wrote his article, he recognized that companies were unable to use IT for such strategic purposes—and he was right. When companies become Service-Oriented Enterprises, however, they will be able to do just that. At that point, then, IT will matter.

BUILDING METAPROCESSES

In Chapter 4 we discussed the automation paradox: The more a company attempts to automate its processes, the more it must focus on handling the exceptions to those processes manually. In other words, the more we automate, the more manual work we have. The reason for this paradox is that companies traditionally try to automate business processes by building them in a rigid way, tightly coupling systems together and making many assumptions that the process won't change, requiring them to handle any adjustments or exceptions to those processes outside of the automation mechanism they have created.

Service Orientation fundamentally changes this poured-concrete situation. Through Service-Oriented Processes, people are now able to compose and recompose processes out of Services as needed. People can manage exceptions using straightforward approaches that are inherently part of the process itself, rather than through separate, often manual means. Although this promise of agile, flexible processes sounds like just the thing that organizations need, it is still out of reach for most companies that still are struggling with simply getting their systems to communicate with each other in a tightly coupled way, let alone in a Service-oriented, loosely coupled way. However, by this point in the book you are now able to break down this vision of Service-Oriented Process into elements that companies can tackle as a straightforward part of their SOA initiatives. The first step in breaking down Service-Oriented Processes is to distinguish between business processes composed of Services, or what we call *composed processes,* and *metaprocesses* that specify the way we deal with those processes.

As we explained in Chapter 4, a composed process is made up of one or more Services and then exposed as a Service—the essential innovation of Service Orientation that enables the creation of increasingly complex processes in a loosely coupled fashion. Business users should be able to compose Services into business-level processes, which they can in turn expose as Services. The loosely coupled nature of Services makes such processes flexible regardless of how complex they become.

A *metaprocess,* however, is a process for dealing with processes. In essence, a metaprocess describes all the activities people do to manage processes, but does so in a way that a system might be able to understand. A metaprocess might involve a number of different actions that people might take with respect to the processes they work with, including creating, managing, revising, improving, combining, or retiring processes.

Although we've heard of the concept of business process for decades, the notion of metaprocesses rarely comes up today because metaprocesses are usually human workflow-intensive and, as a result, very difficult to automate. Most of the existing business process technologies and tools on the market today are capable of making some manual metaprocesses easier, but typically they do not take the responsibility for metaprocesses out of the hands of the analysts who are called on to execute them. In other words, metaprocesses are on the very-difficult-to-automate end of the automation spectrum.

Here's where the game-changing nature of Service-Oriented Process enters the picture: It is the challenge of automating metaprocesses that offers the greatest promise for SOA and the broader business movement to Service

Orientation. Take a closer look at how people handle exceptions to auto-mated processes, for example. One good case study in exception manage-ment involves merchandising processes—say getting winter coats on a store's racks. One early cold snap can cause a spike in demand that throws a wrench into the most carefully laid forecasts, and now people have to step into an otherwise automated process and deal with the situation.

This unexpected change in the process results in people doing all sorts of unpredictable and sometimes undesirable things to get the business back in compliance with the business process. When these exception managers adjust or revise an existing process to deal with the problem, they are exe-cuting a metaprocess—an activity that they almost always handle manually. Sometimes those metaprocesses are specified in some handbook, as part of some training, or just through general experience. But some process excep-tions are completely unpredictable and as a result throw management for a loop.

Let's say, however, that the company has SOA in place, and the pro-cesses it is dealing with are Service-Oriented Processes. In addition to simply specifying the basic, normal flow of business in a business process, the process for dealing with exceptions is also a Service-Oriented Process. As a result, when the unexpected cold snap occurs, the managers can now select from any of the available Service-Oriented Processes or make on-the-spot modifications to those processes to deal with the exception. They can com-pose those processes in a flexible manner to reallocate IT resources as needed. They are still executing a metaprocess that might involve significant manual intervention, but as part of that metaprocess they are composing Service-Oriented Processes into new Service-Oriented Processes.

Metaprocesses and the Service-Oriented Enterprise

Now let's take another look at the solution provider we discussed in Chap-ter 4 that develops an exception management system that automates the metaprocess of composing Service-Oriented Processes to respond to unex-pected events. This solution provider's customers can now handle exception management as if it were just one more set of automated processes. This new system is sophisticated enough to compose processes on the fly to respond to a range of exception conditions. From the customer's perspec-tive, this tool provides a "manage exceptions" Service that appears to the business as a single activity, although in reality it represents the dynamic composition of various processes—the essence of a metaprocess.

Consider some other examples of metaprocesses that companies even-tually should be able to automate once they're Service-Oriented Enterprises:

- Today's marketing campaigns might include several different activities, such as doing market research, creating packaging, developing and running TV ads, putting together print ads, generating leads, speaking and executive presence-building, and many other activities. Putting together such a campaign is a metaprocess, since the individual activities are processes. A Service-Oriented Enterprise might have a "create marketing campaign" Service that handles this metaprocess automatically and deals with exceptions explicitly.

- Acquiring a company involves many different steps, from ordering new business cards to combining the financials to renegotiating leases. Large companies that perform frequent acquisitions often develop a formal plan for handling these events, which is essentially a metaprocess. A Service-Oriented Enterprise might be able to create an "acquire company" Service for handling this metaprocess.

- An automobile manufacturer wishes to streamline its ability to move from one model year to the next, enabling the company to change the model more efficiently as it moves to the upcoming year. Typically, this move involves a significant amount of change to the procurement and assembly processes every time a new model is offered. Now that the firm is a Service-Oriented Enterprise, it can automate the metaprocess of reworking its core business processes, developing "update procurement process" and "update assembly process" Services.

- Every time there's a change in regulations, an insurance company must rework its policy underwriting processes. Instead, Service Orientation enables the company to automate the "rework underwriting process" metaprocess into a single Service.

Sure, we've overly simplified things and made the idea of more easily automated metaprocesses seem pie-in-the sky. No one can reasonably expect companies to automate such metaprocesses any time soon—but the whole point is that Service Orientation offers an overarching philosophy of the relationship between business and IT that offers an approach to solving these sorts of problems.

Thus, we stretch the goal of SOA beyond simply replacing brittle, tightly coupled systems with loosely coupled ones to the notion that Service Orientation should alter the way we deal with unpredictable change as a whole. The real point we're trying to make is that Service Orientation opens the door to automating such metaprocesses. Today, after all, people don't even think of metaprocesses as business processes in their own right. As Service Orientation takes hold, however, the heretofore manual work of creating, managing, and evolving processes will become simpler and more straightforward. It's only a matter of time, therefore, before companies begin automating these metaprocesses as well.

CONNECTING THE DOTS: SERVICE ORIENTATION, OUTSOURCING, AND THE INDUSTRIALIZATION OF IT

Let's take a quick break from the heavy concepts of bringing your organization closer to Service Orientation by stepping back in time—way back. Every technology shift has a social and environmental movement associated with it. Case in point: the evolution of steel making in the Industrial Revolution. Since the dawn of the Bronze Age, humans have made implements out of metal by taking raw ore, heating it up a few thousand degrees, pouring the resulting molten metal into a mold, and then pounding on it until it's the desired shape. Every town required an entire industry of specialists to make the implements of daily life, such as nails, horseshoes, spoons, plows, and swords. The blacksmith rapidly became the revered craftsman and artist who was key to the town's success and livelihood.

In the late 1700s and early 1800s, things would change dramatically for the blacksmith. The Industrial Revolution introduced a rapid pace of new innovations, such as steam power, the railroad, and new construction that required ever greater quantities of metal, at increasingly more predictable and refined measures of accuracy. Suddenly the artisan craft of the blacksmith became more of an impediment to innovation than an enabler of it. How could companies even hope to build thousands of miles of railroad track, utilize thousands of steel girders for their bridges and buildings, or thousands of parts for their new inventions if we relied on the poor city blacksmith to make it all a reality? Indeed, one of the biggest changes of the Industrial Revolution was not just the new technologies and innovations, but rather the change of the whole metals industry.

Why are we talking about blacksmiths and the Industrial Revolution here? Just as the Industrial Revolution limited the days of the village blacksmith, so too are the days of the artisan craft of IT quickly coming to an end. Indeed, the movement to Service Orientation introduces such a significant change to the way people make, consume, and purchase IT that it will have as dramatic and irreversible impact on the IT industry as a whole as the Industrial Revolution had on blacksmithing.

SOA and Outsourcing

In order to understand the fundamental change that SOA represents, let's first take a look back at an idea we surfaced back in Chapter 7: outsourcing. Outsourcing part or all of a business process makes the most economic sense when the company can achieve quantifiable business results from taking a core, critical business process and putting it into the hands of a third party. Outsourcing is not simply subcontracting or the normal business relationship of a vendor and a supplier. Rather, the outsourced task is one of critical importance to the business that it would otherwise have implemented in-house; the business chose to outsource the task to a third party for economic, liability, or strategic reasons. With *Business Process Outsourcing* (BPO), for example, a third-party firm manages an entire business process, such as accounting, procurement, or human resources.

Outsourcing also represents significant risks to businesses, in particular, the risks that it will introduce quality problems, increase customer and partner dissatisfaction, and create new business and legal liabilities. Nevertheless, companies have long seen the benefits of outsourcing various parts of their business. As companies grow and specialize, they no longer wish to maintain staff for many parts of their organization, such as accounting, product assembly and fulfillment, logistics, and sometimes even product design and development. Now there is also increased pressure to outsource various parts of the IT department as well, ranging from the data center to the application developer.

Concurrent with the desire to outsource certain business processes, companies are also looking to improve their own enterprises through Service Orientation. Specifically, the movement to SOA is actually a movement to create IT business process components that people can assemble efficiently to meet specific requirements. At the same time, the movement toward outsourcing offers the growing realization that although IT is a core necessity to the well-being of any company, companies do not have to build their own IT business processes from scratch. Increasingly, companies desire the ability to source from third-party suppliers components that they can readily assemble into business processes themselves, or have third parties assemble and deliver to them on a custom basis.

It's becoming clear that the economic value that companies seek from outsourcing closely matches and reinforces the economic benefits they see from implementing SOA. Furthermore, in order to outsource IT resources properly, companies must approach their IT assets from a Service perspective—applying the right level of abstraction to make sure their outsourcing dreams don't turn into nightmares. Effective outsourcing necessitates effective requirements definition, communication, and abstraction of the third parties' processes. At the same time, building an effective SOA mandates the abstraction of IT capabilities as well. By virtue of their abstraction, these Services must have implementation, location, and presentation-independent definitions. A well-designed SOA assumes nothing about where or how companies implement the Services; they might as well outsource them.

If companies can define abstracted Service interfaces, the details of who implements those Services and where those Services reside are basically irrelevant. SOA provides an abstraction layer on top of existing technology resources, allowing third parties to provide those resources more easily, with business users ideally being none the wiser. In fact, as companies move to increasingly represent assets as Services, they will be less concerned with the implementation details of those Services and instead will seek to outsource them. So, SOA not only makes outsourcing simpler, but it in fact motivates companies to consider outsourcing as a viable alternative when it might not have even been possible in the past.

We can take the SOA/outsourcing combination to a logical extreme and assume that eventually companies will outsource most or all of their critical business processes in the form of Services that they can purchase on a licensed, subscription, or transaction basis from third-party vendors. Today only a small subset of the Services a company might be interested in purchasing, such as customer relationship management, finance, and supply chain management solutions, are available as Services. In order for companies to leverage third-party Services as an alternative to outsourcing, a market must first emerge for a wide range of available Services a business would be interested in—and such a market is still quite nascent.

However, custom-built outsourcing and ready-built Services aren't the only two options for companies looking to leverage the possibilities the combination of SOA and outsourcing offers today. Rather, the movement to SOA offers a company the opportunity to outsource functionality to a group of companies, industry-run consortia, or marketplaces that can provide access to a wide range of capabilities critical to a business. For example, companies might be able to pool a set of shared Services into a community that provides access to core supply chain or purchasing capabilities.

SOA and the Industrialization of IT

The combination of the SOA and outsourcing trends reflects the maturation of the broader IT industry. Before the industrial age, companies built products and tools on a one-off, customized basis; with the emergence of powered machinery, improved technologies, and new methodologies, companies were able to mass-produce all manner of goods. Analogously, SOA and outsourcing are actually both essential aspects of the movement of IT toward increasing industrialization.

Industrialization embodies a number of major concepts: the mechanization of production so that the mass assembly of components provide significant improvements in efficiency and cost, the improvement of the infrastructure around such products to simplify how people build and sell them, and a fundamental change in the way that people buy and consume them. For example, it wasn't individual innovations such as steam power or the mechanical loom that caused the Industrial Revolution, but rather the development of efficient sources of power, effective means for the transportation of goods, and the evolution of an economy where people sought to buy the shirts they wear rather than have their family knit them on an as-needed basis. Such industrialization caused broad, significant changes to the structure of the family, the city, and the economy as a whole.

The convergence of the outsourcing and SOA movements illustrates this industrialization of IT. In many ways, SOA represents the technology required to mass-produce reusable IT components. Outsourcing reflects the increased desire of companies to stop custom-producing their own IT components. In this regard, SOA and outsourcing really are two aspects of the same macroeconomic trend toward the industrialization of IT.

The combination of SOA and outsourcing will become even more established as the value proposition and technologies for implementing SOA continue to mature. As companies seek to gain the benefits of business agility, they will realize that the SOA/outsourcing combination provides options they may never have had before. For example, outsourcing business processes today means cutting off big, inflexible chunks of the business and simply handing them to third parties; with SOA, businesses will be able to take a much more agile approach, outsourcing the components of greatest strategic value.

SUNSET OF LEGACY

Let's switch gears now from the inexorable trend toward industrialization to another of humanity's most persistent aspirations: the quest for immortality. We are all too conscious of our mortality and seek some religious faith, fountain of youth, or cryogenic miracle that can sustain us forever. Nevertheless, immortality is an unattainable goal. Therefore, we shift our ambitions for endless life to the things we do control: our IT systems and solutions that we implement in hopes they stay alive forever. However, as we discussed in Chapter 1, building something to last means that by definition it will become obsolete, given the constant, unpredictable changes in both business and IT.

Service Orientation, however, promises to change this definition. By building inherently flexible systems, perhaps we finally have a way to unlock the shackles of legacy. The fact still remains, however, that no company will be able simply to throw out its old applications and systems once it becomes Service-oriented. On the contrary, SOA enables you to get more value out of legacy, actually making it more practical to keep such systems around, as we explained in Chapter 10. So, with Service Orientation we can keep the old stuff around longer, but the new stuff we build is flexible enough never to become old stuff. The question then is: Will we ever be rid of the old stuff, or does SOA simply create a new form of legacy?

No More Legacy in the Service-Oriented Enterprise?

One of the paradoxes of legacy is that for most enterprises, legacy systems are too old to justify ongoing improvements but are nevertheless too important to retire. As a result, companies must continue to maintain legacy systems even though the returns they receive from those systems diminish over time, in spite of the fact that there must be significant value in the systems to continue using them in the first place. Each legacy system traps some core business logic or functionality, hopelessly awaiting some new technology to free that capability and allow the organization finally to retire their ancient systems.

Given that an important goal of Service Orientation is to shift the IT assets from brittle, tightly coupled systems to agile, loosely coupled Services, then legacy should eventually come to an end. After all, if business users are in control of the application, and the application doesn't depend on legacy systems, then when do we need those legacy systems at all? At the very least, the concept of legacy will transform in the Service-Oriented Enterprise. The hope is that the continual emphasis on composing new Service-Oriented Processes and consuming third-party Services will squeeze greater efficiency out of IT and help to retire systems that have outlived their usefulness.

Fundamental to Service Orientation is a separation between the business requirements and logic, defined in the form of business processes, and the technology, consisting of the infrastructure that underlies the Services layer of abstraction, including all legacy applications and the business logic they have locked up inside them. In a properly architected SOA, business Services represent the data available to the business and the core functionality of the underlying systems. Businesspeople then compose those Services into Service-Oriented Processes, configure the processes based on the applicable business rules and policies, and then expose those processes as Services that other people can compose into new processes.

The important point to understand is that Service-Oriented Enterprises gradually retire the business logic in their legacy, so that eventually the Service-Oriented Processes contain *all* of the business logic in the enterprise. Although certain logic will remain in the software infrastructure that supports the business Services available to the enterprise, none of that logic should be *business* logic.

Do we really believe that Service Orientation will lead to business logic belonging entirely in the hands of business, rather than in legacy applications? Probably not in the short term, because it will take some time for this IT vision to become a reality, and there are many roadblocks along the way to realizing this vision. However, in the long term, the only way to gain the business agility companies need is by making this shift.

For this vision of the sunset of legacy to become a reality, however, we'll have to wait until companies gradually retire the legacy stuff in favor of fully Service-oriented approaches. However, because Service Orientation makes it easier to get value out of legacy systems, we're suggesting a gradual evolution of IT instead of a quick but difficult fix that companies will need to rush into. Eventually, however, business logic finally will be entirely in the hands of the business where it belongs, and IT simply will enable those processes to work as intended and respond to unpredictable change.

Will Service Orientation Create More Legacy?

Whether you buy our prediction that Service Orientation will lead to the gradual retirement of today's legacy systems and applications or not, there still remains one important question: Will today's Service-oriented approaches be tomorrow's legacy? If anything, a Service-Oriented Enterprise risks thinking of business processes, contracts, policies, and semantic metadata as legacy over time. Companies will continue to invest in processes and metadata until they no longer need them or the costs outweigh the benefits of their use. Many Service-oriented organizations might indeed continue investing in legacy processes beyond their anticipated shelf life, shifting the idea of legacy from the underlying systems to the processes themselves.

However, Service Orientation *done right* offers more than simply shifting legacy from one technology stratum to another. It offers a way for companies to think differently about legacy in the first place. If companies can replace applications easily whenever they desire, then the applications will never become legacy. Indeed, if legacy means that a technology is difficult to replace, then certainly Services in an SOA can never become legacy, because they are *meant* to be replaced and altered. Services need never become legacy, because it doesn't cost much to replace them. In essence, SOA allows us to replace applications without the pain and cost associated with replacing legacy. If we can achieve replacement without any real penalty, then there really needn't be such a thing as legacy at all.

Challenges of the Sunset of Legacy

Although the total elimination of legacy sounds good in theory, the fundamental change of the concept of legacy poses significant problems for those in IT management. First, budgeting for legacy systems is fairly straightforward. In many cases, IT managers can simply budget a flat fee or percentage of system cost on a year-by-year basis and plug that number into their planning spreadsheets for many years on end. This predictability provides some comfort when other IT projects continue to grow beyond their own scope and budget. However, a continuously evolving SOA project offers no such solace. No IT manager can place a fixed cost on Service development and continuous evolution, which causes even more discomfort for those people already struggling with how SOA will change the very nature of their jobs.

In addition to the budgeting challenge, legacy systems allow companies to develop deep and long-lasting relationships with vendors. These relationships rely on the trust between companies and their vendors, because the legacy systems are so core to the business that it can't afford to implement a system unless it trusts the vendor behind it. After all, companies make each legacy investment with the assumption that it will be around for a long, long time.

However, you should make no such assumption of longevity for Service-oriented systems, so companies will have to change the way in which they work with vendors. Services and processes can change at a moment's notice, as will the vendors they choose to work with. Therefore, it becomes more important to trust the architecture itself and the professionals who support that architecture rather than the vendors that provide underlying technology.

All of these changes in how legacy impacts the organization are a natural extension of the shift in IT culture, technology, and organization that Service Orientation represents. We're now able to replace the legacy that we know and love (well, at least that we know) with ongoing change. As companies come to accept this shift and realize the benefits of agility, eventually they will scorn legacy as a detriment to their business.

VISION OF THE BUSINESS WEB

Throughout this book, we have planted in your mind the notion that the long-term vision of Service Orientation clearly goes well beyond IT. Although IT is the very thing that enabled the Information Revolution, the business world of tomorrow needs more than just IT to keep it competitive. Through the industrialization of IT, the rise of automated metaprocesses, and the sunset of legacy technology, we finally have a glimpse of the business world of tomorrow, and that vision has more to do with the way that people work with IT than with the technology alone.

In particular, it's clear that the boundaries between technology and business are going away. Service Orientation and the increasing automation of metaprocesses empower individuals to focus the efforts of their work on increasingly productive tasks, those tasks that humans are uniquely suited to perform. Whereas before only those within the IT department were able to effect change, now those who are most intimately familiar with the business process at hand can directly impact change on the company.

However, the wider view of Service Orientation holds that the divisions between one company and another are arbitrary and become increasingly irrelevant to the day-to-day activities within the broader global economy. When an individual or a team requires a business resource that it doesn't have internally, there is no significant technology hurdle to finding and using a resource, regardless of whether that resource comes from an office next door at the same company or a different organization on the other side of the world. As a result, business capabilities and information flow freely, with the infrastructure that handles the policy issues of security, remuneration, and responsibility working so well it fades from view. And so the only real divisions that remain are the organizational and cultural ones that govern relationships from a human perspective.

We call this long-term view of the world of business the *Business Web*. In the Business Web, any company can do business with any other in a seamless, automated fashion. The divisions between teams, departments, companies, and countries blur, as loosely coupled, policy-driven interactions become the norm throughout the economy. Global business becomes so agile and efficient that we are able to build great wealth where before, inefficiencies sucked up so many of our resources.

Competition drives innovation, and innovation drives our daily work. Competition also drives our ongoing efforts to become more agile and efficient. The most successful business efforts, therefore, will be both the most agile and the most innovative. After all, innovation affects all companies. Although we can leverage our ability to innovate better or faster than the competition, in the big picture, such innovations even themselves out. Therefore, if we were to rest on our laurels and decide we didn't have to continue to drive the business, then our competition would quickly eat us for lunch.

The Business Web is still mostly science fiction, but that doesn't mean that you can't create a few business webs of your own. Implement SOA to make your IT agile, and think through how your business can better leverage its IT resources as they become more flexible. Work with business partners, customers, and suppliers as they Service-orient their companies to build your own business web. As these other companies leverage your Services and you leverage theirs, you're on the road to the Business Web.

Just as the Internet led to a Web of human communication, Service Orientation will take that Web to the next level. The World Wide Web transformed most industries and led to entirely new business models of its own—not the ones that sprang up during the dot-com boom but, more important, the ones that survived to flourish after the crash. Now, we're not predicting a Service Orientation speculative bubble—there are no indications that such a thing is in the offing—but we are predicting the same sort of business transformation and creation that we saw in the 1990s. It will likely take longer, as Service Orientation is difficult and complex, but there is a sense of inevitability about it that is impossible to deny.

This sense of inevitability comes from the fact that we see no alternatives to Service Orientation on the horizon. It seems that every company today is somewhere on the road to Service Orientation. Many are still in the planning stages; others have begun the journey. There are, however, no apparent forks in the road. And although today, much of the effort falls within IT, because that is where the biggest problems lie, the true promise of Service Orientation is on the business side. Previous business transformation efforts have largely fallen short due to the limitations of technology; today IT is finally reaching the level of maturity where it's possible to build truly agile organizations.

WHAT DOES IT ALL MEAN?

We know that we've given you a tall order in this book. Will Service Orientation fundamentally change the way business leverages the power of IT, leading to heretofore unknown levels of business agility that companies will be able to achieve far more than they ever hoped to in the past? We can understand that you'll be skeptical. We don't expect companies simply to take us for our word and implement the ideas in this book and expect change to happen immediately. After all, the cultural and organizational challenges to Service Orientation are substantial. However, we have laid out a step-by-step roadmap that begins with changing the way you think about IT. If other parts of the business can facilitate agility, so too can IT. Agility requires a fundamental change in IT, and that change is on its way. Companies that can negotiate this change successfully will have significant advantages over their lumbering, inflexible competition. Those that can adopt SOA successfully will thrive and flourish, and those that don't will be doomed.

Index